The Table

The Plague

The Table

SEASONS ON A
COLORADO RANCH

LARA RICHARDSON

WESTERN PRESS BOOKS
GUNNISON, COLORADO

Western Press Books
1 Western Way, Gunnison, Colorado 81230

Library of Congress Cataloging-in-Publication Data
Names: Richardson, Lara, author.
Title: The Table / Lara Richardson
Description: First edition. | Colorado : Western Press Books, 2024.
Identifiers: LCCN 2024939947 | ISBN 978-1-64642-638-6 (softcover)
LC record available at https://lccn.loc.gov/

Design & cover photo by Mariel Wiley.
Editor: Steve Coughlin.
Managing editor: Jonathan Rovner.
Western Press Books intern: Dylan Roth
Wheat design by Jack Hebert.

https://western.edu/program/english/western-press-books/

Western
Press Books

For Andrew

"To understand the fashion of any life,
one must know the land it is lived in
and the procession of the year."

Mary Austin, *The Land of Little Rain*

Contents

Invitation

Spring
47

Summer
117

Fall
195

Winter
241

Recipes
275

INVITATION

Chapter 1

It's a frigid January afternoon, and the kids will soon be home from school. My husband, Andrew, is out feeding our cows in the blizzard that blows, and I am inside, putting away Christmas until next December. A pot of beef stew simmers on the stove as I open the two antique trunks that bookend the red loveseat along the windows in the living room. Though the weathered wooden trunks are empty, their lingering aromas of candles, ruddy cinnamon sticks, fat pinecones, and sprigs of juniper berries swirl with the warmth that glows in the windows of the wood-burning stove.

As I listen to "O Holy Night" one last time, I tuck away the stack of children's Christmas books and gather the seven stockings that hang from the mantel behind the stove—Andrew's and mine and our five kids'—Grace, Naomi, Abe, Life, and Esther. At 23, 21, 19, 17, and 7, the stockings are still the first thing they go for on Christmas morning, digging down to find a plump pomegranate nestled at the toe. I store boxes of ornaments, balls of white lights, rolls of ribbons, and bundles of candles. I pack the fragile nativity that sits on the table next to the oil lamp, under which lies a long red and green plaid table runner.

The wooden nativity sits motionless each December day until sunset, when its four red candles are lit and their heat rises and spins the wheel of wooden wings that turns a rod which brings the nativity scene to life—Jesus, Mary, and Joseph at the center—and the wise men, who travel in endless circles on their way. I pack the tattered song sheets, whose edges the kids browned in the flames as we sang carols around the table, candle light flickering on our faces and the holy family journeying round and round.

This story, these pages in your hand, are about that table—the table that sits in the dining room of our farmhouse on the edge of a hay field on our family's cattle ranch at the outskirts of the small town of Salida in the middle of the Colorado Rockies. From the farmhouse, across pastures and beyond the highway to the west, the land slowly inclines through piñon, spruce, pine, and aspen trees to the massive mountain range that spreads north and south.

This story is about my family who gathers around the table—and the ranch where the table sits. The ranch looks west to several 14,000-foot peaks named after Ivy League schools such as Princeton and Harvard. They host the Collegiate Peaks Wilderness Area and blend into the Sawatch Mountain Range. The magnificent Sawatch Mountains not only display peaks named for Ute tribal chiefs such as Mount Shavano, which towers 14,231 feet above sea level, but they are also home to the Continental Divide—which sends snowmelt and rainfall either east to the Atlantic or west to the Pacific. On the Atlantic side, 7,000 feet lower than the summit of Mt. Shavano, sits the high-mountain valley that holds the ranch—and the table.

It is a tumultuous time to be a rancher in America. Ours is one of the last remaining farms in this valley where we raise over 300 head of Hereford cattle and produce over 30,000 bales of hay each summer. As a Colorado rancher and mother of five, this is my invitation to you to settle into life on our family ranch, to see both the peaceful and poignant facets of the inner workings of a livelihood that is becoming scarcer with each passing year. It's an invitation to enter into the seasons and the rhythms of the ranch while exploring the stewardship of life—including land, body, and soul.

I have learned, and continue to learn, many lessons through marriage, motherhood, loss, and adoption, while experiencing times of renewal, hope, and adventure through landscapes near and far. Through the stories in these pages, I invite you to pause and connect with this place and its people.

This is an invitation to our table.

• • •

The table, which Andrew crafted ten years ago one autumn afternoon, is made from an Engelmann spruce tree and seats fourteen without brushing elbows (sixteen if we squeeze).

I love this table for all that it offers and represents.

What began as five thick lengths of rough-cut lumber screwed together side-by-side took shape when we brought in the hand planer and orbital sanders from the barn and fired them up. Blond sawdust spun and circled and settled to the smooth wood floor of our dining room. We opened doors and windows, welcoming the late fall air—a mingled mix of split firewood, our overgrown garden, and the sun warming the earth, frozen the night before. Barn cats peeked in the doorway and ran under the table, searching for crumbs. Their thin whiskers gathered sawdust flakes, and their padded feet made a map of tiny tracks.

We sanded, squished wood putty into the cracks and imperfections, and then sanded some more. Our hands, arms, and elbows purred along from one end of the table to the other as the orbital sanders spun round and round, their hum filling the house. Blunt corners were soon smooth and waves became level.

When we turned off the sanders, the quiet was wonderful . . . so soothing as the dust settled in the lowering sunlight. Stiff, we stood up straight, stretched our arms and backs, and removed our safety goggles, smiling at each other like happy raccoons. Sawdust was everywhere, along with quiet little cat tracks . . . like pawprints in the snow. I swept the table and the floor.

Our fingers felt along every plank and edge, checking for rough spots and snags. We sanded more and checked again. Soon the whole table was smooth. We wiped the wood with wet rags, admiring its new softness as the sun warmed the windows.

It was finally ready.

Andrew shook a can of stain, pried open its lid with a screwdriver, and set the can on some newspaper in the middle of the table. We brushed the deep chestnut color across the wood grain, each plank absorbing the rich hue into the fibers of its soul, forever changed. Stroke after stroke, the table took on a whole new character as the intricate designs of the tree were revealed.

We stood at the open door, admiring the table and breathing the fresh air. We circled around, looking at every inch from every angle to see how the grain had taken the stain. After touching up the lighter areas, we let the slow breeze blow across the planks while we ate lunch on the back porch stairs with the garden, corrals, and Mt. Shavano for our view.

After lunch came the first topcoat—the smooth finish upon which many meals would be served and enjoyed—whose sheen would reflect the light of our oil lamp for many years. We laid pages of newspaper on the floor to catch any drips, and I tilted the can: a slow wave spread like warm honey across the dark, dull wood, illuminating tiny details in the grain. Newspaper crinkled under our feet as we brushed thick strokes of shiny satin from one end of the table to the other, around each edge and corner. Imperfections became beautiful character. We delighted in the tree rings unique to each plank—a map of time rolled out as a table. We eventually applied four coats, waiting for each to dry completely. This took days, and we protected the table, like a newborn, from the kids and from any fast cat that might slip in.

A few days later, we woke and ran downstairs like kids on Christmas. Our palms tested the dark sheen: it was dry and smooth as an old church pew. We celebrated with coffee, hesitant to set our mugs on the flawless surface. The table was gorgeous.

• • •

Ten years later, on this cold January day, while onions, garlic, carrots, potatoes, and beef simmer and tender together in a pot on the stove, I gather Christmas and think of how we all have our raw, rough edges. When we meet and mingle our lives together, like a garden harvest softening in broth, we are transformed at the table of life. As we sit together and share our lives and our stories, we are seen, heard, and known—something each human craves. At the table, where we all have a voice, our opinions, intricacies, and character are revealed.

The table is where our family comes together—where we gather to hold hands and bow for a moment of prayer before a meal. When you hold the hand of another, you feel their strength or fragility; soft or weathered skin; thin fingers or thick, calloused hands. You feel a hand that is cozy and warm—or freezing cold. Smells of hay, manure, diesel, sawdust, soil, and soap drift in and out of the chain of linked hands. In that moment, when we pause to pray—when sweaty ball caps and worn cowboy hats come off, and when tired bodies sink into their seats and sigh—thanksgiving and dependence settle in, reminding us of our humanity and our need for community and sustenance.

I pack the forest-green cloth napkins, the snowman plates, and the cookie cutters. As I store away the last of the glass goblets engraved with little white spruce trees, I think of Andrew's mom, Ruthie, and how many of our Christmas traditions came from her. The year before lung cancer stole her from us, she made her famous Christmas Eve Yule log, as usual, though nothing was usual. Having lived a life of riding horses, skiing slopes, hiking mountains, biking trails, and rafting rivers, the shocking cancer made her bones ache as her strong body deteriorated more each day. Those days were similar to, though painfully different from, the way a child grows up before your very eyes.

In her green holly and red berry apron, Ruthie spread the chocolate batter onto a jelly roll pan lined with parchment paper. While it baked and warmed the winter ranch house with its aroma, Ruthie read stories to the littlest grandkids cuddled on the couch in front of the crackling wood stove. When the kids got too squirrely, she set them up with Legos or helped them make paper snowflakes and special name cards for the table. With the ding of the timer came the sound of little shoes scampering across the worn wood floor as the kids hustled to the kitchen where Ruthie helped them sprinkle the spongy cake with powdered sugar.

"Now, watch Grammy," she'd say, as she covered the cake with a thin white dish towel and rolled up the cake from one short end to the other, peeling off the parchment as she went. She lifted the fragile package and unrolled the cake onto a silver platter and removed the towel. Eager eyes watched as she whipped together cream, cocoa, and sugar and spread the sweet layer across the delicate cake. Little fingers swiped the edges of the bowl. She rolled it up one last time—into a log—letting the kids give it one more dusting of powdered sugar and a drizzle of chocolate syrup. I can still see her standing in her apron, silver platter held by hard-working hands, soft auburn hair curled alongside her smile, looking for the best spot to hide the Yule log for her grandkids to find on Christmas Eve.

• • •

But things are not always so simple and beautiful. With life comes hardship, tragedy, and loss. Strong family relationships are a shelter in the midst of the winter storms we all encounter at one time or another, and those relationships are nurtured when we gather together. The table offers a place to recover and reshape as we look to lead more purposeful, peaceful, and healthy lives—lives that are not centered merely on ourselves. As we all share a common hunger and thirst for food and water, the table is a place that not only nourishes the body, but it can be a place that helps nourish the soul.

I place the last of the Christmas decorations in a trunk, lower the old lid and flip the locks down. There is something satisfying about closure. I look out the window and see the dim glow of the sun to the west as the snow blows sideways across the hay fields. The winter day is waning, and soon the kids will be home and hungry. I see the frosty cows lined up in the snow along the path of bright green hay trailing behind Andrew's tractor. Tearing into summer's harvest, the mother cows are ravenous as they are not only feeding themselves but also the calves growing in their bellies. Snow piles on their red backs and blows in their white faces as they fill their stomachs for the long, cold night ahead. I am reminded that the different seasons of life hold their own struggle and beauty while moving toward change and growth.

At the stove, I lift the heavy iron lid from the simmering stew and breathe the steamy goodness. Stirring the hearty cornucopia with an old wooden spoon of Ruthie's mother's, I let broth fill the spoon for a taste. The flavor is good. I'm excited to share this with my family as we gather together and talk about the day and what has happened since we sat together at breakfast.

I remove the glass chimney from the oil lamp and strike a match to light the wick. Its soft glow spreads across the table as the windows darken with the dwindling of day. I shake the match and replace the glass. In the kitchen, I open the big drawer of plates and run my fingers down the smooth white stack, counting seven. I set one at each place along with a folded white napkin and a silver fork. As the temperature drops and the snowflakes slow and settle, I know winter's stars will soon appear. Andrew is still outside, tucking in the ranch for the night—checking on all the animals and their feed and water. It's going to be a cold one, once again.

Chapter 2

Before building the table was even a thought, and before Andrew and I moved to Salida, his parents, Ted and Ruthie, retired and bought the ranch. Composed of two different home places separated by a county road and a few neighbors' fields, the ranch holds much of this valley's history. The original owners of Ted and Ruthie's place along the Arkansas River were Thomas and Elizabeth Cameron. One of the first pioneer families to live in this valley, the Camerons arrived in 1868, eight years before Colorado officially became a state. Purchasing 160 acres for two hundred dollars through the Land Act of 1820, the Camerons also established one of the most senior water rights in the valley. The Cameron Ditch is fed by the North Fork of the South Arkansas River in Maysville and still travels its nine miles to irrigate the ranch today.

In 1868, with the end of the Civil War only three years behind them, the Camerons arrived in the Arkansas Valley where they found no schools and no town. Occupied by the Utes, who had inhabited the land for centuries, the valley was virtually free of fences, farming, and roads—and railroads had not yet reached Colorado Territory (which itself was only seven years old). In the year 1868, Louisa May Alcott published the first volume of her novel *Little Women*; Vice President Andrew Johnson, who succeeded to the presidency after the assassination of Abraham Lincoln, was replaced by Ulysses S. Grant; and John Wesley Powell spent the winter with Ute leaders in Colorado's White River Valley, learning their language and customs.

What became one of many unfortunate steps towards the tragic displacement of the Utes onto reservations, the Ute Treaty of 1868, also known as the Kit Carson Treaty, was signed. The treaty required that the Utes relinquish any claim to land other than the newly established Confederated Ute Territory, which consisted of a large portion of Colorado Territory from its southern border up through Pagosa Springs and onto land near Gunnison, Crested Butte, Basalt, Steamboat, and west to Utah.

It was the beginning of the end to the freedom they had known—a people who, for generations, had camped, migrated, and lived off the land—developing a sacred relationship with their surroundings that was steeped in respect and honor. The land was their source for nourishment and sustenance, and movement and freedom were crucial to their culture and their way of life.

In this valley, cradled by mountains and a river (a boundary line for the Louisiana Purchase), the Camerons created a home for themselves where they raised ten children. With no general store from which to buy supplies, the Camerons built their lives from the ground up. Eventually entering into the cattle business, the Camerons established themselves as a well-known family whose home was a place of shelter for weary travelers—at a time when travel was dangerous and rough.

I think back to when Andrew and I joined Ted and Ruthie on the ranch—how we packed up a U-Haul filled with our belongings, buckled newborn Grace into her car seat, and drove the three and a half hours on smooth roads from Fort Collins to Salida. What a different world it was when the Camerons' long and risky travel took them to an unknown place. But it felt like we were moving for similar reasons—to start a family and a new life in a place where the land would become part of us.

As a fifth-generation Colorado rancher, Andrew has always had a love for the land in his blood. When his landscape architecture career in Fort Collins turned into a farmland development job, we weighed the pros and cons on a paper napkin one night over a chocolate sundae at Denny's, and we made the decision to go. We made the decision to leave the stable nine-to-five job and try a life of ranching.

We moved in, temporarily, with Ted and Ruthie so that we could remodel the other home place about a mile away—the old farmhouse with single-pane windows and no insulation, where you could see your breath inside on a winter's day. Ruthie welcomed me into her home with all my boxes and suitcases. Along with idealistic dreams for my family, I also toted a white plastic bucket that would soon be full of putrid vinegar water and dirty cloth diapers. She shared her laundry room with me—the place where she did her ironing and hung her fun fall sweaters to dry—the place where I dumped the stinking diaper bucket into her clean washing machine every couple of days.

Ruthie became more than my mother-in-law when we moved to the ranch—she became my friend. I thought of the women who had been there before us, and how they must have needed each other just as much, if not more. With a newborn, sleepless nights, mastitis, and no friends in a new place, Ruthie got me out on a walk each day. We'd drive over to see Andrew's progress on the old house, and then she'd help load chubby Grace into the baby carrier strapped to my swollen chest, and we'd walk across the hay fields and hike the steep hill to the top of the mesa. Endorphins—and especially time with Ruthie—helped set my day straight. So began our friendship of walking.

• • •

Tall, thin, and fit, Ruthie taught me how to cook, and eventually we traded-off making dinner each night. I learned how to sauté and how to sip red wine while cooking with it. I learned how to cook without a recipe, how to make savory soups and gooey whole wheat cinnamon rolls, and how to roast a huge homegrown rib roast rubbed with rosemary, garlic, and thyme. I learned the art of grinding whole wheat flour and baking beautiful loaves of brown bread. I watched Ruthie use her worn wooden spoon to stir the yeast as its tiny bubbles rose to the top in a cup of warm water mixed with a smidge of honey. I learned how to use butter instead of margarine, how to fill a stir-fry dish with veggies from the garden, and how to add fresh spinach and garlic to lasagna and spaghetti.

Ruthie liked to pick her garden zucchini tiny, about the size of a pickle; however, I can still see her with an armload of massive zucchinis the size of t-ball bats that had somehow escaped her and would be put into bread. The small squash, both yellow and green, she'd sauté in a dollop of butter and a splash of olive oil until the tender circles were just lightly browned. She'd give her salt and pepper grinders a good twist over the pan and top the garden masterpiece with soft curls of freshly grated Parmesan cheese.

I learned about thread count in sheets, thick towels, and good shampoo—how reading to my daughter was imperative, and that there's truly an art to storytelling. She showed me that a woman sets the tone for her home, and I soon discovered her main tools: she worked out each morning, read her Bible, and prayed before she greeted the world.

I listened to the times when Ruthie stood her ground, and I also watched as she let harsh words, aimed her way, fall short . . . words that she could have easily grabbed and stored to let fester deep within her soul. She introduced me to tea parties, real cream—and the best hairdresser in town—where, even though a rancher's wife, she still had her hair cut every six weeks. I laugh as I think back to how Ruthie and I walked and talked about anything—including sex—and what she learned from the latest *Cosmo* magazine while waiting in line at the grocery. I was so thankful for the times when Ted, with little Gracie sitting in the crook of his arm, would take her on a tour of his yard, letting her tiny fingers examine dangling crabapples and her soft nose sniff tender lilac blossoms, while Ruthie shooed Andrew and me out the door for the night.

After a year and a half of living under Ted and Ruthie's roof, Andrew, Grace, and I moved into the little farmhouse. We settled into our new place and into our new routines. Even though I loved having our own home, I missed living with my in-laws, though they were only a mile away. Thankfully, Ruthie and I still went on our walks.

She often invited us for dinner, and it was something I looked forward to all day. No matter the mess in the world or the mess in my life, there was something settling about walking through her door. The smell of slow-cooked pot roast with sautéed garlic and portobello mushrooms would greet us, along with her voice—so cheerful and welcoming—so full of love. She made everyone in her life feel important and cherished.

This gift of hospitality spans generations and cultures—and also seems to run deep in ranching tradition. In their incredible book about the history of the Arkansas Valley, *Under the Angel of Shavano*, George G. Everett and Dr. Wendell F. Hutchinson, historic ranchers themselves, describe Elizabeth Cameron's table as a well-known place of respite for newcomers and folks passing through:

The Camerons' dining room was fairly large. The table was wide, made of rough cut lumber, but had been hand-planed and was long enough to seat eight people on each side and one, sometimes two, at each end. Then a long bench made of native lumber was on each side and a short bench at each end. At most meals the table was full and at times a second table was set.

Decades later, on the same land, Ruthie brought family together—her four children and many grandchildren—at her own table. Whether it was Easter egg hunts with platters full of ham, an enormous Thanksgiving turkey with the reading of Abraham Lincoln's proclamation, or the Christmas Eve Yule log, she taught us that family is important. One of seven siblings herself, she knew that family conflict could strong-arm love and eventually win. She was determined that a family that can gather, pray, and eat together will more likely stay together, making the words "Family Dinner" represent more than just a meal.

Each caught somewhere between harmony and conflict, we would all show up: brothers, sisters-in-law, husbands, wives, and cousins. When we walked through her door, we not only kicked off our boots, but we kicked off the pride, the hurt, the resentment, the anger, and the comparison—and came in as family. Somehow, she let us know that there was something bigger than our pain—that life had more meaning to it than finances, possessions, status, and emotions. She had this way of greeting us at her door and seeing the looks on our faces and judging what the car ride over was like. Her persistent love, unending joy, and wise perspective somehow dissipated awkward moments and distracted us from disagreements.

Hungry and thirsty people coming together for a meal provides common ground—a place of need from which none of us are exempt.

As we gathered around her table, Ruthie's prayer for the meal always ended with the words, "And Father, keep us in Your ways, and make us hungry and thirsty for You."

Over the years, Ruthie's prayers also saw me through the birth of three more babies. She continued to be my friend and mentor as I grew up and created my own home and habits. She taught me to pack up my then four kids under seven and take them on hikes to high mountain lakes to help combat the monotony of motherhood. She would leave little treats along the trail—a rainbow of Skittles for chubby little fingers to grab and gobble.

As Andrew and I got busy with serving at church, she warned us not to be too busy doing good things that we left our own family in the dust. Taking walks, riding horses, baking, bike riding, attending soccer games and kicking the ball around, and reading hours of stories—I watched her make her own family a priority, connecting with each of us in her own special way.

• • •

Ruthie's roots of hospitality and love for family were cultivated at her parents' table on their ranch just over the Continental Divide in Carbondale, Colorado, where they raised seven children, tons of hay, and hundreds of cattle for over sixty years. Breakfast was served at the same time every morning, and if you missed it, well, you missed it. Lunch would eventually come. At breakfast, Ruthie's parents, whom we all called Gammy and Gan, had their routine. Gammy, an older version of Ruthie, flipped pancakes on the griddle plugged in near her end of their long table, and Gan read from the Bible at his. Anywhere from two to twenty others filled the space in between, along with hard-boiled eggs, Boneset tea, sausage from the latest buck or bull elk, hot cereal, and always a berry smoothie.

They were the strongest team, bookends at their table, who together created a legacy of ranching for their family. Gammy followed along in her own Bible, spatula in hand, as Gan's gentle but
strong voice shared wisdom from the fragile pages he turned with his
thick fingers, gnarled from decades of holding an irrigation shovel
and tending to generations of calves. His head was two-toned: pale
and bald on top, as if forever shielded by his cowboy hat, and well-
weathered from his nose on down to the collar of his striped Western
shirt with its pearl snaps.

Conversations were lively around their table, with opinions being
thrown every which way and old ranching stories never in short supply—like the one about the time when Gan roped a runaway cow from
the hood of a police car in downtown Denver during the National Western Stock Show. Not only were they full of crazy stories, but they were
also full of sound advice. Married for over sixty-six years, they preached
the three Cs for a strong marriage: communication, commitment, and
consideration—words Andrew and I have reminded ourselves of many
times over the years.

Sitting at Gammy and Gan's table fed both body and soul, and the
time spent with them continues to inspire Andrew and me every day as
we try to live out the love, hospitality, and kindness they shared with
each person who walked in their door and to each animal who grazed
their fields.

One of the people who visited their ranch annually was an elderly
Norwegian man named Leif Hovelsen. In his eighties when we met,
and always in a bright blue-and-white Nordic sweater that matched his
eyes, Leif stayed at the ranch with Gammy and Gan for a month each
winter. A sort of peacekeeping ambassador to the nations, he studied
and wrote in his room upstairs with a breath-taking view of snow-
covered Mt. Sopris.

Though the spelling of his name looks as if it would be pronounced like the English word "leaf," the Norwegian pronunciation of Leif actually sounds like the English word "life." Andrew and I loved hearing Gan greet the jolly, white-haired, red-faced man as he walked down the stairs: "Good morning, Leif!" As if he were welcoming the new day itself.

As a young man during WWII, Leif worked with the Norwegian underground resistance against the Nazi regime. Betrayed by a coworker, Leif was arrested by the Gestapo for smuggling radio parts out of Norway and was taken to two prison camps. Leif's time of imprisonment was torturous and included four months in solitary confinement. In his book, *Out of the Evil Night*, Leif tells the story of when the Allied forces arrived and liberated the camp. There was a short time of transition when the guards became the prisoners and the prisoners became the guards. Leif found himself guarding the men who had made his life miserable. During that time, on a particularly hot day, a former captor pleaded with him for a glass of water—so Leif brought a bucket of water and threw it in the man's face, causing all the former prisoners to cheer.

But, deep down, Leif was not proud of what he had done, and his conscience eventually won:

> *I wanted to fight for right and justice, but this was lust for revenge. I got to thinking about the Gestapo agent who had treated me the worst and it suddenly came to me: 'Tell him you forgive him.'*
>
> *When it came time for my guard duty, I summoned him and we stood face to face. He knew me and his glance was uneasy. I looked him in the eye and said the words that had come to me. He shook all over but did not say anything, and I put him back in his cell. Later he was condemned to death and executed.*

In a 2001 letter to one of Andrew's cousins, who asked Leif exactly what his job was, Leif wrote:

My main job is working with people for the sole task of bringing reconciliation and peace to our torn and conflict-filled world. If you want to change the world, the best place is to start with yourself! Thus, I had to start with myself. It is never easy but always a necessity. It took a long time for me to realize that the evil in the world is also in me, in my own human nature. When I recognized the bitterness and hate that I had in my own heart against the Germans and particularly the Gestapo officer who had tortured me, I realized that I had all the evil forces of violence and war within myself as I had accused and condemned the Germans of.

When I learned to forgive, I became a free man.

The key to reconciliation, I have learned, is to forgive and be forgiven. Thus, the major task I am trying to fulfill is to bring the experience of reconciliation, peace, inner freedom, joy, and love wherever it is needed in the world and wherever I can be used. It is a work that demands unlimited patience, unlimited care, and unlimited love. Thus, for me, it cannot be done without the Grace and sustaining power that God is daily granting me.

Leif's joyful countenance, his faith, his efforts at peace, and his story all inspired Andrew to name our youngest son after him. While pregnant with Life, and away for an anniversary trip while my mom, also named Ruth, and my stepdad, Rodney, kept the other kids, Andrew and I discussed this change from the original name we had picked if the baby I carried was a boy.

"But Ben is so normal and easy to spell," I told Andrew.

"Then let's make it easy to spell. Let's just spell it like it sounds."

And Life was born.

When a child comes into this world, his parents do not know what his story will be—what joys and sorrows will come his way. We had no idea that Life's childhood would be marked by tremendous physical pain.

When Life was born, the questions began—along with the tilting heads and drawn eyebrows—as people asked twice, clarifying his name. When he grew into a toddler and adults leaned over to ask Life his name, he'd answer, "Wife."

Recently, I asked Life if he likes his name and he told me, "I do. I like it because everyone knows who I am."

And I like it, too, because it continues to tell one man's story of hope and forgiveness that began in the horror of the Holocaust. And it's always fun to tell Life good morning when he comes downstairs to sit at the table.

Chapter 3

Before the table came to be, Andrew and I grew our family in the old farmhouse. I love that old house. My water broke in that old house; we brought brand new babies home to that old house; we raised our two boys and two of our girls in that old house; we buried our first dog, Moses, under the old cottonwood tree outside that old house; our grandparents, who have all since passed on, visited us in that old house; and we learned how to farm and ranch while living in that old house.

Eventually, the old house grew smaller and smaller as our family grew bigger and bigger. With four children and one bathroom, it felt tight. Naomi, then eight years old, spoke for us all when she said, "I can't even poop in peace!" When a deal on five acres adjacent to the ranch came up, we grabbed it.

Andrew and I began designing our dream home together. Each evening, after the kids were all finally tucked in for the night, we'd roll out our house plans on a hand-me-down dining room table and reassess our design, making little adjustments here and there. We were thrilled at the thought of having a big house where our kids could invite their friends and where we could have company come and stay. And so, less than a year later, we had our dream home.

But it didn't start out so dreamy.

On the cold, gray January moving day, when anyone from our church with a truck had come to help, I sat, alone, on the empty wood floor in the girls' bedroom at the old house—surrounded by nothing but dust bunnies and random under-the-bed things like hair ties, curled-up stickers, and hidden candy wrappers. I was sad to leave. That old house had memories.

That old house and I, we had history together.

I cried as I swept and mopped (hiding from the big new house across the field—with all its bathrooms and empty walls and piles of boxes to unpack). My dad, Frank, and his brother, my Uncle Dan, were moving into the old house from the place they rented in town, so I knew it would be in very good hands. But I was overwhelmed. I wanted to stay back, but my family was no longer there, and they were my life. Besides, I had a beautiful new house to move into. I knew I had to grow up and leave. We would all need beds for the night, and at some point, dinner. I was being sentimental and ridiculous, and I knew it.

I stood and dusted myself off. I finished cleaning, said goodbye to my old friend, and closed the door. As I drove west along the edge of the hay field toward the brown stucco three-story house, with the same enormous mountains for a backdrop and its new driveway filled with trucks and people unloading box springs, mattresses, dressers, tables, and chairs, I looked in the rearview mirror. I couldn't help but think that I had left part of me behind.

The new house stood tall, unfriendly, and unknown. My dream-house? Sort of.

The kids loved the space, and, I had to admit, having more than one bathroom was amazing. We settled in. Silverware found drawers, clothes found hangers, and pictures found walls. I washed the row of tall southern windows in our big dining and living room and looked out at our new yard of rough dirt littered with tile scraps, drywall paper, insulation fluff, plywood splinters, and roofing debris. Beyond lay the clean hay fields, wide-open and free, with the gorgeous snow-covered peaks in the distance. I often looked back across the field from our new front porch. I missed the spruce trees that grew in the big yard inside the white picket fence—the ones planted in honor of the birth of our, then, four kids—Grace, Naomi, Abe, and Life—all two years apart, from eleven years old down to five.

With each passing day, the new house began to feel more like home.

• • •

And with each year that passed, Salida itself began to feel more like home, too. Unless you've lived there your whole life, it can take a while to feel as though you are "from" a place.

With almost 6,000 full-time residents—close to the same population in the 1800s when newcomers came to the area with hopes of making a go at farming, ranching, or mining—Salida has become a place where many now come to get away from the daily grind. Salida, whose number one industry is now tourism, offers some of the best mountain climbing, fly-fishing, mountain biking, and whitewater rafting in the West.

Highlighted by *Sunset*, *Outside*, and *Vogue* magazines, Salida has been "found," once again. And for good reason. This town has award-winning schools, an historic downtown filled with art galleries, Monarch Mountain ski resort only twenty minutes up Monarch Pass, and endless recreational opportunities. The Continental Divide Trail winds along the tops of the towering mountains to the west, and the Arkansas

River flows right through Salida's famous water park where the nation's oldest whitewater festival draws thousands each summer.

With only four stoplights, Salida has a new hospital and is host to a Colorado Mountain College campus. Many people are moving to this valley because they can work remotely; or others, like us, come to start a business of their own—like the famous Sweetie's Sandwich Shop, or the charcuterie specialist The Biker & The Baker, or Mo Burrito—all three started by one family; or the paddleboard company Bad Fish; or The Beekeeper's Honey Boutique (some of whose bees we are lucky enough to host on the ranch). Retirees are coming to build their dream homes in this small town, and families are flocking to Salida with its four-day school week and Friday ski bus to Monarch.

With Colorado being one of the fastest growing states, and Salida recently deemed Colorado's fastest growing town, property values have increased exponentially. Just west of town sits our family's 750-acre ranch, which makes up one-third of the irrigated pasture in what is known to area realtors as the "Golden Triangle," the shape created by the two mountain ranges and the river. Amidst all the good growth, however, there looms over this valley a shadow that's building—and it's getting harder to ignore.

• • •

One fall a few years back, on a twenty-three degree morning, a nasty wind was howling when Andrew blew in the door and shut out the cold. He took off his wool cap with ear flaps, revealing his white forehead and weathered cheeks, just like Gan's. He'd been feeding hay to the calves we'd weaned the week before on another horribly blustery morning when we met up with Andrew's brother, Seth, and his wife, Susie, and their family who, after we were ten years in, joined us in the ranching business.

That weaning day, bundled up in Carhartt jackets and muck boots, we all met at the corrals at the old house and went out on foot, horses, and ATVs onto a 300-acre pasture. We talked and joked as we gathered our, then, herd of 175 pregnant mother cows, with last year's calves still at their side. We separated the protesting mamas into one pen and their raucous calves into another. It was a deafening process as they called for each other. We let the mamas back out into their pasture and moved the calves into an adjacent field—the two separated by a woven wire fence. This "gentle weaning" allows them to touch noses as the calves gain their independence and the mamas' bodies give their energy to the new calves growing inside their big bellies. With strong maternal instincts, the constant calling from the herd filled the valley for three days and nights, each calf echoing their mama's desperate calls. Eventually, all quieted down as the calves took to the hay and water, and the mamas' milk bags finally stopped filling.

A week later, when Andrew came through the door, the ranch was again peaceful except for the howl of the wind. I was cleaning up the breakfast dishes and the kids were at school.

"You won't believe who bought Willy's," he said, his glasses fogging up as he set his work gloves on the counter.

Willy's was a 380-acre ranch between our place and town—one of the few remaining working ranches left in the Golden Triangle. A big chunk of land, with one finger extending alongside a portion of the south edge of our ranch, Willy's place had been for sale for months, with a four-million-dollar price tag. Several years before, when Willy lost his wife, whose family's roots ran deep in Salida's ranching community, his heart for ranching began to wane; but he continued on, working alongside his dad who had grown up ranching in the valley.

Then, a few years later, when his dad passed away, Willy realized his life of ranching was coming to a close: "I couldn't ranch with my wife and I couldn't ranch with my dad—and I knew I couldn't do it alone." Having no children of his own, and two stepsons who did not want to run the ranch, Willy told me, "I could stay and ranch, and not make any money, and work hard knowing that when I die it'll be sold the next day."

When Willy's place first went on the market, we thought to pool Andrew's four siblings together and gather the $400,000 it would take to buy the finger and keep a developer from lining the edge of our hay field with houses. However, between our four families, there are seventeen children to raise, and hopefully send to college, so the thought of combining checkbooks was short-lived. The $400,000 was in no one's budget.

The $400,000 was in no one's budget except for the developer who has been buying up Salida's land for high-end or high-density subdivisions. Often with no history or emotional ties to a property, a developer can come in and make millions beyond the asking price by dividing and developing what others have cared for and poured their lives into.

When you spend time with a place, take care of a place—and the place takes care of you—its pulse becomes part of yours: the way the sun sets and rises in a slightly different place with each season; the way a spring storm blows in with a fury and leaves just as quickly; the way the soil cracks with drought and sighs with water; the way the land provides shelter and sustenance for the animals; and the way peace and solace are offered for the worried, crowded soul.

"People asked me why I didn't just develop it myself, but I couldn't. For so long, we'd made so many sacrifices to keep it—I just didn't have the heart to do it," Willy told me. "I got a check, and that was that."

When I asked Willy why he didn't first apply for a conservation easement—an official way of preserving agricultural land forever—he told me he had tried. But after investing eighty-thousand dollars and two years of his life in the process, Willy was told that a conservation easement on his place would not bring full market value because it could not be annexed into the city of Salida.

With value based largely upon the development potential of the land at stake, conservation easements can provide a fair compromise between concerned citizens wanting to conserve agricultural land and the landowners themselves. Non-profit land trusts all over the nation are working to conserve farm and ranchlands and wildlife habitat. One of our local land trusts, the Central Colorado Conservancy, "works with ranchers to help them continue their operations and ensure they can pass it on to the next generation. Ranching requires tremendous physical endurance and smart business planning. We help ranchers find alternatives to selling their land for development." Similarly, sponsored grant writers, new funding, and large tax credits have recently become available to landowners to help offset the average $70,000 ticket-price for creating an easement.

Conservation easements pay ranchers to give up any future developmental rights of the acres put into an easement, while still allowing the ranchers to own and work their land. Ranchers are paid good money for these easements, often providing financially for one more decade of the lifestyle they love. The money made from conservation easements can also be used to "buy out" other family members who may want the value from the land they don't personally use. As always, things are never clean-cut and easy, especially when multiple family members are involved—as is usually the case with farms and ranches. Everyone comes to the table with differing perspectives, timelines, needs, ideas, and emotional ties.

Unfortunately, when land is put into a conservation easement, its resale value often drops drastically since that land can no longer be developed. Some local ranchers we know regret putting their land into a conservation easement years ago. They had no idea this area would grow as it has and that land values would increase so dramatically. The amount they made from their conservation easement is a small fraction of what they could sell their place for today. To help avoid that scenario, some ranchers are putting large portions of their land into conservation easements while keeping the prime development acres separate.

I have to admire the folks organizing and raising funds for these land trusts. Their desire to preserve open space, working lands, and wildlife habitat is commendable. The more the shadow builds—the more agricultural land is developed—the more I am thankful for the time, energy, and money that is being invested to protect the way of life that I cherish. But there still lives the real struggle of remaining in agriculture while knowing there are millions that could be made by selling out. It's not an easy decision, and I am glad that our family has not yet come to that crossroad.

Though I know one day we probably will—as our family's ranch is owned by varying combinations of the four adult siblings, their spouses, and all the kids. Maybe someone in the family, someday, will ask, "Are you guys done playing cowboy yet? Can I get my cut from the ranch? Have you seen what it's worth?" They are partly right, and partly wrong. While we have been "playing cowboy," we have also been protecting water rights, preserving land, and increasing the value of the family investment. It's easy to see how conservation easements can help soothe tensions between families when some want to stay and ranch while others would, understandably, like their cash for other endeavors.

• • •

Having known, from afar, Walt Harder of Harder Real Estate and Development since our kids were little, I felt comfortable walking into his downtown office to ask him a few questions about his new development at Willy's: Timber Creek Ranch. I wondered what he had planned for the land and how he could reconcile in his heart and mind the development of some of the last agricultural land in the valley. Was there even any reconciliation to be had—or was it all about the money? Walt was out of the office, but one of his kind co-workers suggested I email him.

Walt emailed me back within the hour—giving me a better understanding of how he can accomplish so much in such a small town. With several high-density developments inside the city limits, Walt is changing the landscape of Salida as we know it. In his email, he said he would be happy to meet with me. I laughed out loud when I reached the end of his email where his pronouns read, "Your Majesty/His Royal Highness."

That figures, I thought to myself.

Additionally, the John Muir quote beneath his business logo helped fortify the growing judgments in my mind: "And into the forest I go, to lose my mind and find my soul."

It's interesting when people bring conflicting ideas and philosophies to the table. Deep-seated beliefs give rise to heated conversations. Politics, religion, climate change, money, and morality—such topics can quickly stir the most sedentary of conversations into hours of passionate pleas and speeches by those wanting to be heard and understood. In the absence of listening, as we plan and interrupt with our next words, it's all too easy to see the other side as wrong and flawed.

Regardless of our preconceived notions, we must give each person at the table a voice—it's the hospitality of humanity. Motivated by my morning reading that day, "A fool takes no pleasure in understanding, but only in expressing his opinion," I drove to meet Walt, in an effort to better understand the perspective of a developer.

He welcomed me with a kind smile, and I followed him past a huge conference table where I saw a bowl of my favorite Andes Chocolate Mints. I didn't even consider taking one. As a rancher, I felt as if I had truly entered enemy territory. Surprisingly, Walt's office felt very homey, filled with pictures of his family and the places special to them.

Sitting across from each other at his desk, we revisited our families, realizing we both have adopted daughters. I winced as I dug unsuccessfully in my bag for a pen and was horrified that I had to ask to borrow one of his.

"Sure," he said, handing me a pen, "I've got lots of those around here." I flipped open my notebook, thinking of all the treaties and contracts that have been signed over the years by pens—some good and some destructive.

"So, Timber Creek Ranch. I'll start at the beginning for you," he said, leaning back in his chair.

Walt went on to explain the process of purchasing the 360 acres from Willy for three million dollars, after having had it on the market at one time for as much as five million, with no takers. "Willy told me that I should just buy it—that I'd make millions—but the idea of developing it twisted my stomach."

I listened.

"I bought it right before Covid hit, and it turned out to be the best deal I've ever made in my life. I wasn't sure what to do with it at first, so I moved to the land. I loved walking it, riding it, feeling it."

He went on to explain that he tried to apply for a conservation easement with Colorado Parks and Wildlife (CPW), as CPW and Willy's place have a shared history with the need for irrigation water from the historic Harrington Ditch. Wanting enough money from the easement to buy Willy's ranch and live in peace, Walt invested "mountains of paperwork and tons of time and money, but, in the end, CPW simply didn't want to pay for it."

So, Walt came to a happy medium he could live with: a conservation subdivision.

Sounding like an oxymoron to me, I learned that a conservation subdivision allows a developer to create higher density housing than is usually allowed, in return for preserving an equal number of acres. Normally in an area where only two-acre lots (or larger) are allowed, Walt created a cluster of 68 one-acre lots while preserving over one hundred acres of irrigated land. Each lot will have its own septic and will share a well with three to four other lots. As Walt explained the layout, the idea of almost seventy new septics that close together was a little nauseating, especially with all the future wells so close in proximity.

He printed off a copy of the land plat for me and set it on his desk, facing me. As I oriented myself on the page, I found the circle of the center pivot—and the sixty-eight new lots, looking like little Scrabble pieces all pushed to one side of the board. I asked if the homes would be identical to each other, or if the design was up to the owner. He explained that each homeowner would be able to choose their own design: "Although we don't want to see ugly—we want to keep it western ranch prairie, with colors found in nature." I thought of Walt's high-density developments in town, with their uniform, tightly-packed units, and asked how his development ideas could differ so dramatically from one place to another.

"It depends on the feel and the culture of the space you're working in. Those are high-density lots served by municipalities. Here we are working towards the preservation of a farming and ranching culture," he said.

As I digested the information, Walt explained that during his preservation efforts, he and CPW eventually came to an agreement about the water. "They have a passion for the land like I do," he said. Knowing there had been a water relationship between the 360 acres and the local fish hatchery for decades, Walt said he and CPW both realized that "I couldn't do it without them and they couldn't do it without me." Through the balancing and sharing of their water rights based upon seasons and usage, a sweet spot seemed to have been found.

In his effort to increase the amount of irrigated land, Walt installed gated irrigation pipe and removed rabbit brush on old fields, bringing back to life many acres of open space that had not been irrigated for years. Farthest away from the clustered lots, that newly irrigated land borders the long finger of land that reaches along the south border of our ranch—where Walt also created 5 thirty-five-acre lots overlooking our hay fields, one of them being his own. "Those five lots essentially paid for the whole ranch," he said.

I thought of the $400,000 we tried to come up with to buy the finger, and I wished we would have made some sacrifices. But then again, it was hard to justify investing that kind of money into something with little or no return, as we would not have bought the land to develop it—and its topography doesn't lend itself to being an irrigated hay field.

In an effort to preserve the ranching tradition of the land, Walt replaced the old center pivot sprinkler from 1971 with a new one and contracted with a local rancher to irrigate, harvest, and graze the conserved land. Ranching operations will continue as usual, it seems, on about half of the historically irrigated ground. And the rest . . . it will be filled with houses and septics and streets. And lights at night.

It is a bittersweet compromise.

I thanked my new neighbor, shook his hand, and left his office with mixed emotions. Walt was kind and honest and he answered all of my questions and more, giving me a lot of his time. Though I wasn't excited about it, I came away with a better understanding of the project and the heart behind it.

It just is what it is.

The land was up for sale, and Walt bought it at the perfect time for a fantastic price. Now he's doing what he feels is the best for the land—while making millions—just like Willy said he would. Walt's porch light shines at night in this peaceful valley, as does mine; however, it's hard to picture over seventy more porch lights between here and town, in what has mostly been a dark space beneath the brilliant night sky.

As I drove home, I thought of the changes this valley has seen, how there used to be no ownership of land at all, no sections, townships, ranges, deeds, or titles. No grid across the native soil—a land as open as the sky. And I thought of all the changes to come, all the new mailboxes that will go up, and how this valley will look in twenty, thirty, forty years from now. I know I am not the first person who has wondered if, in the future, we'll still be able to see the stars at night.

But who am I to complain? Were Andrew and I not on the road once, with our possessions packed—ready to begin a new life in this valley—ready to live off the land? Although the exodus these days feels different, as no one can feasibly afford to buy land on which to make a living farming or ranching in this valley anymore—the prices are just too high. It's a different sort of living off the land that people seek now: there is a need to find new life in the land, to breathe deeply amidst the open spaces and wide skies, to play in the river and explore the mountains, while making a living through other means.

I slowed around a biker who waved as I passed. Our hay fields came into view where the herd grazed, not a care in the world. A hawk flew and found a perch on top of a power pole. My thoughts were quieted by beauty.

Chapter 4

On the town-side of Willy's, until recently, was Ron and Jo Jones' place. Coming from town, the Jones' was the first ranch to greet drivers and bikers and runners as they passed Frantz Lake and entered the agricultural corridor between town and the mountains. Ron and Jo had raised fifty pairs of Texas Longhorn cows on their eighty acres for over forty-five years. With thick horns that spanned almost eight feet, those bovine mamas were quite a sight—all spotted brown and white, balancing their burdens as they grazed.

The year before, Ron and Jo surprised us all and sold a thirty-five acre portion of their ranch to a group of developers, and soon after sold the rest of their historic home place to a single buyer who divided it up himself. On every trip to town, I see that looming shadow of development crawling closer to home as more wells are drilled and more foundations are dug.

I wondered if the Joneses were sick or tired or dying or broke—or some combination? What else would cause such dedicated ranchers to sell out? If they needed the cash, I wondered why they didn't apply for a conservation easement?

In the first months following the Jones' sale, a fence went up, dividing the home place from the coming subdivision. One side held the massive Longhorn cows with their miniature copies, grazing and running and playing in the summer grass; while the other ground, no longer irrigated, began to wither, brown, and die. A new sign appeared: *Heritage Properties for Sale on the Longhorn Ranch Subdivision.* The sign displayed the lay of the subdivision with its new road winding past the fifteen lots for sale. That week, someone monkey-wrenched the sign's wooden legs, and it fell flat on the dying ranchland. A fancy metal sign soon stood next to the repaired wooden sign. Then a realtor's sign appeared. Next popped up a big metal box, host to fifteen new mailbox slots.

I used to play small-town volleyball with Jo, a scrappy tough woman with a smile as wide as the horns on her cattle. Jo was a part of the "Fanatics" team, and on the other side of the net, Ruthie, Susie, and I played on the "Wranglers" team—with our unofficial t-shirt mascot being a saddled horse with a caption that read, *Does this saddle make my butt look big?*

Jo and Ron bought hay from us for years, as they used their irrigated ground for year-round rotational grazing; and before my first-ever flock of chickens started laying, I bought perfect white eggs from Jo for a dollar a dozen.

I dropped by to visit one day, parking near their tall, historic home. Rumored to have once been a stage stop, tiny sunshines of dandelions bloomed across the thick lawn and into the hay field. Laundry flapped on Jo's clothesline as she greeted me at the door. Donning her trademark visor and wide smile, Jo declined her usual hug as she was protecting a shoulder she'd broken while out with the cows the week before. I followed her and her cattle dog into the living room where Ron sat in a big easy chair, his oxygen machine pumping and hissing in the corner. The clear tubing traveled across the room to his nose where a cannula rested like an equator between his glasses and his cotton-ball mustache that adorned his smile. Jo offered me a seat next to her on the couch. The couple who sat before me looked gray and frail as ashes—but I knew better. Ron had just returned from a Rotary meeting to which he had ridden his recumbent bike, oxygen and all, and Jo had just come in from checking their cows in the field.

They asked about Andrew, the kids, and the cows—as if they were interchangeable. We talked archery season, chickens, and eggs (which now bring six dollars per dozen). Soon, talk of the sale surfaced.

"Well," Ron said, "I retired five years earlier than I should have from being a dentist, and my health, well, I couldn't keep up with the eighty acres of irrigating with side rolls. That's a lot of work. We're getting old. Up until a few years ago, you couldn't sell land around here. The local ranchers may have paid one hundred dollars an acre for it, maybe not."

"It was hard for me," Jo said. "We heard from everyone: 'That was a terrible thing to do. You ruined the whole area.' They asked us what right we had to sell our land."

I was feeling ashamed for the hard time I had been giving them in the confines of my car.

"I'd say, 'It is our private property.' And they'd come back at me, and pretty soon, I'd say, 'Well, go to hell.'" Ron laughed.

When I asked about a conservation easement, they explained that they had tried a while back, but the details and costs of the easement were insurmountable. The land trust they were working with had tried to tie their small request for an easement to the larger one that Willy had been pursuing for his place at the time; unfortunately, red-tape and finances stalled the entire conservation process for both ranches.

"Did you ever wonder, 'What will the neighbors say?'" I asked Ron and Jo.

Jo shook her head. "Can you imagine how prohibitive that would be for private property owners if our neighbors could decide whether we could sell or not?"

Ron chimed in: "I'd say, 'If you don't like it, give us the money and you do what you want. Oh, and don't forget to irrigate!'" They both laughed. "Everyone says, 'But it's so pretty!' Yeah, it's pretty because we irrigate it for three hours a day all summer."

"We're out there raking or harrowing or irrigating, and 1,900 bikers go by and then there's the joggers, and they're lovin' it, and they wave at us," Jo waved her hand. "They love it for the view, and they love to see us out there working."

I thought to myself that I am one of those bikers, joggers, and wavers who love the view.

"We're workin' for them," Ron said.

"We've laughed at how many people stop out here and take pictures of our cows. Hundreds of people. We even had an art class in our driveway. They asked permission and stuff, but anyways, someone said, 'Jo, don't you wish you could charge for that?' Well, how in the heck could I ever do that?"

"Something needs to be done to help keep us around," Ron said. "Agriculture is just falling by the wayside. Someday, somebody's going to get hungry and say something."

"Yeah. Where's the beef?" Jo said, and we all laughed, because sometimes that's all there is to do.

• • •

I left the Jones' place and headed west toward home—past the Longhorns, past the repaired sign, past the new neighborhood road—and my thoughts were a little softer toward the sale by my neighbors. I thought about how my own porch light was once a new light, too, in this valley. Thoughts of our family's ranch, my graying hair, and our future retirement grazed in my mind as I passed the growing lines of new mailboxes along the dirt roads. I thought of when our mailbox was new.

Andrew and I were once newcomers here, too.

I drove past Willy's, so open and free, knowing it would soon be changed forever. I looked up at Mt. Shavano and Mt. Ouray, both steady and unchanging. I thought of the Ute chiefs for whom they were named: how Chief Shavano stood firm against the invasion of the pioneers, and how Chief Ouray—who worked to make peace between the Utes and the federal government—had signed the Kit Carson Treaty in 1868.

I thought of what the valley must have looked and felt like before the Pony Express was even an idea. Before porch lights shone in the night. Before roads crisscrossed the land. Before dams held back the rivers. Before horse-drawn plows turned up the soil. Before miles of irrigation ditches were dug. Before the people who migrated through this valley never returned. Before those who once called this place home were displaced. Before we arrived.

Growth brings turmoil of varying degrees, and it always brings change.

• • •

One day, soon after my visit with the Joneses, I sorted through the mail on our kitchen counter and noticed an official-looking letter addressed to the legal name of our family's ranch. Someone had researched our place on the county database.

My skeptical fingers opened the envelope. A "Land Specialist" from a Fortune 500 company, along with "one of the world's leading power companies," asked to meet with us about leasing or selling the ranch to use as a solar energy farm. Offering up to $1,500 per acre, we could lease the fields for well over half a million dollars each year with no work on our part. The company was working to be completely carbon-free by 2050 (80% carbon-free by 2030), and they wanted us to partner with them.

I thought of the awesome technology behind solar power and the capability it has to make a huge impact on the energy crisis faced by our nation. I shuddered at the idea of looking out to see a field of solar panels shadowing the ground instead of cows and alfalfa plants. I've driven through agricultural communities and come upon fields I had thought, from a ways off, were patterned with beautifully plowed furrows of rich soil—only to drive closer to see black rows of a massive crop of solar panels.

The letter in my hand reminded me of the hemp grower who had recently offered us $90,000 each year to grow hemp on two of our fields—and how hard we work each year to match that.

The dollars can be tempting at times.

However, Ron Jones' words ran through my head: "The character and quality of this lifestyle makes it worthwhile. If you can put food on the table, I think most agricultural folks are happy with that."

Another local rancher, same vintage as the Joneses, had recently sold fifteen acres of his land to a solar company. I was curious to see what it might look like if we took the Land Specialist up on his offer, so I went for a visit. Bordering Highway 285—which is lined almost completely on both sides by previous ranchlands now developed into subdivisions—the fifteen acres was part of one of the last working ranches along the highway. With the towering mountains to the west and trophy homes to the east, the ranch looked claustrophobic. I was starting to relate.

I parked next to the "solar farm" under construction. I was surprised when the sight made my chest tighten—surprised to feel my deep-rooted emotions about land manifest themselves physically. Several men in hard hats scurried up and down the rows of solar panels that stood about five feet off the ground. The shade on the dirt beneath each panel felt part of the larger shadow of development. The new crop of technology, with roots of black cables hanging down, would soon be planted into the grid.

Oriented flat and looking straight up during construction, the panels were designed to follow the sun as it moves across the sky, like a field of sunflowers. A perimeter of tall posts stood ready for an eight-foot high wire fence. The whole sight was too bright on the eyes—and too dark on the heart. Though I had often praised the idea of solar energy, I hadn't realized how its physical presence could change the aesthetics of a landscape so close to home. The nearest house in the subdivision bordering the acres of solar panels was just the width of a dirt road away, and it had a For Sale sign posted out front. Its view, once pastoral, was now marked by giant-sized computer chips, all organized like a game of *Memory*.

I drove up the driveway at the north end of the ranch, about a half mile away, to see if anyone was around for a chat. Bret Collyer waved from his yard. I introduced myself and asked about the solar project.

"Come on in."

I followed him through his yard and past a donkey standing in the grass. Bret opened the door to his old cabin and apologized, "Sorry for the mess. We live outside." I smiled and nodded, as I knew that struggle well.

Bald and about my age, Bret runs cattle and raises hay together with his wife's family. He explained how his own family used to ranch on the other side of the highway—until the drought of 2002 hit hard—

and they were forced to sell. That former ranch is now a subdivision almost completely built out. Bret offered me a seat in his living room, and soon his wife, Jenna, joined us.

"We talk all the time about how sad it is to see all this [development] happening," he told me. "And the kind of people who are moving here, most seem to have no appreciation for it. They must think we are just supposed to maintain their open space while they pedal their bikes up and down the road in their spandex and cuss at us when we're driving our tractors."

I listened, as both a rancher and a biker.

"That subdivision goes in, and that subdivision goes in," Jenna said, pointing east and west. "It's like we're getting squeezed out." She looked at Bret and said, "But then I suppose my family contributed, too, because they sold that to the solar farm." She turned to me. "They had medical bills piling up, you know. People are just trying to make it work."

"You can't own a view," Bret added.

"When you look across your fields to the solar panels, they don't bother you?" I asked.

"Not at all," he said. "It was an unproductive field that used to be green, but with all the wells drilled for the subdivisions around here, the ground water is drying up and there's no more seep to keep that field green." Bret looked straight at me. "It's better than more neighbors."

He explained that for a very brief time their closest neighbor had been shooting their horses with paint balls and setting off fireworks, which sent the horses through the barbed wire fence. I winced at the thought. We talked about our cattle, the recent snow, and the new coffee shop in town.

As I walked back outside, past the donkey, and through the gate to my car, I eyed the paintballer's place just over the fence. It was so *close*.

Building upon building and toy upon toy, it looked like its own small community. I looked back across the fields to the solar panels glaring in the sun.

The whole valley—in all its beauty—felt like it was unraveling.

• • •

It's easy to wonder how neighbors can get along, how agriculture can be preserved, and how newcomers can still be welcomed into this valley. Since I've lived here, the face of downtown Salida has changed drastically. Once a slow street with some vacant storefronts and not much draw, the main street is now the heartbeat of the area. Concerts, art festivals, galleries, hip restaurants, yoga studios, bike shops, and busy retailers all meld together to create this thriving community. Trail systems have expanded and are well-maintained, and the river park is a magnet for both locals and tourists in the summer. The newcomers have brought some new life to the town, shining a bit of sunlight through the looming shadow.

Thankfully, amidst all the expansion and change, there are some encouraging steps being taken by this community to grow well. In 2014, the Chaffee County Commissioners added an article to the land use code called, "Right to Ranch." The article begins:

> You're living in farming and ranching country. You've chosen to live in one of the most beautiful places in Colorado. The farms and ranches that are your neighbors are a big part of what makes this a great place to live and add to its value. This brochure intends to tell you more about those farmers and ranchers and responsibilities you have to them and their responsibilities to you.

As our ranch has over twenty-three miles of irrigation ditches to maintain, this code has greatly helped us when we have been yelled at for a beaver building a dam in one of our three ditches, causing it to overflow and flood a new million-dollar home. Likewise, the code has also helped us on that same ditch when we were yelled at for maintaining it to help prevent the flooding of a different dream home. Thankfully, Chaffee County's protection of water rights is backed by the Colorado Supreme Court: "Ditches are important to Colorado. They permit a landscape, economy, and history in which fertile valleys prosper. Without them, properties adjacent to or distant from watercourses wither."

Realtors are becoming more educated as they sell subdivision lots that were once agricultural properties and are now homesites whose backyards still have ranchers' ditches running through them. Andrew recently sat on a four-rancher panel before one hundred local realtors and answered questions about ranching and agriculture in the valley.

Following in the commissioners' "Right to Ranch" footsteps, Envision Chaffee County was created: "A county-wide community effort to help maintain our natural beauty, special sense of community, and rural landscapes as we grow and prosper."

With all the differing opinions, perspectives, and backgrounds represented in this valley, I am encouraged to see many in the community working together toward a common goal of preserving the feeling of *place* here in Salida. With so many new people coming in, just as Andrew and I once did, there is a danger of diluting the essence of this valley. There is a danger that this small town could turn big-city—that it will one day become the very thing people are leaving when they move here. The very thing Andrew and I left when we moved here.

It does not escape me that before this town was born, and before there was ever one electric light shining in this valley, the people here must have felt something similar—though on a grander, more intrusive and more destructive scale.

At least there is a conversation being had today.

Maybe the bikers and the ranchers are really more similar than we think: that deep down, we really do value the same things. I don't know how future development will ever fit itself into my life's puzzle—if it ever will—but the Joneses and Willy both found a necessary spot for it in theirs. This makes me want to hold fast to the roots of our land, appreciate the life I have while I have it, and protect the open spaces for the wildlife and the cattle who are nourished by the same land that nourishes my soul.

• • •

That night, as Andrew and I sat at the table with our kids, there was big talk about Willy's, solar farming, subdivisions, and conservation easements. Vacations, college funds, future careers, new cars, and the future of the ranch all dropped into the conversation. The oil lamp that illuminates our winter evenings flickered and reflected the young faces who shared their thoughtful ideas and bold opinions. They each had a voice.

But in the end, when the dishwasher whirred and the kids dispersed to do their homework, and when the lamp light was turned down—Andrew and I sat by the fire and sipped tea. As the night winds howled against the windows, we discussed the things we could do with money like that. We eventually concluded, before we opened our books to read, that at this point in our lives, we would only buy the life we already have.

SPRING

Chapter 5

"Ranchers are midwives, hunters, nurturers, providers,
and conservationists all at once."

— Gretel Ehrlich, *The Solace of Open Spaces*

Calving season on the ranch bids winter adieu and welcomes spring, though they overlap in many ways. Tender green tulips poke through the thawing ground to warm in the sun, only to be buried in snow that night. Bluebirds appear, flashing blue and white from fencepost to fencepost, then seek shelter from an instant March blizzard. Fierce, house-shaking winds come and go, and the mountains receive their final dumps and dustings of what will soon be water in the rivers, streams, and irrigation ditches. The time changes and the days lengthen; the earth awakens—stretching and beginning its thaw—giving new energy to all living things.

Everything, and everyone, is ready for the change.

Thick ice warms and trickles in the ditches. The dogs and horses shed their fuzzy winter coats. Sleepy hay fields wake to the patter of little hooves as the newborn calves run and race, skip and buck—and the herd doubles in number.

Each year, we sell our calves when they are about a year old. Other ranchers buy our heifer calves to start or add to their own herd of mother cows. Beef producers buy our steer calves (born bull calves until castration on branding day) to fatten up and eventually sell as beef. We hold back a few steers for our own grass-fed beef, ensuring our family's freezer is filled with roasts, steaks, and burgers that feed us all year long.

Calving weather is not always ideal. A lot like life, the days are not always warm, calm, and sunny. Often a blizzard sets in overnight. Having gone to bed with a spring breeze blowing through our bedroom window, we wake to quiet snowfall and a white world on the other side of the frosty glass. Calves born on frozen, snowy nights get sick more easily, and they can suffer from hypothermia as they enter the world slick and wet—their black, curly hair instantly frozen by a biting, dark wind. Some calves, born on the coldest of nights, will even lose the edges of their soft ears to frostbite. It is on those shocking, frosty mornings that we have had calves in the bathtubs. Gan always told Andrew that a warm bath is the best way to warm a calf's core.

One spring morning, as the kids were getting ready for school and I was shouting orders to brush teeth and find backpacks, Seth came in—holding a new calf—both of them powdered with snow as the wind blew a drift through the open door. School and schedules blown away by the blizzard, I followed Seth's boot prints up the stairs to Abe and Life's bathroom. Dressed for school and actually brushing their teeth, their eyes widened at the sight of their Uncle Seth and the calf and they moved out of the way. I pushed through and started the warm water in their tub.

"His twin's in the truck," Seth told us, lowering the black calf into the filling tub. "And another one besides." I counted tubs—that meant Andrew's and my tub would be used, too. Naomi peeked in just as Andrew appeared in the hallway with the other twin, a tiny heifer calf, so cold she wasn't even shivering.

"Looks like you're gonna be a little late this morning, kids," I said.

As his glasses fogged up and his coveralls defrosted and dripped, Seth held the new bull's head out of the tub and I followed Naomi to her bathroom where Grace was curling her hair and where Andrew stood with the heifer calf. Naomi started the tub. Andrew slid the slick black body, almost lifeless, into the warm water, careful to keep her head clear.

"Naomi, hold her head while I get the other one," he said. Naomi dropped to her knees on her bathmat and took the cold, slippery face from Andrew's leather-gloved hands. "Grace, turn the water off once it's to the calf's neck," he said.

"So, are we not going to school then?" Grace asked him, unrolling a curl in the mirror. But he was already down the hall.

Before any of the kids were old enough to drive to school, they loved the days when school took a back burner to calving. It was a legit excuse for our ranch kids when I called the school, the secretary nodding on the other end of the line saying, "I'll let their teachers know."

I cringed when I walked to my bathroom, following the boot prints on the carpet I'd just vacuumed over the weekend. The third calf was lying still in my once clean tub. Surrounding the black fur that waved in the water—manure, remnants of afterbirth, and a fleshy umbilical cord floated in my place of evening relaxation. Then I heard the little life try to bawl and I was reminded that this barely breathing baby was in need of help. Andrew massaged the cold body under the warm water as I held its thick head whose long, wet lashes were motionless, eyes closed.

I stuck two fingers in the calf's mouth—his prickly purple tongue was cold—and it grew even colder as I felt farther back in his mouth.

"How's he doin'?" Seth came in to check on us.

"He's not looking good," Andrew said.

"He's pretty cold," I said, rubbing the calf's tender ears, trying to work some warmth back in. "How are the twins?"

"Naomi and Grace are with one and the boys are with the other. Time will tell."

• • •

The twins made it, but the bull calf did not.

Piled in the pickup with the heat on high, we drove through the frozen white field and found both frantic mamas, blowing billowy clouds in the cold morning air with each desperate call for their calves. Andrew and Seth unloaded a big black plastic sled that held the motionless bull calf from my tub. The two mamas rushed over and sniffed at his body, licking the frozen peaks of black fur. They each gave their gentle calls to him to see if he was theirs. No response. Undaunted, they continued, eagerly following the sled as it trailed behind the pickup, tied with baling twine, bumping along the frozen cowpies through the pasture back to the barn next to our house. The mamas followed right in step, lowing and trotting the whole way, full milk bags swinging with each anxious step.

Back inside the house, the kids had the twins warming on some old sheets on the rug by the wood stove in the living room. Delighted, they sat on the floor, running their fingers through the soft new coats and feeling the thick yellow wax that covered each sharp hoof like a shoe. A protective design to prevent the hooves from tearing the inside of the mother during labor, the wax would wear off once the calves ran around in the field for a day or two. Brother and sister, a big bull calf and a little heifer calf, once warmed up, would soon start trying to stand and find their mother as their instincts would kick back in. It's astonishing to watch a newborn calf stand for the first time and bump its soft nose around the warm belly of its mother, looking for tender teats full of colostrum, the mother's first milk.

"It's hard to believe these were both inside one mama," Naomi said, holding the little heifer in her lap.

"Remind me never to have kids," Grace said, sitting next to her.

"This little one won't ever have kids," I told them, feeling the heifer's warm ears.

"Why not?" Life asked, petting the bull calf's blocky head resting on his leg.

"Well, when male and female twins share the same womb, the heifer is always sterile. Something about exchanging hormones with the opposite sex."

"That's kinda sad," Abe said, sitting with his knees tucked under him, petting the heifer's furry back as she laid in the morning sun that warmed her through the windows. "What about the bull calf? Will he be sterile, too?"

"No, just the heifer. If twins are both males or both females, there's no problem." The fire crackled in the stove as the chaos of the morning settled like fresh falling snow on the fields.

"Mom, do we still have to go to school?" Grace asked.

I looked at the time. Ten o'clock, and there was still work to do. We needed to finish warming the calves and get them up and walking again and outside to the barn where we would get them nursing. They each needed an ear tag, and we had to get water and feed to their pen.

"We'll see," I said, floating my fingers through the feathery fur of the bull calf. He lifted his heavy head and blinked his long lashes, then lowered his head back to Life's lap and closed his eyes.

• • •

As we all warmed by the fire, Andrew made ear tags for the twins with the same number as their mama: 13-21. The mama was born in 2013, and she was number 21 in her group. One calf would be 13-21A and the other 13-21B. The heifer calf's tag went in her right ear—I remember this since "girls are always right"—and the bull calf's tag went in his left ear. A big bell that clanged from a cow collar was put around their mama's neck, and the three were put in their own special pen in the corrals near our barn. They would bond there for a week or two, the calves nursing and learning the sound of their mama's bell.

Cows and their calves have a distinct call all their own—a mother cow can call for her calf across a field and the calf will come running. Likewise, mother cows are always listening for their calf's call. But with twins, things can get complicated. Once the three are moved back into the nursery pasture with all the other mother cows and their calves, it's easy for the twin mother to set off across the field for water with only one twin following and the other left behind, napping. When the sleepy twin wakes up, its mother is nowhere to be found. The cow's mothering instincts are satisfied by the one calf at her side and she doesn't call for her second calf. The bell is a way that both twins can keep track of their mama.

Usually, cows are good moms. But once in a while, especially with twins, a cow will completely abandon a calf: then we have a bottle baby on our hands. On a really bad day we will lose a mother cow to any number of causes: disease, illness, complications with labor, or natural causes—all resulting in an orphaned calf who needs milk. Bottle babies are adorable, but they are a lot of work. They must be fed a large bottle of warm milk morning and night—a chore the kids love, for the first week, until it gets old and becomes Andrew's and mine.

If a calf dies near the time we also have a bottle baby or twin calves, we prepare for the possibility that the twins' mother will abandon one of her calves. If we have a bottle baby, or if a twin is abandoned, or if the twins' mother doesn't have enough milk to support two calves, we try to "graft" one calf onto the lonely cow whose calf died.

If that mother and her original calf bonded for days or weeks before the calf died, it can be hard to make the sneaky switch with a twin or a bottle baby. Often the confused mother will kick the new baby, who was already abandoned by its own mother (or whose mother died), sending it flying across the pen. Grafting can be a brutal process. To help the bonding go more smoothly, we use a powder called "Orphan-No-More," or another, called "Adopt-A-Calf." Both are salty, manure-smelling concoctions that cows cannot get enough of. We sprinkle the powder along the calf's back as the mother cow watches us, sniffs the air, and swings her heavy head from side-to-side to see what we are doing. We step away and she moves over to the calf and smells, licks, snorts, and licks again—eventually, hopefully, bonding with her new calf.

In some instances, the cow will still reject the new calf. That is when we take the hide from the cow's original, dead calf and create a sort of "coat" for the replacement baby. It's a gruesome-looking process—skinning a dead calf—not to mention seeing a calf walking around with the dead skin of another on its back.

In that case, Andrew hangs the dead calf upside-down with baling twine from a rafter in the shade of the lean-to at the barn. He sharpens his knife and then methodically starts at the top and cuts the soft hide away from the body, revealing the translucent casing around each muscle, ligament, and tendon. The hide dangles as Andrew peels it away, making careful, angled cuts with his knife. Leaving the tail attached to the hide, he carries the finished product in two hands like rolled pizza dough.

Back in the barn with the replacement baby, Andrew makes four slits in the thick, slippery hide—two in front and two in back—and then lays the odd coat over the calf's own hide. Holding the calf between his legs, Andrew slides the kicking calf's bony legs through each hole in the hide. The mama watches, wide-eyed, stepping away to give the peculiar rancher some room. He ties the hide under the calf's belly with more bailing twine—not a very pastoral sight. However, the cow, less concerned with aesthetics, takes two tentative steps toward the calf and sniffs—then licks and lows—glad her baby finally made it back home.

Who ever said motherhood is easy?

As ranchers, though we are raising a product that we, and many others, will eventually eat to nourish our own bodies, we have a code of animal husbandry by which we live. It is motivated by respect. We honor the calves' lives and respect them, caring for them in the most ethical ways we can, knowing that their lives will soon be taken so that many may live.

Chapter 6

"There are two spiritual dangers in not owning a farm.
One is the danger of supposing that breakfast comes from the
grocery, and the other that heat comes from the furnace."

— Aldo Leopold, *A Sand County Almanac*

Cattle are not the only species to calve. Aardvarks, antelope, bison, camels, elephants, elk, giraffes, hippos, moose, rhinos, whales, and yaks are among those who also bear young called calves. In the Arctic, reindeer calve, as do glaciers, whose pale blue freshwater icebergs crash into the Arctic Sea.

When people learn that Andrew and I raise beef cattle, there are often mixed reactions: some will ask us if we sell our beef, and if so, do we have any available, while others toss a quick word our way that beef is the main problem behind today's climate crisis.

As permafrost thaws—revealing age-old animals previously frozen in the ice age—as we hear of glaciers melting away, and as we watch sea levels rise, more and more research reveals the global warming crisis at hand.

Randy Sage, an old-timer who grew up in the old house across the field, remembers when Salida's former sale barn was located where NAPA and McDonald's now sit; when Absolute Bikes and the pawn shop were both feed stores; when Salida hosted five dairies and milk delivery was the norm; when there was still a herd of over fifty wild horses running free up Ute Trail; and he remembers when Salida was consistently covered in two or three feet of snow all winter.

"Once Halloween came and went, you'd better batten down the hatches, 'cause the snow was comin' and it'd be there 'til May," he told me. They fed their dairy cattle with a horse-drawn sled because the snow was so deep and the wind made drifts ten to twelve feet high. These days, we are lucky to see one snowfall of eight inches on the fields—and even luckier if it stays long enough for me to cross-country ski a loop around the ranch before the wind takes it all away.

Though there have been historic trends of cooling and warming over the ages, the changes we see happening in our time, however, seem to be more human-induced. Fingers are being pointed across the globe, wanting someone, or something, to blame. We want someone to take responsibility and change the trajectory of our future without drastically inconveniencing us. Many are searching for immediate ways to reverse the damage done while preventing further harm. We are realizing that efforts such as recycling, carpooling, clotheslines, and reusable grocery bags are not making the big impact we had hoped they would.

In this search for a scapegoat, the beef industry has been found.

In her book, *Great Tide Rising*, Kathleen Dean Moore argues that we have a moral obligation as humans to be good stewards of the planet we've been given, and that our lifestyles must change—and I whole-heartedly agree. While enjoying the benefits of the Industrial Revolution, we have ravaged our natural world. It is shameful that we have literally trashed the planet that was designed to help us breathe, drink, eat, work, and enjoy.

All that said, however, my horns lock with Moore's when I read these words of hers: "If I am repelled by climate change, I can't eat beef cattle, those blowsy blowhards."

In 2021, the US commercial beef industry processed just under thirty-four million cattle. How much does the production of thirty-four million cows contribute to the annual greenhouse gas emissions that are warming our planet? Can we ethically eat beef any longer?

Moore is not alone with her thoughts that the beef industry is the main culprit of the global warming crisis (although she strongly blames the oil industry). One of the pleas set before us is the idea of eliminating—or at least limiting—our intake of animal products. Another predominant voice promoting this idea is Jonathan Safran Foer, author of the book, *We Are the Weather: Saving the Planet Begins at Breakfast*.

Foer writes that, "according to one estimate, electricity use accounts for 25 percent of annual greenhouse gas emissions. Agriculture accounts for 24 percent, mostly from animal agriculture. Manufacturing also accounts for 24 percent. Transportation: 14 percent. Buildings: 6 percent." Many of Foer's statistics come from two controversial and conflicting reports: the United Nation's 2006 report, "Livestock's Long Shadow" and The Worldwatch Institute's 2009 report, "Livestock and Climate Change."

"Livestock's Long Shadow" claimed that the cattle industry alone was the main producer of greenhouse gasses at eighteen percent. At an even higher percentage than attributed to transportation, the study led to attacks on beef as the biggest contributor to global warming. Since then, consumers have been encouraged to reduce their beef consumption in order to "save the planet."

Eleven years later, in 2017, the livestock study was found faulty and inaccurate.

University of California scientist, Dr. Frank Mitloehner, who discovered the misinformation, found that "meat and milk production generate less greenhouse gas than most environmentalists claim." He went on to say that limiting beef and dairy production creates "more hunger in poorer countries," and he suggested the focus should move to "smarter farming, not less farming."

A study by the Environmental Protection Agency (EPA) in 2016 found that direct emissions from the US cattle industry accounts for only two percent of our nation's total greenhouse gas emissions. Globally, beef emissions account for six percent of greenhouse gas emissions. Notably, in the cattle industry, only fifty percent of the animal is used for beef—leaving the other half for use in many other products such as leather for our shoes and couches and food for our pets.

In 2019, the USDA completed a comprehensive study in which researchers measured "the use of fuel, feed, forage, electricity, water, fertilizer and other inputs to raise beef cattle throughout the country— from birth to slaughter."

As a beef producer, I appreciate this study because it addresses some of the most common concerns regarding beef and the climate crisis. I want to know if my livelihood is one of the main contributors to global warming.

The study reveals that "beef cattle production accounted for 3.3 percent of all U.S. GHG emissions (by comparison, transportation and electricity generation together made-up 56 percent of the total in 2016 and agriculture in general 9 percent)" and "were not all that different from what other credible studies had shown and were not a significant contributor to long-term global warming."

Support for the idea that responsible ranching and livestock grazing actually help capture carbon is gaining strength and numbers as scientists and ecologists such as Allan Savory are finally being heard. Instead of pinning the blame of climate change on the cattle industry, scientists are discovering what Savory has claimed for years:

> *Most grazing lands should have more livestock added, because their movement and their waste and their relentless chomping stimulate grasses to grow. When grasslands restore themselves, they sequester carbon; so, increasing the density of cattle and other grazing animals not only restores the environment, it protects against climate change.*

Education is one of the most effective weapons in combating climate change. Ranchers—who have historically been devoted to land ethics—are continuing to learn new strategies for better feed and grazing practices, water usage, land management, biodiversity, and manure management. Many cattle producers have moved to providing consumers with solely grass-fed beef instead of the corn-fed beef product most Americans are used to consuming. Additionally, ranches such as White Oak Pastures in Georgia are marketing their grass-fed beef as "carbon negative," since their animals help sequester more carbon in the soil than they produce.

It is important that the world be properly educated regarding the false perils that have been attributed to US beef production. Not only do inaccurate studies harm the agricultural communities that supply our nation with protein, but according to Anne Mottet and Henning Steinfeld, two agricultural scientists from the United Nations' Food and Agricultural Organization, misinformation harms others around the world:

Wealthy consumers, in both high and low income countries, who are rightly concerned about their individual carbon footprint, have options like driving less or choosing low carbon food. However, more than 820 million people are suffering from hunger and even more from nutrient deficiencies. Meat, milk and eggs are much sought after to address malnutrition . . . and negative press about livestock may influence development plans and investments and further increase their food insecurity.

In the United States, most people are insulated from hunger as a daily reality. But in the 1800s, when ninety percent of Americans lived on farms, the daily struggle for food was very real. Gardening, canning, hunting, milking cows, making cheese, churning butter, gathering eggs, and raising livestock for meat were commonplace practices. Today, only one percent of Americans live on farms. As a nation, most of us are detached from our food sources and are dangerously dependent upon others to provide our food. It is imperative that we are accurately informed about agriculture in the United States and that we support responsible agriculture before we further jeopardize the very industry that feeds us.

• • •

In an effort to learn more about improving our personal ranching practices, I emailed Marj, one of Ruthie's sisters. A part of the fourth generation of Andrew's five-generation Colorado ranching family, Marj and her husband Bill have spent their lives raising cattle together on their Cold Mountain Ranch, over the Continental Divide in Carbondale, Colorado. One of Gammy and Gan's seven children, Marj is a lifelong rancher and a committed Democrat. I was excited to learn her perspective on beef production and global warming when her email showed up in my inbox.

Hi Lara,

I'm in my rush as usual; we rode all day yesterday and sorted and hauled cows this morning, but here's a stab at your questions.

Bill and I have always been frugal in the extreme. This is both an economic action and a lifestyle choice for attempting to limit our footprint on the planet. I try to limit consumption by wearing my kids' hand-me-downs, reusing everything possible, washing plastic bags, trying not to waste food, and other eccentricities; I try to be efficient in our trips to town and even in how many trips we make to the stackyard when feeding hay, etc.

We have had a solar water heater for 30 years. We have 16,000 kW of solar on our house and shop. I have always used a clothesline to dry clothes. We have never owned a clothes' dryer. That's the gist. I have had a garden all my adult life. We tend to eat seasonally; a lot of asparagus and rhubarb in May, lettuce in June, things pick up in July, down to the last kale, beets, and potatoes in the fall. I can tomatoes and salsa and apricot jam. We eat a lot of beef, especially hamburger, pretty much every day. It's our own beef and it is grass-fed.

I like grass-fed beef because I don't like our calves cooped up eating corn. I think beef is a great product, especially in the Rocky Mountains as cows can basically harvest "sunlight" through grass in an area that is not suited to other crops. The cows climb around in the mountains where farming is impossible. Even our hay ground has too short a growing season to grow much; the quinoa and hemp markets are fairly well saturated. There's only so many radishes the market will bear. Alfalfa is getting a bad rap these days, but it is drought-hardy and fixes nitrogen. We replant one field a year, creating a 7-10 year cycle. We've moved to intensive grazing on our pastures and have improved productivity and the soil.

Grass evolved with grazing animals, buffalo, elk, and deer. I like to think of cows as tools that manage grass. Properly used they can regenerate soil and increase carbon sequestration. They can reduce the risk of forest fire on forest grazing allotments and near urban areas. They release methane, but as part of a balanced evolutionary process.

Carbon emissions are a very real problem. Like everything in life, moderation is required. Right now, societies are emitting way too much carbon and methane. There is irrefutable scientific evidence. The planet is experiencing extreme weather of every sort: hurricanes, floods, droughts, wildfires, tornadoes, too much snow, too little. YES, extreme weather has always occurred, but the FREQUENCY of extreme events has increased dramatically with the rise in carbon dioxide.

Yes, eating meat has an impact and so do plastic straws . . . HOWEVER, the massive increases in carbon are primarily the result of fossil fuel use and this needs to be addressed immediately. We need to keep increasing our use of renewables and learn to live without fossil fuels as well as research methods for carbon capture. Grazing done right is actually beneficial. We value agriculture and think there is a place for grazing. It's all about timing and degree of use.

I am still a fan of flood irrigation. At higher elevations, when fields are flooded, the water is slowly released back to the river in the late season when the river is low, providing a benefit to the river. We apply fertilizer judiciously on some pastures; not most of our land. Mostly we rely on manure from our cows.

We try to produce a natural product with as few inputs as possible. I'm sure we could do better. Our goal is to improve the land and the planet. It's a challenge.

Talk to you soon.

Love,

Marj

Her email is special to me—not only because of her intellect and her love for the land and her cattle—but because every time I see her, she reminds me of Ruthie and Gammy. She looks, sounds, and moves like they did. And I appreciate the practical points she shared—straight from the heart of a rancher.

• • •

Though the carbon footprint of a cow may not be as wide as some once thought, there is always room for improvement. I strongly believe in the push toward Country of Origin Labeling for beef products sold in our grocery stores. We know where our apples, peppers, and blueberries come from, but no one knows where the beef in major grocery stores comes from. I think consumers want to know if their steak was raised in America, or if it is from Brazil, where rainforests are being destroyed at an alarming rate to create grazing lands for cattle.

Similarly, there is room for improvement in the excesses of the American lifestyle, and this can no longer be ignored. Greenhouse gas emissions from transportation are at twenty-nine percent with fuel consumption in the United States at almost 143 billion gallons per year. Emissions from energy production are at twenty-eight percent. Likewise, the following statistics from a retail energy company, Electric Choice, should be seen as a call to action in the United States:

- It is estimated that the United States spends more than $300 billion a year on energy that goes to drafty doors and windows, inefficient appliances and other energy wasters that could be easily remedied. This is more than the United States spends on its military every year.
- Google alone uses enough energy to continuously power 200,000 homes. The amount of energy it requires to conduct

100 searches on the site is the equivalent of a standard light bulb burning for 28 minutes.

- Approximately 75 percent of the electricity used in most American homes is used while the product is turned off. Idle power is a major energy consumer, with the average desktop computer using 80 watts of electricity while turned off.

- American refrigerators consume approximately the same amount of energy as 25 large power plants produce in a single year.

- Every minute, enough sunlight hits the earth's surface to supply the entire world's energy demands for a year.

As Marj wrote, we need to learn how to live differently.

• • •

One cold spring morning a couple of years back, we woke to find a new calf, frozen and dead in the field. It had been completely eaten away—only the spinal cord, ears, and tail remained. We assumed a coyote, or more likely, a mountain lion had come in the cover of night. Its mother, udders full of milk, was left bawling as she stood at the remnants of her new calf.

The following day, we put down a mother cow, whose calf had come in the night—whose birth we had especially been waiting for. Months earlier, we noticed that the mother cow had developed "cancer eye." Even after a surgery to remove the affected eye, the cancer still spread. In her condition, she would not be able to sustain her calf, and a sick or diseased animal is never sold for beef.

That morning, as his own breath puffed in the cold air along with hers, Abe, seventeen at the time, shot the mother cow.

The ground was frozen solid, so he could not bury her; instead, with chains and a tractor, he pulled her 1,500-pound body into the trees at the edge of the ranch, leaving her for the birds and scavengers. Maybe she would help stave off from the rest of the herd whatever animal it was who had eaten the dead calf overnight.

There are some rhythms on a ranch that are beautiful, like the planting, irrigating, growing, harvesting, and grazing of the fields. However, there is also an underside to the glorious tune: the heartbeat of life silenced by death.

Raw and rough were the two realities facing us that spring day: a mourning mother with her bulging milk bag, and a hungry orphaned calf—both bawling incessantly. Andrew paired them up in the barn, and thankfully, they took to each other right away.

Things are rarely ever that easy.

Esther, who was five and a half then, spent every hour she could in the barn, singing to the calf, just wanting to be near it. The mother cow was gentle, allowing Esther to stay and be.

"The little calf is so glad she has a mama, isn't she?" Esther asked me, as we sat together in the barn, watching the big red cow lick the little black calf who sucked and nursed, wagging its happy tail.

I stroked Esther's shiny, long black hair and thought of when she came to our home, and how I came to be her mother.

Chapter 7

Unlike the mother cow Essie and I watched together, I had other children to care for.

Four to be exact.

Officially done with having any more, Andrew and I were not looking to adopt a child. We were thrilled with the freedom that comes to families who grow past sleepless nights, nursing, pacifiers, diapers, wet wipes, car seats, boosters, board books, nap time, sippy cups, and tantrums. The kids were 10, 12, 14, and 16 then, and we were finally skiing and rafting together as a family.

I remember the first ski run we all took as a family: no squiggly toddler wedged between my knees or Andrew's, trying to teach French fries and pizza—going and stopping—with their skis. No freezing tears wiped away by a cold and naked hand as we sat on the ski lift, mourning the tiny black mitten resting on the steep slope far below our swinging skis. No looks of bewilderment as ski pants slowly soaked when we arrived at the bathroom seconds too late, fighting mittens and zippers and snaps. No—everyone was independently skiing, and the kids were taking jumps and showing us their fancy moves as we swished down Monarch Mountain. Andrew and I had finally recovered from the exhaustion of parenting lots of little ones. Things were starting to seem more manageable, and parenting was getting more fun.

Then one night, we got a call at 2 a.m.

• • •

One of our six nieces had moved to Salida earlier in the year to live with her dad, my brother, Ted. She was sixteen and pregnant with a baby girl. Wanting a new start for the two of them, she left the Navajo Nation, where she had grown up and had been living with her mom. She wanted to raise her baby, and I wanted to help make that transition easier for her in any way I could. Since the father of the baby was no longer in the picture, she and I attended labor and delivery classes together and painted her room pink—her room she would share with her baby.

My beautiful niece, half Navajo and half Ted, was trying to make a life for herself and her coming baby. Tugging at her was her former life of alcohol, drugs, and partying, but she fended off those who pursued her—keeping safe and healthy her baby who grew in her womb.

One evening, when the baby's due date came near, when all the little onesies from a baby shower had been washed, folded, and tucked into a dresser drawer; when a hospital bag was packed and waiting; when the crib was set up and made cozy, Ted called.

"Can you meet us at the hospital?" he said, his voice urgent and nervous.

The next hours were spent breathing and praying by my niece's side. I tried to remember all the ways my mom and Ruthie had helped me as I gave birth to my four kids. I felt like I was giving birth again as

I breathed right alongside my niece; I had to remind myself not to push as we labored into the night.

I reminded her that the pain was going to eventually bring her baby into the world. As I watched her cringe and cry with each contraction, I thought back to the first time I saw Grace's eyes when she was born: to finally see the eyes that were created in my womb, to feel her tiny fingers wrap around mine—it was miraculous.

In the dark of early morning, Esther Hazel was born. I watched the new little life open her mouth and cry for the first time. It was a desperate cry, one that I've recognized from that very moment each time it surfaces these days with a skinned knee, a stomach ache, or exhaustion. The doctor, who had also delivered Naomi, Abe, and Life, placed 8-pound, 10-ounce Esther on her mother's chest.

Their next weeks were filled with breastfeeding, diapers, and little else, especially sleep. When I went over to get them out for a walk, as Ruthie had done with me, I carried Esther's tiny body next to my heart as we walked down the road along a little creek.

I could tell my niece was getting restless.

At the weekly home-nurse's visit, I listened to her as she told the nurse that she was really struggling. With a quivering chin she said, "I don't think I'm ready to be a mom."

In response, the nurse recommended to the Department of Human Services (DHS) that Andrew and I officially become part of a "safety plan" for Esther in case her mom found herself in a bad situation. Knowing things between her and my brother were not going well, and knowing that she needed help learning how to be a mom, we asked if she and Esther would move in with us. She thanked us for the offer: she would stay where she was and would make good choices.

Then, at 2 a.m., into the middle of our new season of fun and manageable parenting, the call came.

"Lara, it's Nicole from DHS. Sorry to call you in the middle of the night, but Esther has been removed from her mother's care, and we need to enact the safety plan."

"What? What happened?" I sat up in bed, wide awake.

"I can give you the details when I see you. Listen, if it's okay, I will be there with the baby in about an hour."

"Yes, yes, of course," I said. "See you soon."

I switched on the light to see Andrew propped-up on his elbow, wide-eyed and wondering.

An hour later, Nicole and two police officers were at our door—along with six-week-old Esther—bundled in her car seat.

At that moment, our lives, our family, and our table, changed forever.

• • •

While our niece continued her efforts, as a teenager, to make the decisions of an adult, we found a crib for our bedroom and a highchair for the table. I picked up Esther's clothes from Ted's house—along with all the blankets, diapers, and her little baby bathtub. Andrew and I prayed that the situation would improve, but circumstances only grew worse. Eventually, Esther's mother was moved to a foster home over two hours away, as there were only a couple foster homes in all of Chaffee County, and they were both full.

Meanwhile, our new status as "kinship" foster parents was expedited. Andrew and I were interviewed several times and completed a series of online classes. I remember being on a trip in Mexico with all of Andrew's family while Mom and Rodney watched Esther for us. Andrew and I would stay up late each night after a day at the beach to watch the required videos and take tests about various subjects such as Fetal Alcohol Syndrome, child abuse and neglect, and foster parent responsibilities. Our backgrounds were checked, our fingerprints were taken, and our entire home was inspected. We covered every outlet with a little plastic plug, put a lock on the closet that held our locked gun safe, installed child-locks on every cabinet, updated our dogs' rabies vaccinations, obtained copies of our kids' grades—and the long, long list went on.

For over a year, Andrew and I attended court each month where numerous lawyers and case workers brought their reports, including the case worker from the Navajo Nation who reported by phone. It is primarily the goal of DHS to reunite parent and child, and the county gave it their best effort.

Also attending by phone from Arizona was a young man who was thought to be Esther's father. Though he was working through current drug charges, the county's goal was also to unite him with Esther.

It was a stressful time.

My jaw is forever misaligned from clenching and grinding my teeth so much. I was exhausted. I was up at night feeding Esther, and then "on" all day with the rest of my family. Emotionally, Andrew and I were drained, as the outcome of the situation changed from week to week.

My walks up the hill on the ranch were therapy for me as I watched the days of spring lengthen and buds swell on the cottonwood trees. When my world felt so unstable, so uncertain, I was thankful for the consistency of the seasons, though they could bring surprises of their own at times, too. I felt the sun warm my back as I climbed, melting my heart that frequently wanted to hold my life, my family, my home, and my table with a closed fist—a closed door.

Frequent phone calls from Mom, who lives three hours away up and over the Continental Divide, encouraged me in the daily tasks of being a mom, a wife, and a rancher. She reminded me of Elizabeth Elliot's wise words to "Do the next thing." Those words played over in my mind as I walked, working it all out with God in my thoughts and my heart.

Keep moving. Keep loving. Keep going.

Don't give up.

Do the next thing.

And, like the seasons, I kept on.

And Andrew kept on, too. Though exhausted from a long calving season, knowing a long summer was ahead—he pressed on, undaunted, into the demanding spring season of foster parenting, ditch cleaning, irrigation, plowing, and seeding. We both kept going, moving forward—doing the next thing—even on those days when we both wanted to quit.

Esther and I drove over four hours twice each week for visits with her mother at the foster home. As I drove alongside the river, through the canyon, and away from the ranch, I felt pulled away from the kids as I entered into the unknown world of foster parenting. It was painful to watch my niece's broken heart surface when she saw Esther. I could see the struggle on her face as she weighed the responsibilities and demands of motherhood. Alone, afraid, and only sixteen—she was not yet ready to be a mother.

As time went by, and as things became more difficult for our niece at the foster home, Andrew and I both agreed that we would adopt Esther if given the opportunity. I distinctly remember asking God to allow us to adopt Esther, as our grand-niece had nestled and settled into her own place in my heart.

When we mentioned the possibility of adoption to the kids, they all had varying responses:

Grace: "You guys can do what you want, but you know you'll ruin your retirement."

Naomi: "Wow, well, I can see why you are doing it."

Abe: "Oh, okay. Can I go shoot my BB gun?"

Then there was Life: "You have to adopt her. You just have to."

Out of all the kids, Life was the one whose birth order would change. No longer would he be the baby.

The rest of the extended family was eventually on board as well—most importantly, Mom and Rodney. Initially, Mom's first reaction was: "You can't do this, Lara. You already have enough on your plate."

And she was right, our plate was overfull and overwhelming. But we knew it was the right thing to do—maybe not the easy thing—but it was the right thing. Mom and Rodney agreed to be our "back up" when we wanted to do things with the bigger kids, like rock climb and raft, that we couldn't do with an infant or a toddler. They were an essential part of our decision, and, to this very day, we cannot do it without them.

Frustrated by the two worlds in which she was trying to live—both parent and child—our niece ran away from her foster home. Her own mom found her in New Mexico and brought her back to the case worker. Weeks and visits later, she ran away again.

Having avoided those who searched for her, she called us from a bus going "somewhere" in the middle of the night. She spoke in sobs we could not understand.

"Where are you? Are you safe?" I asked, sitting up in bed.

"Yes, I'm safe," she said. Through her tears, she asked us if we would adopt Esther. "I just can't do it," she said. "I'm not ready to be a mom."

My mind went wild, and Andrew grabbed my hand.

"Yes, of course," I said, "we love you and Esther so much."

"I know she will hate me when she's my age," she said.

Her words broke my heart, and I assured her that Esther would grow up knowing how brave her mom was—how she had made the right decision. The hard decision.

"It's the right thing to do," Andrew said. "We will take good care of her for you." A sigh of relief came right through the phone.

She thanked us and soon said goodbye.

I set the phone back on the table beside my bed.

The night was dark, and I could see the stars through the window.

Though we had been praying that our niece would come to this decision for Esther's sake, Andrew and I talked late into the night about the implications of adoption becoming a reality.

However, it would not come soon, and it would not come easy.

Chapter 8

When my life feels unstable and inconsistent, the ranch offers a gift: there is work that must always be done. The ranch requires us to leave our fragility behind for a time and focus on the job at hand—and the job usually requires going outside. Working outside, no matter the weather, offers a healthy dose of reality and perspective, reminding me that the world is much bigger than my circumstances, emotions, and struggles. And ranch work usually demands a focused mind—giving reprieve from the things that can weigh me down.

After the late-night phone call, so many thoughts ran through my mind: if we adopted Esther, how would we balance things like toddler nap times and high school soccer games? And family movie nights—would watching *Jason Bourne* turn into watching *The Little Mermaid* again? Would *Settlers of Catan* game nights turn into hours of *Go Fish* and *Candy Land* as our teenagers slowly slink away to their rooms? Would I lose my four kids in the process of gaining a fifth? Was I willing to enter back into the world of potty training, play dates, sippy cups, and learning to tie shoes and read? Was I ready to feed a family of seven each night at the table? If I thought of it all too much, it pulled me down and stopped me from functioning.

But the ranch doesn't lend itself to malfunctioning for long. Instead, Mom's soothing reminder to "do the next thing" entered my thoughts and pulled me from myself like a lifeguard; and that "next thing" during spring on the ranch, after the calves are all born, is branding.

Written on the calendar for weeks, it's a day the family knows they need to set aside. In preparation, Seth, Susie, Andrew, and I all have our lists. Andrew and Seth research and order vaccines and new needles, fill the propane tanks for heating the branding irons, update and print off the latest cattle spreadsheet, and hose down the corrals.

One of the things on my list, and Susie's, is the food—one of the most important components of branding day. The menu is a family tradition: it's always chili, passed down from Gammy, our ranching matriarch, who served chili on branding days and at lunch breaks on cattle drives from Carbondale to Snowmass since the early 1940s. Andrew wanted to carry on that same tradition when we had our very first branding day for our first ten calves—whose Hereford mothers we bought from Gammy and Gan—and it's been chili ever since. Along with cheese, Fritos, and sour cream, Susie and I have added a few traditions of our own: watermelon, Texas sheet cake, lemonade, and cold Coors beer.

• • •

As our pots of chili simmer on the stove, everyone meets at the table for breakfast burritos to go over the plan for the day. Diagrams are drawn to show the latest idea for bringing in the herd—which pen they will start in and who will sort the calves off from the cows. Gangly teenagers in worn cowboy boots, faded jeans, and long-sleeved shirts lean in and try to understand the early morning ideas sketched on paper.

A spring day outside can be any sort of weather in Colorado—we've had blizzards and warm sunshine, howling wind and stinging sleet—often all in the same day. Rain is the only weather that requires rescheduling branding day, as the brands just don't work when the calves are wet.

Bellies full of breakfast and plans made, we all look out the window and layer for the weather. Leather gloves and straw hats are pulled from the pile on the counter by the door and cowboy boots are pulled on, worn by work to the exact shape of each foot. Young backs bend and pull bootstraps with no thought, while older backs pull and grimace at the thought of the work ahead.

Branding is a loud and multi-faceted process as we bring in the herd from their pasture. Some of us are on foot, others on an ATV, and the lucky ones are on horseback. The mother cows start talking as soon as they see us heading toward their pasture. Calves sprint and play as their mothers try to corral them and we spread out to move the whole herd to the corrals. The herd of large and small bovine bump and crowd into the barbed-wire alleyway that leads to the large pen in the corrals at the old house—the noise growing louder and louder as each mother calls for her calf and each calf calls for their mother as they walk in circles, bellowing and listening in turn.

We let a small mixed group into the alley and sort off the calves from their mamas. Eventually we end up with all the moaning mothers in one pen and all the cranky calves in another. The air is filled with dust and the deafening din of disturbed cattle as they holler back and forth across the alley—a thick fence of old wooden planks keeping them from each other until they are reunited again. The propane heater growls like an angry bull as it heats the branding irons—adding intensity to the cattle's cacophony.

Scattered throughout the corrals, family and friends, both young and old, set to their tasks: whether it's manning a gate, moving a group of calves further down the line, filling vaccines, working the chute, roping, flipping, holding, recording, vaccinating, castrating, or branding—it takes everyone focusing to get the job done. When the kids were little, they congregated in the dust with cousins, roping each other and sneaking away with dirty fistfuls of stolen cake, but as the kids and our backs have grown older, the next generation has become an integral part of branding day.

There is a certain progression to the branding process, starting with getting a group of eight or so calves to line up single-file in a long, narrow alley where they wait their turn. Moving the calves down the line can be a rough and painful job as the calves can climb on the back of another and try to twist and turn around or send a mighty kick straight back to a person's unsuspecting shins—a situation that has sent both Life and Abe searching for soccer shin guards mid-morning.

One by one, the calves push and crowd along the wooden alley where they eventually see the end that leads into a spacious corral. Some hesitant calves will stop at the edge of the alley and look around before they take that first step out into the open, and some will see the open space and run as fast as they can to escape. Either way, our kids and their cousins are waiting to rope the calf's front feet and then the back feet, bringing it to the soft dirt where the ropers hold the fighting calf on its side, tight and still. Wranglers and Levi's get caked with dirt, mud, and manure; and varying sizes of hand-me-down boots dig into the dirt as the kids hold the squirming calf with everything they've got so they don't get kicked.

Each calf is branded, given two vaccines for respiratory and intestinal viruses, and, if it's a bull calf, castrated with a band. Our brand is RCC, for Richardson Cattle Company. The calves are given this mark to determine ownership. As our cattle go to several different pastures in the high country each summer, neighboring cattle often get in, or ours get out, and the brands, along with color and breed, help determine whose cattle are whose at the end of summer—or when we get those calls from the sheriff wondering if it's one of our cows out on the highway. Likewise, cattle hustlers, who long ago used to be hung from the old hanging tree, are still very active, and a brand is hard to argue with since it is not as easily switched as an ear tag.

Like a couple of Charlie's Angels with (vaccine) guns in hand, Naomi and her cousin approach the calf. They administer the shots under the calf's skin just in time to scoot out of the way as Seth or Andrew appears, holding the long branding iron with the red hot RCC at its tip.

"Look out boys," Andrew says, as Abe and Life tilt their wide white hats away from the calf. They close their eyes and hold their breath as Andrew presses the iron to the calf's furry left side. Fur singes and smoke swirls as the hide is branded and forever marked. Like a teenager getting their first tattoo, the calf grimaces and groans until the sharp pain dissipates like dust kicked up by the spring winds.

Susie and I are often the castrators. I'm not quite sure how we got the job, but we are both good at it, and we laugh and make bad jokes as our teenage boys hold the calf and squirm at the idea of castration. I drop my knees in the dust at the bull calf's hind end where Abe, sitting in the dirt, holds one of the calf's legs with both gloved hands and he presses the other leg firmly with his boot. I find the furry sac between the calf's taut hind legs and feel for two fleshy marbles, careful not to let one slip back up into the calf.

"Make sure you get 'em both, Mom," Abe tells me, his white straw hat tipped back on his head and his big toothy smile sporting a line of dirt.

With my free hand, I squeeze the handles of the metal bander together, stretching the green Cheerio-sized rubber band to the diameter of a plum, and slip it over the sac and release the band back to its tiny state. I wiggle free the bander and declare, "There ya go, big guy."

Life watches on as he sits at the calf's head, waiting for me to get my job done. "Nice, Mom," he says, flashing his own gritty grin as Grace, holding her pen and clipboard, checks the calf's ear tag number on the spreadsheet. The kids take turns, switching out with cousins and friends as they work each calf that comes down the line.

When we have a large group of calves who have been branded, sitting in the sun, recovering from the whole process, we open a gate to allow them to meet back up with their bawling mamas. On a recent branding day, when Abe asked why we kept moving the branded calves instead of waiting until the end and moving them all at once, Jim Clark, our faithful neighbor who helps us in every season on the ranch, answered, "Abe, if we gave you two shots, branded you, and cut your nuts off, you'd probably want your mom, too."

Jim's wife, Gina, cackled and said, "Yeah, Abe."

The dust, the smoke, the loud herd, and the laughter of family and friends working together swirl together to make a memorable day. Sometimes a calf tugs loose from the rope, a needle pokes through the jeans, a kid gets bored with their not-as-fun job, a mother cow gets past the gate, or a dad loses the patience he strives to keep—but the work does its magic—it dominates the mind, giving us all a little reprieve from our personal worries and anxieties.

When the sun is high overhead, glistening off the bright white of the peaks to the west, everyone's exhausted and hungry, though we still have more than fifty calves left to brand. Regardless, it's lunchtime, and if the crew's gonna keep going, they need to be fed. Coated in dust, dander, and dung, we leave the corrals and gather together on the spring grass at the old house—a rancher's picnic table. We circle up and pray under the wide-open sky, thankful for the fullness of the lives we've been given. We grab bowls of chili and kick back on the grass, extending stiff legs and leaning on tired elbows. Dirt-coated mouths laugh and remember the morning's events as we forget our worries for a day and work hard together as family and friends.

Though work on the ranch can distract from the worries and hardships that life can bring, there are times when difficulty and change are not avoidable and they are consistently present in everything we do. Like carrying a new baby to branding day and having to leave early for naptime—or carrying news of a recent cancer diagnosis in your body and having to sit in a chair to watch all the action going on around you—the ranch still gets us up and out and into the life we love.

Whether we gather around a table or eat in a group on the grass, it's sharing life together that draws people in. These short breaks from hard work offer us the chance to catch our breath and share our stories, whether they are harebrained, hilarious, happy, or heartbreaking.

◆ ◆ ◆

And small towns, they are full of stories.

When I hear some news my kids never thought I'd find out, they wrinkle their eyebrows and ask, "How'd you know?"

I lift my eyebrows and smile and say, "It's a small town!"

While raising kids in Salida, where most everyone knows everyone, it's not unusual to get a call from another parent asking where the kids are—or do I know what they are doing, or, (and this one's the hardest), "I would want *you* to call *me* if it were *my* kid . . . that's why *I'm* calling *you*."

Groan.

In a small town most everything gets found out, eventually; and in this small town, we share life together. When our soccer team wins a championship, the whole community comes to watch the playoffs, and when a family is hurting from the loss of a loved one, the community hurts with them. When friends of Naomi and Grace lost their father—and much of Salida lost a friend—the huge white "S" on "S Mountain" downtown was transformed into a "B" that shone over the town in honor of the family.

And in this small town full of teenagers, a group of moms decided to cook lunch together each week—a big lunch where the high schoolers could gather around tables and share a meal, and their lives, with each other.

In the stainless-steel kitchen at church, Susie and I, along with a handful of other moms, spent every Monday of the school year together chopping and assembling the day's ingredients. We loved preparing these free Monday lunches together. Our own high school kids, along with over fifty other students, walked across the street each week for "Church Lunch," or what is now known as "Chunch."

We tried to learn each kid's name as they came through our line and grabbed a warm, home-cooked meal handed to them with a smile. We wanted the kids to know they were loved and that there was a church always open to them. We wanted them to know where the door is—and that there is free counseling for anyone. In times when school shootings, loneliness, and suicide have become the status quo instead of rare and isolated events, we wanted to love on our kids and their friends.

As we gathered around the kitchen's shiny steel island covered with cutting boards, sharp chef's knives, green celery, white onions, bright orange carrots, and smooth ivory garlic, Monday lunches grew into a gift for us moms as well. We laughed at what had become our weekly "therapy sessions," slicing and sharing together while the huge old soup pot simmered a bit of butter on the big black stove, awaiting our veggies. We went around the circle, telling the latest of our lives. The triumphs came first and came easy while the wounds of the week wound their way to the surface—like hard words with a spouse or a teenager, or hard words with oneself. As we assembled meals of lasagna, burritos, chicken noodle soup, or one of the kids' favorites, homemade mac 'n' cheese, we bore each other's burdens. The things that overwhelmed us—we put them on the table for all to see—where we worked together to slice and dice them into a size that was easier to manage.

Some Mondays, before the cutting boards even came out, any one of us would arrive, overwhelmed with life, and the tears would escape. We would get to work peeling, chopping, and mixing while we listened and nodded, asking questions along the way. Soon the smell of garlic, peppers, and onions sautéing in butter filled the kitchen as we worked through problems together. Struggles softened and became translucent, taking on a new shape and perspective from their raw beginnings.

Other Mondays were light and less dramatic—weeks when life was easier. We'd turn up the music a little louder and fill the kitchen with singing and laughter. Favorite songs from our kids' playlists echoed through the church as we cooked away to Taylor Swift's "Shake It Off" and diced to Mumford and Sons' "Awake My Soul." Cooking together brought us, and many kids in our community, together. The church's kitchen, and all its tables, became a place to share and listen—a place to be seen, known by name, and loved.

But, as life reveals to all of humanity, no one is immune to hardship.

The newest addition to the group of moms, Suzanne, who had recently moved to Salida, announced one Monday that her non-Hodgkin's lymphoma, from over twenty years earlier, had returned.

We grieved with our new friend as though our cancer was back. She started treatments and eventually didn't feel well enough to come on Mondays—but we still grabbed what time we could—a cup of coffee or sitting with her at the hospital as chemo flooded her veins. We walked through those days together, and we prayed together. Suzanne fought and endured, and when the news of her clean scan came, we all celebrated together as if it were our scan that was clean.

Suzanne shined: she had been given a second chance at life, for a second time.

Chapter 9

One day, during the spring of 2020, Andrew came in for lunch from the hay fields where he had been harrowing and breaking up the thawing winter manure with a wide web of metal prongs that dug and bounced behind the tractor. The cape of heavy chainmail dragged along, awakening the earth. The harrowed field looked newly vacuumed—no more mounds of manure and exhumed prairie dog tunnels stippling the sleepy spring ground. The harrow had broken that morning, but the fix was routine: grab a new bolt from the barn and replace the old one.

We ate our lunch at the north end of the table, while at the other end, in the light of the southern window, there sat dozens of containers of dark soil with just the tips of cantaloupe, pumpkin, basil, cilantro, and zucchini plants beginning to surface. I sat with Andrew that day because I was not rushing around as usual. Our schedules and routines had been dug up and turned on end. The halo of the Coronavirus was slowly shrouding the globe and had finally reached our country.

We discussed the new restraints placed upon our society—seeing even our lunch through new lenses.

I listened as he told me that his grandfather, Gan, used to straighten nails. Born in 1918, Gan knew wartime rations. He knew empty nail bins at the hardware store and reusing as a necessity, not an environmental effort. Sparse shelves at the grocery store made us wonder what unsettling circumstances tomorrow might bring.

With each day of the new war being waged against our world, we were losing more of our elderly generation—the nail-straighteners who had once endured battles against enemies that could be seen without a microscope. As the virus claimed more of society's grandparents and great-grandparents, adding aged and frail bodies to the daily death count—we were losing the stories, wisdom, and reminders of yesterday—stories and wisdom we would no longer be able to hear firsthand.

Early on in the pandemic, an 89-year-old resident in Salida's nursing home contracted the virus and died. It was disheartening to think that entire populations inside nursing homes could be completely erased.

My own dad would turn eighty-one that spring. Until the year before, when he moved in right next door, he had lived in the old house with Uncle Dan, who would soon turn eighty. They have both had open heart surgery and have smoked for much of their lives, until recently. Uncle Dan tells the same stories over and over every time I see him. And Dad doesn't hear well—he nods and smiles like he hears me—but I can tell he doesn't always. I hear about old Navy days, about the time when Uncle Dan dated Miss America, about how Dad's latest insulin is or isn't working better and about the most recent news from his DNA testing.

Until the pandemic, I hadn't had time for listening. I'd been too busy to stop and listen—too rushed to sit and stay and repeat myself so that my own dad could really hear my words. I was often too consumed with my own schedule to take a minute to stop by and let them know how the kids were handling online school, if I'd started my garden seeds yet, and when the cows would be heading to the high country for the summer.

But with the arrival of the virus, things were different.

When I pictured them on ventilators, struggling for each breath—not being able to stop and visit them—it changed things. I wanted to listen. I wanted to hear those same stories again. I wanted to see their faces as they awaited my response to the one about the hurricane with ninety-foot swells that crashed on Uncle Dan's aircraft carrier, the *Lake Champlain*, when he was the only sailor on deck. Or the one about the time when a Navy jumper landed on top of Dad's parachute mid-air and danced along the top—how their strings got tangled—and how they barely untangled before landing.

Though they told stories from the past in vivid detail, they had started struggling to remember if they had been to Walmart yet that day. Or was it yesterday? Walmart is their main social outlet, and they refused to let it go when the virus came. At least they had started wearing masks on their outings—even if, along with Wranglers, western shirts, cowboy boots, and cowboy hats, their red and blue bandanas added to their already strong personas of Butch Cassidy and the Sundance Kid.

When I thought of them not being there, not waving with one hand and holding the hose and watering their new grass seed with the other; not offering my dogs a biscuit every time I came by; not hearing their stories—when I thought of them not being there—it changed everything.

That Covid spring, before they moved next door that fall, I walked across the harrowed field to the old house and knocked. They came outside for a visit, during which I lingered and listened. I was ashamed that I had been so occupied with being busy—ashamed it took a pandemic for me to become a better listener. They asked about the kids and if they were healthy. Dad shared the latest numbers of the virus—it turned out he followed them as closely as Andrew and I did. Uncle Dan said the virus reminded him of an old girlfriend. And when I asked, Dad told me he had enough insulin on hand for three months.

Though the days of the virus brought much upset, grief, and uncertainty, they also brought perspective. Though the doors to the nursing home were closed to visitors, I was thankful that Dad and Uncle Dan were on the outside, still accessible, still here. I was thankful for the time I had with them during the early days of the pandemic—even if it was six feet apart in the spring wind.

Standing outside, his slippers on the cold earth, Dad was getting chilled, so we said goodbye and gave our air hugs. As I walked back home across the field, my boots crunched the sharp stems sticking up from last summer's hay crop. But underneath, tender blades of spring grass were pushing through, growing taller each day. I took a deep breath and savored the walk, the air, and the visit. I was thankful that, even during the vulnerable times of the pandemic, there grew a tendril of hope—while the harrowing virus clawed, trampled, rearranged, and broke apart life as we knew it—the dormant soil was slowly warming, ready for a new season of growth.

• • •

It was the first Sunday our church had ever been closed. And school wouldn't start again the next day. It would have felt like a normal Sunday morning, except for nothing was normal anymore. Like waking up with grief and remembering the one you have lost—waking up in those early days of the pandemic required remembering that our world, too, had drastically changed. Though we filled our pantry and prepared for uncertainty, life on the ranch felt insulated.

And that morning, the rooster still crowed.

Regardless of the pandemic newsfeed, mornings on the ranch still remained all about feeding—feeding the cows, the calves, the heifers, the bulls, the steers, the pigs, the chickens, the rooster, the teenagers, the toddler, and the hungry rancher. That morning I was thankful for the routines that are so easy to take for granted: there were eggs to collect, bacon to turn, and pancakes to flip.

In the kitchen, I was distracted from the griddle as I glanced at my phone. I was waiting to hear from Grace who had been studying overseas in Jordan where she had just caught one of the last flights out before Jordan closed its borders to protect its citizens from the pandemic. She was flying from Amman to Dubai, to New York, to Denver—where we planned to meet the next day. No word yet. I took a deep breath and a sip of coffee, and, to curb the inclination toward being anxious, I remembered to "do the next thing" and piled pancakes from the griddle to a platter.

The rest of the kids were all outside in the cold spring wind helping Andrew with the morning chores. I scooped more batter and poured six perfect circles. They sizzled, spread, and stopped. I found comfort in the hot rectangle of order—when the world seemed so out of order. Watching for the tiny bubbles to appear in the circles of batter, I waited for Grace's text from somewhere on the other side of the globe.

On a normal Sunday, we would rush to get to church on time, but not that Sunday. *Normal* had quickly become a thing of the past. That March morning, we took our time and lingered at the table.

After breakfast, we moved to the living room and sat by the warm wood stove with our seconds of coffee and tea. There was a nervousness in us all. Like guitar strings tuned too far, we were ready to pop. School closing, homeschooling beginning, summer rafting jobs pending, soccer canceling, family time increasing, the market dropping, the virus creeping, and Grace flying—we were all wound up, tight and tense.

We needed to be outside.

Knowing this, Andrew suggested, "Let's walk to the Eagles' Nest for church today."

Near an actual bald eagles' nest on the ranch, this picnic spot of sorts is tucked in a circle of cottonwood trees that overlooks the hay fields. On that chilly spring Sunday morning, after the virus had changed life as everyone around the globe had known it, our family walked a mile together for church in the trees.

We peeled the kids off the couches, except for Esther, who was bouncing around the house like Tigger. The rest rolled their eyes and complained. They wanted to stay where it was warm and comfortable instead of heading out into the cold wind again.

"Isn't the Sabbath supposed to be a day of rest?" Naomi said.

Life rallied and looked for his Tentsile (a three-sided tent that hangs high off the ground), because there's a perfect triangle of trees at the Eagles' Nest from which to hang it. Abe followed suit and found his hammock. Naomi flopped back onto the couch—disgusted—hoping we would change our minds.

But we didn't.

Andrew, leather Bible in hand, and I, Esther's little hand in mine, followed the big kids across the field toward the Eagles' Nest. The gray wind was howling, but everyone was energized by being outside. Abe and Life ran ahead to set up their hanging church pews. I watched Naomi flick her hood on and tuck her chin to her chest as she walked past the massive eagles' nest built high in the bare cottonwoods. I saw the mother's white head, laser eyes, and yellow beak peek over the edge of the architectural masterpiece where she kept her eggs warm. The father chirped from a branch above her.

He knows us—and he didn't fly away.

We turned and followed the row of cottonwoods that led to our sanctuary. Hundreds of cottonwood trees, all waiting to leaf out, sheltered us from the wind with their limbs. The kids tied their church pews to neighboring trees: Abe's hammock was a blue banana—swaying with the wind—and Life's mesh green tent was a floating triangle, five feet off the ground. Esther ran everywhere, grabbing sticks and hitting trees, and I wondered how we were ever going to pull off a church service of our own.

Life reached up and made a few more adjustments to the straps at each corner of the triangle and then unzipped the eye-level tent. He intercepted Esther and dumped her in. She laughed, bounced, and rolled, making the trees sway. Life jumped off the ground and hoisted himself up—like getting out of the deep end of a pool—and joined the giggle-monster who immediately attacked him. Naomi took a running start and launched her torso into the tent—kicking the air with her feet and sending her shoes flying. Esther, whose static hair floated like a halo, saw her chance and body-slammed her sister who screamed and wiggled in, joining the precarious pew in the sky.

"Come on, Mom!" Life's blue eyes and rosy cheeks bid me to join them.

I was worried the whole screened contraption was going to fall, but since the kids had embraced the outing better than I had expected, I took a deep breath and jumped up, adding myself to the crowded tent suspended in air. My body folded with the sagging floor as I braced myself on nothing, wondering when the three straps would fail and how bad the drop would be.

"Look out guys, here I come!" Abe said, taking a running leap.

We all screamed and threw our arms up to protect our faces as he dove in. The tent swung and sagged, and we all slid to a pathetic pile in the middle. Somehow the thing held. Andrew, his cowboy boots planted firmly on the ground, laughed and told us to smile for a picture. We stuck our haloed heads through the rainbow opening, electrified hair swaying in the wind.

I tried to get comfortable—but there were elbows and knees poking everywhere—and Life's stinky socks were too close to my face. I wedged my cold toes under his rear just moments before I, too, was body-slammed by Esther—who dissolved into a pile of giggles. Naomi played one of her favorite worship songs on her phone. Like winter's lone last leaf letting go and floating to the forest floor, the slow melody of the guitar settled us all.

I thought of Grace.

I wondered where in the world she was at that moment, and I wondered if she was scared. My head rested on Abe's taut belly as I stared at the gray branches blowing in the wind up high. The blue sky was trying to push through the cold March day, and the sun was hidden somewhere far away.

Andrew pulled himself out of Abe's hammock and called his congregation to order. He stood tall and handsome in his cowboy hat, flannel, Levi's, and worn leather belt and boots. Now married for twenty-six years, we are growing older together, graying together. When he laughs, the laugh lines remain.

I love this man.

And that day, I loved that he had brought his family outside for church.

He opened his Bible—turned a few thin pages—cleared his throat and read, "My dear brothers and sisters, be quick to listen, slow to speak, and slow to get angry."

I laughed because I knew he was prepping us for the weeks to come, prepping us for sheltering in together. It was hard to know who was more anxious about it—the kids, or us.

"Okay, I'm next," Naomi said. Andrew handed her the Bible across our jumbled limbs. She searched and read, "For God has not given us a spirit of fear and timidity, but of power, love, and self-discipline."

The words were a balm to my soul.

Naomi handed the Bible to Life, who tried to prop himself up on his elbow, only to sink back into the mushy mess. He held the big book above him with both hands and sorted through the pages, clearing his throat.

"When you pray . . ." he began, and I watched him as he read. I was amazed that the kids were sharing verses full of meaning, instead of pulling some random passage from the Old Testament about foreskins, circumcision, or battles. He continued, ". . . Your Father knows exactly what you need even before you ask him."

Esther could no longer keep still, and she began squirming and rolling over everyone. Andrew grabbed her from the tent, and she was thrilled, as she, too, had had enough of us. They swung in the hammock together as we tent-dwellers heaved a collective sigh of relief.

Abe sat up, displacing my head. He grabbed the Bible, flipped through a few pages, cleared his voice, and read, "Do not worry about everyday life—whether you have enough food and drink, or enough clothes to wear . . . ."

As he read, I thought of the extra beans, canned peaches, and spaghetti I had bought that week. Our pantry was full.

"Isn't life more than food, and your body more than clothing? Look at the birds."

I thought of the eagles.

"They don't plant or harvest or store food in barns, for your heavenly Father feeds them. And aren't you far more valuable to him than they are? Can all your worries add a single moment to your life?"

He closed the Bible, resting it on my chest. I picked a short verse, as the sermon had already gone too long and I knew the congregation was antsy to leave. I turned to the Psalms and read, "The Lord gives his people strength; the Lord blesses his people with peace."

Naomi volunteered to close us in prayer. She asked God to protect our family—to give us peace—and for Grace to make it back to us safely.

For a moment, I had almost forgotten about it all—about the new normal of staying home and the new routine we would need to create. I had almost forgotten that a whole generation was dying in Italy. I had almost forgotten that my daughter was flying across the world and sitting in international airports—sharing air with hundreds of travelers from all over the world. Being at the Eagles' Nest on our ranch in the middle of Colorado, I had almost forgotten.

Being outside—immersed and surrounded by the natural world—gives me a sense of peace. When I see the design and harmonious way it all comes together, I am reminded that I am not alone and that my life is not a mere chance happening set on its own course of fate. I am reminded that I have a Creator who is intimately involved and invested in my life.

Church was dismissed, pews were disassembled, and the teenagers headed home, as if they had somewhere important to be. Esther threw rocks, swung sticks, and kicked dirt into gopher holes as Andrew and I took our time walking back. We talked about what life was going to look like—how we would need to quarantine as a family once Grace got home—how it was possible someone we knew and loved could get the virus and not make it through. We talked about how the numbers seemed so far away, so foreign.

We discussed the cows, and how if things got really bad, we could help feed our community for a while. But mostly, we talked about our family, and how time together—the sort of Sabbath from life as we knew it—might contain some blessings. With two kids in college, we realized it would be one of the last times all seven of us would live together for an extended time, just as us.

My phone chimed with a text and a picture from Grace. She had made it to Dubai and was in line for virus screening before she boarded her flight to New York. I showed Andrew the picture of the hundreds of masked travelers, all waiting, just like her. I looked from my phone to the snowy mountains and the open fields around us—with no one else in sight.

My heart tightened when I thought of how far she had yet to travel. But the chosen words from the morning washed over me, and I shared them with Grace.

I breathed, and we walked on. "It'll be good to have her home," Andrew said, taking my hand in his.

Back in the kitchen, I thought about lunch, as it is always about feeding. I wondered how long my pantry stores would need to last?

I was reminded not to worry.

It's just so easy to forget.

I was thankful for the full fruit bowl that adorned my kitchen counter, at least for that day. Naomi and Life joined me, each grabbing a Cutie.

"That was actually pretty cool, Mom," Naomi said, leaning against the counter and digging her thumb into the peel, sending a citrus spritz her way. "I'm glad you and Dad dragged us all the way up there."

Having just spent the fall semester backpacking the jungles of Papua New Guinea with a medical missionary team, Naomi knew that church was not about a building.

Life hopped up on the counter and said, "Yeah, we could do that for church every Sunday." He smiled and popped a sliver of orange in his mouth.

As I wondered how many Sundays would pass before we went back to church in town, I was surprised that it didn't seem to matter.

Chapter 10

The earth continued to absorb body after body as the virus spread throughout the world. Our family was on edge from the pandemic and the new culture it had created, and we were already antsy for summer. We needed spring break. Everyone needed spring break—but it was canceled for our family, town, state, nation, and world. Traditionally, we would split spring break with Seth and Susie—one family staying home to take care of the ranch while the other plays—and then vice-versa.

Our family would usually load up for a canyoneering adventure in Moab, Utah. However, in the spring of 2020—when there was no more tradition and no more usual—no one was flying, no one was driving, and no one was leaving their home unless it was for something essential. Though we all felt stir-crazy and a spring break getaway seemed essential to us, only certain businesses were labeled so, such as Walmart, liquor stores, hospitals, pot shops—and thankfully—farms and ranches.

So, we headed to the river.

Having met as river guides in this very valley, Andrew and I started our life together on the water. Loving the thrill of whitewater rapids and the slow swirls of eddies, floating in the current between canyon walls wells up in us a peace that helps put life into perspective. The river awakens our senses and reminds us of beauty, design, and timelessness. The river feels like a sanctuary.

Our place of solace, peace, refueling, and adventure—we obtained a permit to float Utah's Green River through Desolation and Gray Canyons. The plan was that we would float the Green for the first half of spring break, and Seth's family would float the San Juan River for the second half. Even Papa was willing to risk it and join us. We would leave Grace home alone during the pandemic to finish her Arabic classes with her teacher who Zoomed in from the Middle East.

Grace was not happy.

"It's completely irresponsible," she said. "The entire country is in lockdown and you guys are leaving me to go on the river?"

She was angry, hurt, and scared. And I knew what she really wanted was to come along. But she couldn't. She had online finals, classes, and group projects—she still had jet lag from her insane trip home from the Middle East—and she was still technically in quarantine. Nothing about it was ideal. Nothing. I wavered back and forth. Should we cancel? Should we go?

I braved Walmart with my gloves, mask, and hand sanitizer. On the way, I noticed that people were wearing masks while driving—alone—in their cars. I saw masked people walking and jogging the trails.

I took my typical river menu to Walmart and came home with it majorly altered, as there just wasn't much available. Eggs and milk were completely out—and toilet paper had been scarce for weeks. Empty shelves and empty faces filled the aisles.

I froze layers of ice in lasagna pans and brought the huge river coolers down from the attic above the barn. Andrew filled the rafts with air, checked all the nozzles and thwarts, and gave all the technical gear a good once-over. The kids dug past their dusty ski gear to find life jackets, wet suits, Chacos, and shorts. Red sand remnants from last year's river trips fell from overturned dry bags, and sleeping bags were stuffed.

Then, the day before we were to leave, Andrew called off the trip.

"It's too risky," he told everyone.

Seth's river permit had been canceled that morning—the San Juan River was officially closed. One could swim through the tension in the house. I had a deep need for river currents, red canyon walls, sandy beaches, and blue herons. In desperation, I called the BLM office in Price, Utah.

"Yep, we're still open," the ranger told me. "I can't tell you not to come—it's a come at your own risk typa thing."

The trip was back on.

We loaded the horse trailer—which looked essential—with all our essential river gear. I told Grace we would be careful, that we had full-sized spare tires for all the vehicles and the trailer, that we would stop once and pay at the pump for gas on the way there and stop once for gas on the way home—that we had packed all our food and would stop for nothing else.

"Yeah, but the irresponsibility comes when you guys need a new tire, or when someone gets hurt on the river and you pull rescue and medical workers away from Covid patients to help *you* because *you* were recreating. It's just not right." I knew Grace was partly right and mostly disappointed she couldn't go. A summer raft guide herself, and a lover of the river just as much as we are, it was torture for her to stay behind.

Part of me wanted to cancel and just stay home—to sacrifice and show Grace how much I loved her. However, there were four other kids who were equally as passionate about going. If we stayed home, the week would be torturous for us all, with the kids (and me) sulking. If we stayed home, spring winds would have blown cold and strong as the kids helped with new calves in the snow. They would give Andrew and me "the look," the look that would say, "We could have been on the river right now." And me, I needed a break. I needed a break from the pandemic. I needed a break from the walls of the house, the dishes, the meals, the laundry, the bills, the freezing wind, and the dormant landscape.

And so, we went.

As we drove off, I thought of Grace at the table—all alone—and my heart felt like a river divided around a sandbar. We left Colorado, while under lockdown, for the state of Utah, which was not. I thought of Grace, and I felt as empty as the highways.

We arrived in the dark and opened our doors to the cool spring night. The desert stars welcomed us as we left our masks on the dash. We were the only people at the put-in—even the ranger was gone for the evening. As the campfire crackled and its orange sparks mingled with the stars, I began to loosen and unfold, like a sleeping bag pulled from its stuff sack.

The morning sun the next day displayed the beauty we had driven to in the night—a wide, slow river and red cliffs rising into canyon walls downstream. We unloaded all the gear at the water's edge. The gentle warmth of the sun seemed to soothe everyone's nerves. The calm of the river and the desert were finally settling in. We unrolled and pumped up rafts, filling them with coolers and dry bags. We lined up life jackets for the ranger to count, along with our rescue gear, throw bags, and the rest of the required gear for a multi-day trip.

I slipped our permit into the box outside the ranger's house, per the directions on the door. We saw him an hour later when he drove his truck twenty yards from the river's edge where we were checking straps, cracking open drinks, and putting on sunscreen. We waved and watched him survey our scene. He never got out, and he never said hello. River check-off, pandemic-style.

March on the river can be cold, but the days were warm and therapeutic. Our cups were filling, and we were relaxing more and more as mile after mile floated by.

Each camp held gifts of its own—a deep side canyon to hike, cougar prints in the damp sand, and the sound of the current as we fell asleep under the calming night sky. We played games on the beach, made dinner as the sun set, washed dishes by lantern light, and sat around campfires made of driftwood, forgetting that we had left a world infiltrated by an unseen enemy.

We hugged and laughed once again—and the virus that had stolen the world's smile seemed like only a bad dream.

Each morning brought new light on the canyon walls. The soft sound of the stove heating water for tea and coffee kept us company as we read and journaled. There was so much to write about. Our camp chairs made a colorful crescent facing the river. We watched the water currents swirl together the colors of the canyon and sky. A blue heron stood like a statue on a stone where the ebb and flow of the river laid lines in the sand—a topographic map drawn and erased by the current each day. We listened to the many birds, excited with song, as they perched in the tall cottonwood trees that were slowly starting to unroll their tender spring leaves.

For five days, we had seemingly eliminated the pandemic from our lives. As I watched the dawn illuminate the river corridor, I remembered that for many, the pandemic had been more than a mere interruption to community, routines, and traditions—it had been an end. It had been an end to so many lives across the world—and that weight sank deep—like a rock thrown in the water.

The ripple effect of loss makes us hold more dearly those we love. I thought of Grace. In her loneliness, I hoped there lived a little part of her, deep down, that was proud of her folks for persevering and getting away in the middle of a pandemic, in the middle of a lockdown.

I'm glad we took the trip.

My soul had room to breathe in the vast desert with its canyons and rivers. Though the ranch is wide open, there is something about a change of scenery, a change of climate, and a chosen change of routine. Though the planning and shopping were done, there were still meals to make; but mealtimes took on a fun freshness as we all worked together to cook outside under the open sky. Even dish duty under the stars was a novelty—with lively talks that sent our headlamps bobbing up and down as we scraped, dipped, washed, rinsed, and rinsed again.

With headlamps twisted off, the lantern hissed down, and the dish towels tied to a willow branch to dry in the desert air, the kitchen was tucked in for the evening. I walked to the river where the moon made the water white at night. I listened to the calls of the owls I couldn't see. I heard the water in the eddy flowing upstream at the back of the rafts whose round bows rested on the shiny wet sand near my feet. Listening in the dark made things clearer—like closing your eyes when you reach to touch.

I left the river feeling like a winter-weary field that had finally seen the first waters of spring.

Chapter 11

M arch melted into April, and April blossomed into May. The days
warmed, the fields thawed, and the calves ran in the soft spring
green of the pasture. The lockdown languished, but the pandemic persisted. Social distancing was the new way of life, and we saw few people
outside our family.

Andrew and Grace, the two introverts, embraced social distancing.

"I love this—now people don't bug me to go out all the time," Grace
said.

"We've been trying to do this for years!" Andrew said.

But Naomi, Abe, and Life—they couldn't stay away from friends,
despite our protests.

"We're only outside looking at the stars," Naomi said.

"Just dirt biking, Mom, just dirt biking," Abe said.

And Life, somehow, even without a driver's license, still managed
to get out and about through it all. I checked in with friends, mostly
through texts, trying to remember to keep up with everyone's lives when

coffee dates came to a halt. But I still tried to celebrate the important things—like the April morning that Susie and Suzanne came over to celebrate Suzanne's birthday. We had coffee and banana bread on the breezy porch where we cozied up in blankets six feet apart, breathing the fresh air as we caught up and enjoyed each other's unmasked smiles. Suzanne showed us her new mountain bike—as she was thrilled to be living free from cancer once again.

Though the world felt terribly unstable, we continued to find stability in the routines and rhythms on the ranch. Each spring, once calving and branding are over, we introduce the bulls back in with the cows—on or near Mother's Day—a date that makes it easier to remember when Andrew and Seth go to calculate the number of days the bulls have been in. It's hilarious to watch the enormous bulls come to life when they enter the pasture full of cows in heat. Solid masses of muscle, they strut and sniff, throwing their heads high in the air and curling back their top lips. They bellow, moan, and mount as they spend the next sixty days "servicing" their harem of twenty-five or thirty cows. Our kids learned a lot about sex by watching the bulls and their huge, dangling "seed sacks" as they fertilized the egg nestled inside the cow. The kids saw it all—ending with the calves born every spring.

Mother's Day 2020 came, and it was a perfect day.

I woke to Grace and Naomi making heart-shaped buttermilk waffles with berries and whipped cream. Excited for warmer weather, all seven of us ate in the warmth of the spring sun on the front porch. Songbirds serenaded the sun and swallows made countless flights back and forth from the ditch to the eaves of our house, beaks full of mud, busily building their homes.

"Well, Mom, what do you want to do today? It's your day!" Life said, sitting on the warm porch as our mama cat slinked by and rubbed her back against his.

"Hmm . . . well, I do love a good hike to a high lake, but I think it's too early for wildflowers, and the lakes are probably still frozen." I ran my hand over the warm coat of my golden retriever, Molly, who lay by my side—my best friend covered in sunshine. "How about getting on the river?"

I know the kids all inwardly breathed a sigh of relief that I didn't mention yard work—my other go-to when I have their full presence for a day. Normally, a May day on the ranch would be spent up at a summer pasture in the high country, checking perimeter fences and repairing broken wires where the elk had crossed during the winter. Abe always makes sure he's on those workdays so he can search for antlers as he rolls the four-wheeler along the melting patches of snow, stringing and tightening new wire. It's truly a treasure hunt in the forest.

That spring we were making a concerted effort to set Sundays apart a bit more—an attempt to create a day of rest from the long ranch days that easily exhaust us all. Knowing that the day was originally designed to give a break from work, we tried to prepare for Sundays before they arrived by getting projects wrapped up and tools put away. But there were still the daily chores that we could not ignore—the feeding and the irrigating.

We pulled ourselves like Velcro from the sunny porch while the cats stayed and lingered in their warm places, curled up and cozy. Life volunteered to clean up the kitchen and Abe left to feed the cows. The girls gathered life jackets and got themselves river-ready. Andrew, Essie, and I took the four-wheeler to irrigate, and I hopped off along the way to see the eagles. As I walked, I called Mom and texted my friends and sisters-in-law to wish them a Happy Mother's Day. It was fun to have texts chirp in throughout the day with pink hearts and flowers and little snippets about what everyone else was doing. And I remembered

Ruthie—how on Mother's Day we would always plant flowers in the whiskey barrel by her front door.

Chores finished and the kitchen clean, we looked to the river. Abe unfolded his raft on the concrete floor of the barn and flipped the switch of the air compressor, filling the stiff and wrinkled baffles full of air. We scurried around like happy ants as we gathered all the things we would need for a picnic on the river.

Springtime was breathing new life into us all.

We piled in a pickup truck with the raft strapped to the back and drove to the river. We launched and floated past the ranch and Papa's house into town. The kids all took turns rowing, and it was great to be on the water again. Like an unrolled raft, we stretched our stiff white legs, thawing our mid-solstice bodies. We watched hawks leave their cottonwood perches to fly, fall, and climb in the warming spring air. Ducks and geese bobbed in the crisp currents, and a blue heron stood very still on the pebbled shore, watching for fish. The river, once again, was completely soothing—reminding me that there was a whole wild world going on outside my own.

Back home, river gear drying in the yard, Andrew and the boys planted toddler-sized spruce trees they had dug up the day before. Each year, the aspen and spruce at the summer pastures in the high country creep a little closer from the edge of the woods into the fields and the ditches. Andrew brings home any trees he needs to remove and plants them in our yard. They are always a gift.

The girls heated leftover burritos for dinner, and we gathered together again to watch the sun descend from the back patio. When the cool of the evening settled in the valley and once Essie was fast asleep, we frosted the special day with a game at the table.

◆ ◆ ◆

It was at the table, while playing cards, that I got the call.

I got the call at nine p.m., and it began one of the worst nightmares of my life.

One of Suzanne's daughters was on the line, and she could barely speak. She was crying, almost hyperventilating.

"Have you heard about Mom?" she asked.

My first thought was that Suzanne must be in the hospital with some sort of horrible cancer-related emergency. Thoughts of Ruthie came to me—how cancer can suddenly take someone before their time. But Suzanne wasn't in the hospital. She was nowhere to be found.

Suzanne was missing.

Her daughters had been on a road trip to Idaho, and her husband had gone to Denver for a work project that morning before the sun came up. Suzanne had woken up alone on Mother's Day. She had left on a bike ride by herself—and her bike was found—but she never returned. The memory of her sweet smile when she showed Susie and me her new bike flashed into my mind. No one had heard from her all day, including me. She was the only one who had never returned my Happy Mother's Day text.

The call ended and I answered my family's wide-eyed faces.

"I'll stay here with Essie—you guys go," Life said. He has a deep sense of what is needed and frequently offers to stay with Essie when Andrew and I need to get out on a date, visit someone in the hospital, gather loose cows, or fix a flooding ditch. We left him alone at the table with our cards dealt to play. Andrew, Grace, Naomi, Abe, and I all put on coats, warm hats, and hiking boots. We grabbed backpacks and flashlights.

As we drove for fifteen minutes up Monarch Pass, I watched the gray of the western sky as it blackened and joined the silhouette of the mountains. I thought about how Suzanne had been alone on Mother's Day. No waffles on the porch, no float to town in a boat filled with her family, no beautiful spruce trees planted in her yard, no cards played at her table.

Alone.

We all wondered out loud what had happened to one of the kindest people we had ever known. New to mountain biking, we were worried she was suffering from a concussion or a broken arm somewhere in the dark forest.

The eerie glow from emergency vehicles lighted the ponderosa trees that lined the dirt road to Suzanne's house. Andrew pulled off the highway and our eyes flashed with red, blue, and white lights as we came upon a mess of people—some scurrying while others huddled like bugs around a porch light. Dozens of search-and-rescue volunteers, Chaffee County Sheriff's deputies, Salida Police, and a couple of Suzanne's friends and neighbors filled the spaces between the vehicles lining both sides of the dirt road.

"Oh, no," was all I could say, as the seriousness of the situation glared in our eyes. I started to shake and my heartbeat picked up its pace. Andrew parked our car and we all bundled up and headed down the dirt road.

The cool night air only heightened our attention. We found Suzanne's husband standing in the road near where her bike had been found. Andrew and I hugged him.

"You're a good man," he told Andrew.

We stood with him for hours—Andrew on one side—and me on the other. His two daughters arrived just before midnight. We wept and wondered together. A neighbor gathered a small group of us together and, in her quivering voice, said, "I think we need to pray." We huddled together as she prayed for Suzanne to be found. I had no idea that her prayer would be the first of countless others said for our friend and her family.

Frustrated that we were not allowed to join the search, we listened to the emergency radios, watched official search-and-rescue teams filter through the woods, and waited for the search dogs to arrive and hopefully catch Suzanne's scent.

Nothing.

We stood together until 2:30 that cold morning when the teams were called off until sunrise.

As we drove home, we had so many questions: Who had her? Where was she? What happened?

I worried she had crashed and hit her head, had tried to walk home, and had fallen in the creek. I pictured her submerged in the spring runoff—caught under some tree pushed over by the fierce winter winds that often tore through the steep valley.

A week of fruitless searching passed.

Friends, family, and volunteers spread out over the Rocky Mountains looking for Suzanne. Eventually, what began as a missing person case turned into a full-blown criminal investigation, with no declared suspects.

It was hard to fall asleep and hard to wake up. I was in a constant state of prayer for Suzanne and her family. She could have been anywhere after one week. My mind was plagued with horrible thoughts—stories of women kept in basements for decades and women caught in human trafficking. I wondered if she was close by in some weird forest camp held by a madman, or if she was being trafficked in Vegas. I was nauseous at the thought of her being raped and killed or buried alive. Amidst all the awful "what ifs," there were two things I knew to be true deep in my heart: Suzanne was not suicidal, and she would never have intentionally left her family to suffer in the torturous grief caused by her unexplained disappearance.

Andrew and the kids helped in the search, and I helped with the meals. I went each day to sit with her girls. And I had no words.

● ● ●

One morning, the church lunch moms sat in a parked minivan, with twelve long banners rolled like a pile of sacred white scrolls on the floor. Though it had been a long Covid spring away from each other, we sat in silence.

Suzanne had brought us together.

We began to unroll one of the banners along the length of the van floor past flip flops, painted toes, running shoes, and cowboy boots—and then stopped it when the large red letters printed on the white plastic background shocked us all, though we already knew. We sat around the banner and wept.

There was no softening the raw reality that sat before us: one of us was MISSING.

Our wet faces watched as we unrolled the rest of the banner and Suzanne's sweet smile greeted us. As our deep sobs escaped, we somehow managed to laugh that she would like the pictures they chose. We stared at her bougie brown sunglasses, her teal bike helmet, and her thin gold necklace against her tan skin. *Beautiful.* We shook our heads and stared at each other. We knew we must rally. We knew we had urgent work set before us: there were banners to hang because one of us was *missing*. Where do four frantic friends hang the first banner? Walmart.

Our shaky fingers threaded orange baling twine through the gold grommets at each corner of the banner we hung at the front entrance. We tied and straightened and re-tied as if Suzanne's life depended on it. My scattered mind tried to remember how to tie a square knot I'd tied a million times before. I wanted the banner to hold. People stared as they walked by, some stopped and cocked their heads to read with a furrowed brow. One asked, "Did you know her?"

"We do," I answered, without looking up.

Tears fogged my sunglasses. Banner straight and taut, I laughed inside, thinking that Suzanne would never believe she was a Walmart greeter. It felt wrong to laugh, but how do people live life amidst tragedy? Walking back to the minivan, we all realized we were subconsciously peering through the windows of parked vans and cars, looking for her face staring back at us. Looking became a new part of our lives—looking for her on roadsides, in backyards, in basement window wells, in forests, and at rest stops. There was an urgency in everything we did—as if time was running out—as if she were being taken further away with every second.

The minivan door slid closed and we drove to hang the next banner. Questions bounced back and forth as we clarified facts and shared last texts and last words. We made ourselves sick thinking of all the possibilities. With no answers, and only more questions, we quieted down and looked out the windows.

The next week, as the banners hung all over town, we each made meals for Suzanne's family in our own solitary kitchens, with our own solitary thoughts. I sliced and diced red, orange, and green peppers, purple cabbage, and bright green cilantro. I thought about how thankful I was that Susie and I had celebrated Suzanne's birthday on the porch just a week before she went missing—how Grace had juiced a special drink for us. I winced at the thought that I had almost canceled our get-together.

I was almost too busy.

I squeezed the juice of three limes and remembered how Suzanne was so excited about her new mountain bike and how good she had been feeling since her clean scan. I went down the list of things for dinner—was I missing anything? I leaned against the counter and thought of her family and how they could barely stomach a meal.

But the other searchers—I knew they were ravenous and needed the calories.

That week, we cooked and baked and replenished supplies of Gatorade, granola bars, and homemade cookies. It was what we knew how to do—and we needed to do something. The whole church eventually provided meals for the family over the next month.

I had no idea that a week would turn into a month and that a month would turn into years. I had no idea when I woke up to a special breakfast that Mother's Day how perfect the day would be. And I had no idea how quickly perfect would change.

• • •

Though I felt paralyzed and frozen by fear, the ground had thawed.

I went to the garden and got my hands in the spring soil. Andrew rototilled, forming long mounds of gorgeous dirt. We turned over the sleepy soil in the raised beds, careful to work around the soft sprigs of green chives poking through, fresh and full of promise amidst the decay of last year's stringy brown remnants. Life and death commingled in the garden while faith and despair fought each other for my heart and mind.

As I pulled the crinkly tangles of mint from the herb bed, I breathed in the strong, fresh smell and it woke me with wonder. The air filled with anticipation and expectation. The energy of life surrounded me. The earth felt like a bustling building full of schoolchildren—antsy from the long winter—waiting for the last bell of the semester to ring. I was thankful for the wonder that came with the newness of spring, thankful for the promise of growth and change. The barn cats wandered out to curl up on the rich soil in the sun. They kept us company as we placed tiny seeds of hope into the darkness.

Time in the garden is life-giving. I always come away invigorated, with a renewed perspective. Though gardens breathe life into humankind, the planting is always an exercise of faith. Every spring, that one glorious morning always surprises me when I walk out to check the newly planted garden and delight at the tiny green flecks of life pushing up through the dark dirt. The spring garden grows gratitude in me, knowing that one day its harvest will be a gift of nourishment to my friends and loved ones.

• • •

Through the uncertain days of the pandemic and Suzanne's disappearance, gathering around the table as a family created stability for us. When nothing felt normal, right, or balanced, the simple routine of mealtime helped ground us. Joining our hands together to give thanks before we ate seemed to help reset the insanity of the world, even if just for a moment.

Whether I held Andrew's rough hand whose fingerprints were stained with tractor grease; Grace's long fingers that flew over the letters of her laptop as she finished her semester online; Naomi's hand still frigid from dipping it into the freezing spring irrigation ditch to change a tarp; Abe's hand smelling like bar oil from a chainsaw after cutting trees that had fallen in the ditch; Life's hand that smelled like soap after washing off the smell of his 4H pigs after he walked them down the road and back; or Essie's little hand, still sticky from the first popsicle of the season—these hands gave me strength.

SUMMER

SUMMER

Chapter 12

When summer arrives on the ranch, it's hard to believe that I ever wish for things to stop growing in the fall. As the light shifts and spring makes way for summer, I am thrilled for the long, hot days when everything feels alive and well. Once the last frost has come and gone, we dig down and set into the garden soil the hearty plants of zucchini, cucumber, pumpkin, and yellow squash whose seeds we started inside when spring snows still fell. Come June, Andrew's long days spent irrigating the hay fields in April and May finally come to fruition as the grass and alfalfa are tall and waving in the new summer breezes.

The cattle are all paired up, cows with their calves, and they are trucked in semis to the larger pastures over two hours away, or trailered to the smaller, closer pastures. They will enjoy these pastures, rotating grazing all summer, until we bring them home in the fall.

We get two cuttings of hay each summer—one in mid-June and one in August. The alfalfa is ready to cut when its first tender purple blossoms begin to appear; and the grass is ready to harvest when the seed heads thicken like wheat at the end of the stalks.

It's an incredible feeling sitting on a tractor and baling hay. The view is astounding as the mountains on all sides create a valley where the hay fields shimmer and wave in the breeze. In June, remnants of snowstorms linger in the shadows on Mt. Shavano while the rivers and creeks fill with winter's water.

The weather forecast is checked throughout the day, as a week of sunshine is ideal for making hay. With six hundred acres of hay to cut, dry, rake, bale, and stack, the first cutting takes about a month from start to finish. Once the grass and alfalfa are cut and laid to dry for days in neat windrows by the swather—the massive machine with the scissoring knives that click, swish, pull, and cut—one lucky teenager (you, a sibling, or a cousin) rises with the sun to start raking the hay before the baling begins. While the dew is still on the green rainbow of rows that fill the field, the rake spins and grabs two rows, fluffing and combining them into one. The alfalfa leaves cling to the stalks only for those early morning hours before the sun warms the valley. If the rake comes after the dew, the precious protein-filled leaves will fall, lost to the ground.

This summer morning you are part of the baling crew who drives the tractors pulling balers back and forth, back and forth, back and forth over the fluffy green lines of beautifully cut grass and alfalfa warming in the early sun. You watch hawks, crows, and magpies (and if you're lucky, an eagle) swoop in and grab a mouse scurrying for cover from one windrow to the next. Or maybe you'll spy a coyote slinking along the pasture's edge—only to blow its cover when it spies a prairie dog and leaps in the air to pounce on its prey.

Baling days are long and repetitive, but they are also full of team-work and satisfaction. Like vacuuming or doing laundry, you can see the progress of your work as you go along. As you straddle your tractor and baler over the row of hay you are baling, you can look back and see the dotted line of tight and tidy hay bales that follows behind you like railroad cars. You can feel the rhythm of the baler as it collects each flake—and since you've checked the weight, tension, length, and moisture of the bales—they are popping out in perfect form.

You wave when another baler passes you (your cousin, sibling, aunt, uncle, grandfather, mom, or dad), knowing they are listening to an audio book, a podcast, the small-town country radio station, or their latest playlist. You pass another, and you laugh because it's that one cousin whose big smile you can see a mile away—the cousin who waves with both hands off the wheel—her blonde topknot bopping to her tunes. Though you don't think of it often, today you think that the ranch is a pretty fun place to grow up.

Lunchtime comes, and you can't wait for the four-wheeler to come rolling down the open aisle between windrows and stop for you. The lunch barista (usually your mom or your Auntie Susie) hops off with a smile, delivering a sandwich, a stack of salty Pringles, a crisp apple or a bunch of sweet grapes—and if you're lucky, maybe some Oreos or homemade chocolate chip cookies.

You idle the tractor and pause the baler—all in the correct order of things—swing open the heavy door and climb down the metal stairs to the stiff stems of the mown field below. You stretch and twist and realize that you needed a break. You update the barista about the abundant hay harvest and thank her for taking the time to remember you. She waves and speeds off to the next hungry baler. You grab a bite of sandwich—perfect—mustard, no mayo—and look around at the sea of hay bales surrounding you. You look south to the cottonwood trees and see the eagles' nest high in the old forked branch. To the west, you see frail lines of snow in the shadows of Mt. Shavano.

You take off your hat and wipe the sweat from your forehead and then remember to pee behind the huge black tractor tire before you climb back into the air-conditioned cab and get back to baling, eating as you go.

• • •

When I watch my kids, nephews, and niece as they bale hay all summer long, I remember my own childhood. I grew up living near a combination of California beaches and mountains, then a small Colorado mountain town just west of Denver, and then in Denver itself. Having tasted family life for a season before divorce came in and cut my family down like a swather, I knew a few years of family dinners around a table with Mom at one end and Dad at the other. But life for everyone is not always so pastoral. Marriages fall apart. Homes are divided. Dreams, once strong and vivid, are cut to pieces.

I looked forward to my summers away from school, summers filled with church camps, YMCA day camps, and hot days spent at the community pool. Though my newly single parents were persevering through their own struggles with finances, addictions, and relationships after the divorce, they always made sure I was loved and provided for. My two older brothers, Ted and Garrett, licked their own wounds in their own ways, and we did not grow up tightly knit. I gravitated toward friends who had what seemed like "stable" homes, learning a lot about family from other families.

Though childhood for me was not easy, and though it was often lonely, there was a consistent thread of love in my life—from my parents, yes, very much so—but the strongest love came from my relationship with my Creator. This love has been the rock upon which I have stood all my life, no matter the storm raging around me. And the more intense the storm, the more planted I am. If I could go back and exchange a more "stable" and "easy" childhood for my relationship with God, I would not.

Like an alfalfa plant, I grow stronger with each harvest.

• • •

Hours and hours and bales and bales later, you look out the enormous tractor window and realize you've watched the sun span its arc across the entire sky—from the hills in the east to the mountains in the west. You watch as the sky changes, highlighting the dust and the myriad of insects that float and fly around your tractor. You hope the sun is thinking about setting—though you know it's still too early—and you think about how you could easily go to bed.

A few more songs play and another hundred bales are baled as you see a cloud of dust in the distance and squint: is that the four-wheeler again? Is it *milkshake time*? Yes! Your weary baling soul revives as the barista's smile gets closer and closer. Straight from the blender, she pours your empty water bottle full of the most delicious combination of chocolate ice cream and bananas—the best milkshake you've ever had.

Your teeth are covered with green hay slime from baling and grinning all day long . . . because what better summer job is there? You climb back in and look at the sea of hay bales around you. You see your dad or Uncle Seth (and these days, Abe) cruising around the fields in the huge yellow and red stack wagons, sucking up hay bales one at a time—a farmer's vacuum. They fill the 160-bale stack wagons and drive to the hay barn, carefully backing and tilting the huge block of bales until it perfectly lines up and leans against the growing stack of hay stored under the tall metal roof that holds ten thousand bales.

Though it's dinner time all across the valley, the work isn't done yet on the ranch. You wait until the hay boss of the day, either your dad or

Uncle Seth, sends the text to the "hay crew" group chat—letting everyone know it's "time to knock off," as Uncle Dan always says.

Until then, you watch the glorious display of colors unfold as the sun finally begins to lower—and the western sky turns exquisite shades of red, orange, yellow, blue, and purple—a constantly changing rainbow laid out along the horizon made of peaks. The temperature changes in the cab as the sun leaves the valley. No group text comes in, but you see there are only two more rows for you to bale, and you know the other balers across the field are almost done, too. As it cools off, and with quitting time just on the horizon, there's a renewed sense of energy and comradery as everyone stays to finish the job.

You think of how rewarding this job is as you bale the very last bale and turn the tractor toward the barn. You see the other two blue tractors pulling their red balers that way, too, as you all navigate through the checkerboard of hay bales. You think of dinner and a shower as the stars arrive . . . one by one. At the barn you park the tractor, shutting it down in the correct order of things. The hay boss is there to greet all the happy balers with his own green smile: "Amazing job today, everyone—the bales were uniform and tight—the perfect length, weight, and moisture."

Everyone smiles and stares up at the towering stacks of hay—beautiful, perfect, green. You and your siblings and cousins make plans for a family movie and maybe a late-night trip to Sonic for yet another milkshake. You hop in your favorite old blue Ford and head for home. You take it slow and see Venus twinkling above the peaks as you go west. You roll the window down, toss your dusty ball cap on the even dustier seat, and lean out to let the breeze blow through your sweaty hair. In the side mirror, you see your reflection, along with the tiny tip of a crescent moon rising in the east behind you.

At home, you wash up and make it to the table just in time for prayer as your family gathers to close the day with homegrown steaks straight off the grill, creamy mashed potatoes, and a fresh salad from the garden. You think to yourself that things cannot possibly get better than this.

• • •

But the days, they don't always happen that way.

Some days look a little more like this . . .

You wake up late, grab a bowl of cereal, pull on tired boots from the pile at the door, and head out to find a pickup or four-wheeler to drive out to the field. Your siblings beat you to it: all the trucks and four-wheelers are gone, so you are left with walking or riding your bike. You bike, cereal bowl in one hand, down the washboard dirt road and across the field to where everyone is already lubing balers and refilling twine. You're late. Though it's light, the sky is cloudy, and it's obvious that a summer storm is coming in from somewhere. Bed-headed teenagers fill the tractors, and you realize you are left with the lame one—the one with the broken radio and broken air conditioning, whose baler constantly gets jammed with hay—the tractor no one wants to drive.

You lube it up and check the twine boxes. They are close to empty, with only enough for a few bales left. You look around for the orange spools of new twine, but all you see are their empty plastic bags blowing around. You walk to the milk barn and grab the heavy twine and load up your boxes, trying to remember how to tie the knots just right. You tie and re-tie, finally getting it. Your phone buzzes—it's a text from your dad—the hay boss for the day, wondering where you are and why everyone else is baling but you.

You start the tractor and realize you are on empty. You release the emergency brake and drive over to the two big tanks and put the nozzle in and pull the handle. The fuel starts to travel down the hose to the tractor when you realize that the tank you're pulling from is unleaded gas, not diesel. You let the handle go just before the fuel enters the trac-tor. You shake your head and hang the handle back up, grab the correct one, and fill the tank.

A huge gray cloud is already hovering over the mountains. You see your dad driving the old tractor with no cab on the far end of the field—the orange rake bumping along behind him, whirling and spin-ning and throwing windrows of hay together into one fluffy row be-tween the tractor tires. He is cruising, racing the clouds. You know he's done the twist-and-scratch test to see if the hay is cured—the twist-ing of a handful of hay to see if it breaks within three twists and the scratching of the bark of an alfalfa stalk to see if it's dry and ready to bale, or if it's still soft and shaves off with your fingernail, indicating it needs more time to dry. Making sure the hay is properly cured is essen-tial, since customers are paying good money for premium hay (not hay that's baled too soon, turns moldy, and gets so hot inside it can ignite itself and burn down a barn).

You see Uncle Seth weaving through the field like a speedy beetle with a big load on its back, sucking up hay bales, one by one, onto the back of the stack wagon. He zigs, zags, swerves, and lines up just right as each sixty-pound bale enters the wagon and is neatly stacked. The hay barn is full, so he adds to the outside stack that will have to be tarped before the rain hits. You find a raked row of hay and line your tractor and baler up just right. You stop and remember the order of things—because if you get it wrong, the long PTO (Power Take-Off) shaft spinning behind the tractor will twist and break.

You feel like everyone is watching you, and you know your dad is, since the machine you are driving cost the ranch $75,000. If you break it, not only are the repairs costly, but then one baler is out of commis-sion when a storm's coming. You sigh with relief that you chose correct-ly—you got the order right—and you are off and baling.

You look out the huge window, dirty with hay dust, pollen, and dried aphids. You see the other balers pulling along, green bales falling to the ground every twenty seconds or so. Then you remember you are supposed to be counting the flakes of hay as the baler spins, collects, squishes, and ties the flakes into the rectangle bales. As you listen to the *whumpf . . . whumpf . . . whumpf* coming from the belly of the baler, you try to count thirteen repetitions—thirteen flakes—thirteen mouthfuls of hay pushed together to create one bale.

You wish you could listen to music, but the radio's broken and your phone is almost dead. You know you shouldn't listen to anything but the *whumpf* anyways. You drive along and see the clouds building up north now. It's gonna be a big one. You think about how beautiful the hay looks right now—bright and healthy, like a nice green salad. You know that one big storm can come in and dump an inch of rain and ruin the hay, adding a week's more work to the sad harvest that ends with ugly stacks of brown hay. You watch the hay bosses working as hard as they can, and you know they are watching the clouds, too, right along with you.

Then, like a sudden storm, your work day fills with hay jams, broken bales, and knots you tied wrong, making the bale strings tie incorrectly. It seems like at every row you have to stop for some mistake or some stroke of bad luck. For every five good bales there are ten bad ones. You get frustrated and start to drive a little faster as you see the sky turn one shade darker.

You see Uncle Seth cruising faster now, too, with a full load to add to the stack, when you think you see a drop of rain on your windshield. Sure enough . . . another falls . . . then another. You look to your dad, who is on his last row with the rake. As you drive along, the storm fills the whole valley, from north to south, and that's when you see Uncle Seth's last perfect stack fall apart like a sandcastle as he pulls the wagon away. You see him get out and scramble to restack the fallen hay bales in some semblance of order before the water unleashes from the dark clouds above his head.

The sound of rough gravel startles and informs you that you drove past the end of your row and you turn quick and hard, forgetting to turn wide—and it all happens faster than you can think. You hear the thunderous clap of metal snap behind you. Your stomach turns a sickening flip, and you stop and shut everything down. This will not be a quick fix. This is more than just a simple hay jamb.

A broken PTO costs $1,500 to replace.

You hop out and see the twisted, severed arm of the PTO dangling in two pieces like a broken bone. You feel the intermittent drops of rain on your shirt and see the thin, dry blades of grass bow under the weight of each drop. You think to yourself: *things cannot possibly get worse than this.* You take off your hat and run your fingers through your hair. This is way beyond your skill set, and you look to see your dad, headed your way, done with the raking. He stops his tractor near yours and hops out—smiling green—until he sees your face and the PTO.

"Oh," he says, as his eyebrows raise and come together in thought. "Turned too tight?"

You nod.

"Well, we'll figure that out later," he says, staring at the sky, having triaged the situation. "We've gotta get that hay tarped before this storm hits. Let's drive back to the stack and you can help me." He walks back to his tractor and heads for the long stack of hay where Uncle Seth is bracing the bales with long wooden poles.

You look one more time with regret at the broken shaft between the tractor and baler and then climb back inside the cab. Raindrops roll the length of the windshield, dragging green hay dust down the glass. You try to console yourself—*it's almost too wet to bale now anyways.*

The cab fills with the earthy scent of rain wetting the dry fields. You love the moisture as it falls over the ranch mid-summer . . . how it settles the dust . . . how it balances and sparkles on the periwinkle petals of the alfalfa blossoms. You think about how a rainstorm can be both a curse and a blessing—how it can ruin one field of cut and drying hay while watering another filled with thirsty plants growing taller and taller until their time.

The tractor chugs to life and you drive toward the stack. You picture what the next thirty minutes will involve: climbing the tall hay stack that has grown to over one thousand bales, pulling the outer bales up and stacking them the entire length of the middle to create a peak from one end to the other, and hoisting a heavy gray tarp up on top and unfolding it across the whole stack—all while your hair stands on end and lightning cracks in the west.

You park the tractor and race the storm as the drops get heavier and your shirt gets wetter. You climb the stack and stand on the top—surveying the storm as it rushes the valley. You take careful steps to avoid the deep crevasses between bales as you and your dad pull the side bales up, stack them in a neat line, and unfold and tighten the tarp. Out in the field, you see the other balers heading back—it's definitely too wet to bale now. You climb down and secure the massive tarp with thick black rubber straps hooked to shiny grommets every two feet.

You are amazed that your dad still smiles even though the rain taps on the tight tarp, waters the wilting windrows, and shines the sharp steel of the severed PTO. You know his joy and peace come from somewhere deep inside. Though the ranch runs on its routines, there are days when routines, pride, and PTOs get broken—days when the order of things gets fractured, jumbled, and severed—and it's on these days that joy is tested down to its very roots.

Chapter 13

Though we may have our routines, and those routines may bring comfort and a semblance of order to the chaos of life, the unexpected can descend upon us, changing everything in just one moment. One summer, just after Life's eighth birthday, a real whopper came our way. I never thought that a child's wheelchair would be among the chairs pulled up to our table.

As I held the black handles at his back and maneuvered the tall wheels, trying not to knock the heavy orange cast that covered his right leg from his ankle all the way up to where it circled around both of his hips, Life said to me, "Mom, I really don't need to be at the table." He looked up at me with his big blue eyes still bright, even after all the painful tears he had cried. "Really, I'm fine to just eat in the living room or my room."

His "room" had been moved downstairs to what was our office. I knew he was frustrated and in pain, but still I insisted, "No, it's important that you're at the table."

We may not get a lot right, but one thing Andrew and I have gotten right is this—we make family mealtimes a priority. Maybe that's why our table is such a focal point in both our home and our lives. It has provided a place of gathering and regrouping, a place of order in our often chaotic world.

Consistency hasn't always been our strong suit as parents. Our old vaccine records vary kid-to-kid depending on what camp I was in at the time, along with curfews, dating policies, and, in general, what we allow and what we don't. But coming to the table, it helps bring consistency to our lives. It creates a pattern in which we start and end each day, together. At dinner, we often share our highs and lows of the day— and on some days, well, we are just glad to sit down and eat.

I didn't want Life to miss being at the table. He was already isolated from soccer, rafting, hiking—from anything active—and he needed to be with people. And so, I wheeled him as close as I could get him and set a large wooden cutting board on top of the arm rests of his wheelchair, creating his own table. He was already two surgeries into a journey we had no idea would extend to six. The journey had begun two weeks earlier with a trampoline and a helicopter.

◆ ◆ ◆

It was the middle of the summer, and it was lunchtime. Mid-summer on the ranch is exhausting. We had already done so much work: we were three-fourths of the way through the first hay cutting with the second cutting still to irrigate, harvest, and sell—and we had cows to check at the six different pastures in the high country.

Come mid-summer, just like mid-day, Andrew and I pine for naps, the time change come fall, and date nights. Instead, we get up before the eager summer sun and eat dinner way too late. We go hard all day long—him in the fields, ditches, and pastures—and me in the kitchen, garden, laundry room, and office—and on a lucky day, on a tractor, a horse, or walking a ditch. Though under the same roof and doing life together, it's easy to get busy and live separately. It's easy to have our own lists, agendas, goals, and schedules apart from each other. It's easy to disconnect and forget that we are *one*.

And that's how it was on that summer day when Life was eight. Andrew was out in the field in a tractor with, then, ten-year-old Abe, teaching him how to bale hay. In the front yard, thick with new grass, kids and cousins played in the summer heat, jumping on the trampoline while I enjoyed a few minutes alone in the kitchen making sandwiches. As I layered turkey, cheese, avocados, red onions, and tomatoes, I uncovered the layers of stress to figure out why things were distant between Andrew and me.

Finances are always on our minds. We get paid once a year and budget that one check over twelve months. Summer is the time when we work sunup to sundown, often in the dark, to earn our income for the year. Summer is also the time when we tend to forget January's budget talks—when receipts start piling up on the office desk.

Dirty mirrors and toilets that needed cleaning, sun tea that needed making, overflowing trash that needed emptying, baskets of wet laundry that needed hanging, frozen burger that needed thawing, stubborn weeds that needed pulling, overgrown grass that needed mowing, messy rooms that needed vacuuming, and stacks of bills that needed paying—everything added up—layer upon layer—to create one big pile of stress.

As I sliced the last tomato and wiped my hands on my blue apron, I reminded myself that the pantry was getting low and I needed to get to the store for that dreaded huge trip. Exhaustion can easily taint perspective, turning a life full of wonderful things into an overwhelming to-do list. Instead of seeing my cup as full—that I had a home, a healthy family, clean water, a washing machine, a loving husband, and money with which to buy groceries from a store—I was seeing my cup with tired eyes. I filled the counter with colorful plastic plates like a game of Twister and dealt out carrots and apple slices as my list consumed my mind.

I thought about how life is full of lists and always will be. It's how I choose to tackle them that makes life enjoyable, or not. Perspective is everything. I realized what was really bothering me that day was the way Andrew left for the fields that morning—off in his own world— leaving me with *another* list:

1. *Pick up tractor parts*
2. *Where are we in the budget?*
3. *Make appointment to get brakes fixed*
4. *Return hay buyers' calls*
5. *Put a hay ad in the paper*

At that point in the summer, the idea of ever handing Andrew a honey-do list was unheard of. He had so much to think about and take care of that I knew better than to add one more rock to his pile. And, usually, I welcomed his lists. Usually, we worked as a team and I liked to help lighten his load. But on that mid-summer day, I was tired. I felt used up. What I really wanted to do was toss away my apron, tear up every list, and tell everyone to *make their own damn sandwiches*. What I really wanted to do was go for a long run up the road and then take a nap in the sun like our barn cats.

But I didn't.

Though the idea of a nap was laughable, I would run later. I looked out the kitchen window at the incredible mountains, our growing garden, and the fresh sheets on the line, swaying in the gentle breeze. I thought of Andrew and how hard he was working—and was thankful for the life we had together.

Then, one of my nephews came running in, his terrified voice breaking through my manic moment. I whipped around to see his wide eyes and hear his frantic words: "Auntie Lara! Come quick! Life's really hurt!"

I ran outside to the trampoline where Life lay screaming on his side. The sound was animalistic, unlike any I had ever heard before. I reached and tried to grab him, but he yelled me off: "Noooooo! *Get Dad!*"

I heard the ATV racing across the field and saw Naomi bouncing on the back—her arms wrapped around Andrew's waist. She had driven out to get him.

"He's coming, Life, hang in there," I said. His screams turned to whimpers and I began to cry and pray. Andrew jumped off the ATV and into the Suburban. He drove across the yard of newly sprouted grass to the trampoline and threw the car in park. He ran to Life, who screamed louder and louder, "Daaad! Help! It *huuuuurts!*" Huge teardrops smeared the trampoline under his face.

Andrew slipped his arms beneath Life's shaking body and lifted. The sight was nauseating: Life's long femur bone folded in half over Andrew's forearm. I'd never seen anything like it. I ran to the back seat where Andrew placed Life in my lap. Naomi shoved my purse by my feet. "Here, Mom, love you," she said, and she slammed the door.

The hospital is five miles away, and Andrew drove over 100 mph. I was sure we would die along the way. I tried to brace as he didn't slow for the corners. Life's screams grew louder and more intense as his fingernails dug into my arm. I was terrified.

Andrew carried Life into the emergency room where a nurse visually triaged the folded femur, waving us past other mothers who waited with their sick and injured children. They eyed me and my apron as I followed through wide doors and into a room. Life's wailing was inconsolable as we answered question upon question. Andrew pulled traction on Life's leg—separating the broken bones—easing some of the pain—enough so that we could hear the nurse. Another nurse came in and inserted an IV into Life's arm and began pumping his shaking body full of narcotics. Nothing touched his pain. If Andrew moved in the slightest, the screams would intensify, scaring us all.

Andrew had to let go for an x-ray, and it was unbearable. They wheeled Life away on his hospital bed and we could hear his cries all the way down the hall. Soon he was back in the room. I sat at his side, holding his clammy hand in mine. I watched tears flow down his face, and I felt helpless. The IV filled his veins with more drugs as he lay whimpering and shaking on the bed, his crying eyes closed.

The ER doctor soon appeared and pulled up the X-ray on a computer.

"Life has a completely shattered femur," he said, pointing to the jumbled mess of bone fragments. "And, also—something else we hadn't expected—he has some sort of cyst in his femur." Life's high-pitched moaning filled the room as the doctor explained that the situation was very serious. Life was in danger of losing his entire leg and needed a pediatric orthopedic specialist, immediately.

Life's hand gripped mine and he howled. Arrangements were made: he would be transported by Flight for Life (which even then was a little funny) to a Children's Hospital satellite campus in Colorado Springs. It was closer than the main Children's Hospital in Aurora, and time was crucial.

Andrew signed papers. Life's hand tightened again, and he shouted from his narcotic world, jarring us all. He begged me for something to stop the pain, over and over, crying, "It huuuuurts! Mom! Help!"

I looked through my tears to the nurse who was biting her lip as she scanned her records. She administered one more dose. In an instant, Life's heart rate dropped, filling the room with a cacophony of alarms.

His face went white, and his entire body fell limp; Andrew grabbed Life's other hand. I smoothed my fingers through Life's sweaty hair and pumped his floppy hand in mine.

"Life?" I searched his face and saw his eyelids flutter. "Lifey?"

There was no response. I wondered if we were losing him. The nurse injected something into the IV, and soon he began moaning. His heart rate climbed back up.

The helicopter pilot and nurse entered in their navy-blue uniforms. The pilot's handlebar mustache bobbed up and down as he told us the protocol and the plan. No parents were allowed in the helicopter as there was no room. We would have to drive the two and a half hours.

I kissed Life's hand and let go.

"One, two, three," the pilot counted, as they lifted the four white corners of the sheet Life laid on, transferring him to a narrow gurney. He shrieked as his body bent and buckled. They secured him with wide black straps and buckles. Like his leg, he was a jumbled mess of winces, screams, and cries, mixed with brief seconds of silence. We followed behind as they wheeled him outside and down the sidewalk to the black asphalt pad where the helicopter waited, engine purring.

The sun was beginning to lower to the mountains beyond the hay fields where the rest of our kids waited with family on the ranch. The pilot assured us of Life's safety once again and climbed in and slammed the door. The loading was quick—no time for me to kiss Life's cheek or whisper a prayer in his ear. The blades above our heads started to turn and spin—faster and faster. Dust stirred, sanding our faces and tears. We backed away, watching the helicopter lift and leave.

Andrew sped through the mountains as we covered over one hundred miles to the hospital. I couldn't hold still and my hands were clammy as we talked through every possible scenario. We got a call when we were about thirty minutes out—finally back in cell phone range. It was the surgeon himself. The circulation to Life's leg had been cut off by the swelling, and they needed to operate immediately. Andrew drove faster.

I prayed as the miles went by, "Please, Lord, be with Life and give him peace."

It was after-hours at the hospital, and all was silent except for the humming of vending and coffee machines. Fluorescent lights shone on pods of empty couches, chairs, and low tables with their assortment of magazines. We settled side-by-side into two purple polyester chairs with wooden armrests and dated geometric patterns.

We sat in silence. The stark lighting illuminated my running shoes and Andrew's worn, manure-crusted, hay-dusted cowboy boots. His hands, their summer cracks filled with black grease, sat folded on the lap of his grubby jeans. My mind replayed the day from the sandwiches and lists to the trampoline and the x-ray. I remembered the mid-day, mid-summer exhaustion. I remembered being overwhelmed by my list and irritated with Andrew's.

Everything felt so trivial now. I was embarrassed. I was wakened from my selfish reverie by tragedy. I would have given anything to be back home with my lists and the kids outside playing, laughing, and having fun.

Not a super-emotional guy, not one to talk too much or feed on dramatic "what-ifs," Andrew was quiet. We sat, each with our own thoughts, and I wondered what he was thinking.

"Well, I'm gonna go walk for a minute and find a bathroom. I'll be back," he said.

"Okay, I'll stay here in case the doctor comes."

It was just me and the soft hum of machines. I thought back to the scene in the yard, how the kids had pulled the trampoline across the new grass to the base of the massive orange dump truck. I could still hear my nephew saying, "We were just jumping off the dump truck onto the tramp. Lifey jumped—and then I jumped and double-bounced him—and I think he landed on the metal bar of the tramp. I'm so sorry, Auntie Lara. I'm so sorry."

I remembered two months earlier when that same nephew had helped us plant grass seed in the yard. A storm was coming in from the west, rolling across the Rockies like a wave far out in the ocean. As we all held bags of grass seed, the prepared soil felt cold on my bare feet, even though it was a warm May afternoon. We scattered rainbows of tiny seeds across the earth—squishing them in with feet little and big— like farmers straight out of a parable.

Then we all stopped. Standing in the raked dirt, we stared up at the sky that had changed. The early summer sun, in an instant, had been replaced by cool shadows. We watched the wave in the west as it hit the tall wall of mountains that looked over us, and the sound was thunderous. The peaks darkened beneath the charcoal storm as it flowed up and over the Continental Divide and down into our valley. We breathed the tiny water droplets that preceded the rain. As the air thickened, we tossed our last seeds and tamped with our toes.

Lightning lit up the west and thunder echoed its warning to take cover—but the steely silver sky was mesmerizing—and we had to stay. We had to stop and look in every direction. The sky captivated us with its ominous beauty as we bent back our necks and watched waves whirl above us—grays and blacks and whites of all shades swirled like spilled paint from heaven. And then . . . the drops . . . one by one . . . began to fall on our lifted faces as the storm soon hit the yard in full force. The rain wet our bodies as we danced our way back through the dotted dirt to the covered porch where we watched the storm wash over the valley.

· · ·

Andrew returned with two cups of coffee. Soon after, the doctor walked in. He wore a long white coat over blue surgery scrubs. A surgery hat was tied tight to his forehead, and a mask hung from its strings around his neck. Though smiling, he, too, looked exhausted. Andrew and I stood.

"Hi, Mr. and Mrs. Richardson, I'm Dr. Shaw," he said, extending his hand to Andrew first.

"I'm Andrew, and this is my wife, Lara," Andrew said, putting his arm around me.

I smiled and offered a weak hello as I shook the doctor's hand and then put my hand over my mouth, as if to trap all the emotions—the stress, the exhaustion, the fear, and the tension—that had gathered and were ready to let loose. Rerouted, they escaped from my eyes as tears. The doctor looked at me, closed his eyes and nodded his head in sincere compassion, as if to say that he understood—that this wasn't his first experience with a complete mess of a mother in the waiting room.

"Please," he motioned to our chairs, "sit down." He sat across from us and began, "First, the surgery went very well. Your son's in recovery, and you'll be able to see him in about an hour." Andrew grabbed my hand, and I let out the breath I didn't know I had been holding.

The doctor continued, "Secondly, Life's leg broke today not only because he landed on the metal frame of your trampoline, but his leg broke because his femur bone is egg-shell thin. The trampoline only exacerbated the problem. Eventually, any day, his leg would have crumpled just by walking." I looked at Andrew and then back to the doctor. "Honestly, in twenty-five years of orthopedics, I've never seen an injury quite like this before. I put two rods in his leg to help stabilize the shattered femur. He will need a special brace to help hold the bones in place as they heal. I've already measured and ordered it from a company in New York where they are handmade to fit the specific patient. And, lastly," he said, pausing for a moment, "Life's bone is eggshell-thin due to the presence of a bone tumor."

The word tumor sent my hand to my mouth again and filled my wide eyes with tears that overtopped and rolled down my cheeks. The doctor leaned in, folded his hands and rested his elbows on his knees. We leaned in, too, as his words sat in the quiet of the waiting room.

"I took a biopsy of the tumor, and we should have the results back in another twenty minutes or so."

I squeezed Andrew's hand. Biopsy? Tumor?

Cancer?

And to think I was just making sandwiches a few hours ago. I was learning, first hand, that when a day begins, we never know what it will hold. It can hold lists of monotony and chores, it can hold the gifts of joy and magic, but this one—it held catastrophe.

The doctor left us, and we sat together in silence. So many thoughts came in and out of my mind. Mostly, and maybe in a subconscious effort to protect my mind from dwelling on an unknown future, I thought back to the long family hike we had taken up to a high mountain lake just two weeks earlier for Life's eighth birthday.

All seven of us have summer birthdays, and Andrew and I try to make the days special for our kids by drawing a huge birthday sign and hanging it along the wall of windows by the table. We want the kids to wake up and know they are celebrated and loved. We spend our precious early morning coffee and porch time to make the sign—treasured moments normally spent reading, journaling, and watching the sun glisten in the dew drops.

We roll out a long piece of blank newsprint that covers the counter, and we track down all the markers in the house. I resurrect my best middle school block lettering and we fill the big letters and numbers with colorful doodles of rainbows, soccer balls, rivers, mountains, stars, antlers, unicorns, zigzags—and anything else we can think of before six in the morning. We hang the sign and balloons that will eventually greet the birthday kid.

More often than not, our birthdays are spent haying or checking cows, and are then somewhat redeemed with a fun Family Dinner at sunset. But once in a while, if a birthday falls during a rare lull, we can actually do something special to celebrate.

Two weeks earlier, Life woke to his eighth birthday. He came downstairs and saw his sign and balloons hanging at the window and his wrapped presents on the table. We were excited to let him know that he could actually pick what he wanted to do on his birthday—the first hay cutting was over, the cows had all been checked in the high country, and, after chores and irrigating, the day was his.

He chose to go on a family hike to fish at a high mountain lake.

To get ready for the day, much had to be done. Andrew and the kids took care of the chores and irrigating; finding fly rods and reels and making sure they worked; waterproofing hiking boots; making a picnic lunch; filling water bottles; and loading up the car. I put a roast in the oven for dinner and made Life's favorite birthday cake: chocolate with white cream cheese frosting.

Making birthday cakes is one of the things I love to do for my family. As a mom, I feel like I'm the one person to do that. Baking a homemade cake is a gift from me to them—it's a way I let them know I love them and that they are special to me. I pulled the cake from the oven and set it out to cool. I would frost and decorate it after the hike.

The lake Life chose is over an hour's drive from the ranch. The forty-five minutes on the highway that lead to the twelve-mile bumpy dirt road only gets you to the trailhead. The lake is found after hiking along a mountain stream for two miles and then cutting right at the fallen trees at the base of the massive avalanche chute. Void of snow, but filled with tiny strawberry plants, the steep hike up the chute was sweet. That day, the berries were perfectly ripe—red little treats that kept the kids, then ages 8, 10, 12, and 14, climbing up, up, and up some more, until they reached a waterfall that tumbled down the high alpine tundra from the lake above. They knew they were close.

With renewed energy, the kids ran ahead, following the bubbling water whose edges were decorated with a colorful celebration of columbine, bluebells, monkshood, alpine buttercups, Indian paintbrush, bellflowers, mouse-ears, and purple asters. We passed the last of the shrinking trees at the edge of the chute, the ones flagged on one side from the fierce winds and snow, and crested the green carpeted knoll officially above treeline. The view was captivating. Before us, the pure water of the high lake reflected the tall granite mountains that created the hidden place. It felt as though we were the first people ever to see the magical crags on the other side of the lake that jutted up from the lush and spongy tundra, cushioning the soles of our hiking boots like slippers.

The dust and dry of the ranch felt a world away.

We spent the day fishing, picnicking, and hiking a little higher to where the mountains towered straight up to create the stony divide between the Rocky Mountain valleys. After lunch, Andrew and I rested on a smooth rock the size of a pickup truck. The sun warmed our mid-summer muscles, and we delighted in watching the kids as they fished, collected rocks, and waded in the chilly water.

As the afternoon waned, we packed up and started the several-mile journey back to the car. The joy-filled birthday boy ran down the gorgeous green mountainside, leaping from one granite rock to another, leading the way back to the avalanche chute. Tired and happy, we made it home in time to set the table for the birthday dinner, frost and decorate the cake, season and roast the new potatoes, toss a fresh salad from the garden, and slice the roast. Ted and Ruthie, Seth and Susie and their kids, and Dad and Uncle Dan all came over. We shared pictures from our hike, opened presents, and sang Happy Birthday as we celebrated our youngest son turning eight.

Sitting under the bright fluorescent lights at the hospital, I cringed at the thought of Life's leg collapsing in the wilderness as he hopped from rock to rock. With the results of the biopsy determining so much of what was ahead for our family, I was thankful for the day we were given as a family to celebrate Life. Would we stop to celebrate each other without birthdays? Would we take the time to spend a special day together and give a gift? And on normal days, if we didn't protect the tradition of gathering at the table to share a meal, would we just fill our plates and scatter to solitude?

Being together each day helps solidify the relationships in our family and reminds us that we have a place where we belong. As we waited for the biopsy results, I tried not to think of Life's chair being empty forever. Though the reality of death for each of us, one day, is always present, the possible change in its proximity prompts us to cherish each other all the more—and not just on birthdays.

• • •

My phone chimed with a text from Andrew's folks.

"The kids are at Grammy and Papa's—everyone's there tonight for dinner," I told Andrew, looking up from my phone.

"That's good," he said.

I knew Andrew's mind, though primarily thinking about Life and cancer, was also thinking about the ranch. It was the end of July, and he'd left during the hay harvest. He'd been on a tractor, teaching Abe how to bale hay—how to make exact bales by keeping the tractor centered over the windrow; how to go the right speed to create the perfect density; how to count the number of flakes created as the hay gets pulled in—and pushed out—as a bale. Still one of the most dangerous jobs in America, with twice the annual fatalities compared to law enforcement officers, farming is not to be taken lightly. While Abe was living every boy's dream, Andrew was teaching his son to be safe.

"What if it's *cancer*? How do we tell the kids? And the rest of the family? And *Life*? How do we tell *Life* he has cancer?" My mind erupted aloud with questions.

Always practical, Andrew reminded me that we didn't *know* if the tumor was malignant or benign. He was right. I knew better than to forecast grief. I needed to remember to take God's advice and *think on what is true*.

We decided to go to the cafeteria to find some coffee. The place was deserted, and we sat at a table, not knowing what else to do. We heard voices coming down a hallway, and they grew louder as we saw my oldest brother, Garrett, and his wife, Beatriz, walking toward us.

We stood and hugged them and thanked them for coming. It meant a lot to have them there with us to distract us, pray with us, and support us. If they had asked if we needed company, and if they should make the drive from Denver to come be with us, we would have said no, not wanting to disturb their evening.

But they didn't ask. They showed up, and their showing up was a huge gift.

There's not a lot to say, and not much to do in situations like that, but they were there. And that's what friends and families do in times of tragedy—they show up. They keep kids, they make meals, they bale hay, they clean house, they do laundry, and they pray. My mom is a master at this. She sees what needs to be done and gets right to it.

The four of us returned to the waiting room, not wanting to miss the doctor. After filling them in on the story, we caught up on how our nephews were doing.

Andrew looked up and then stood, offering me his hand. The doctor was back. We walked to meet him, and I tried to know our answer by observing his body language, but before he even reached us, he smiled and said from across the room, "No cancer!"

We stopped, and I half-cried, half-whispered, "Oh, thank you, God," as Andrew put his arm around me.

"That's great news," Andrew said. "Can we see him?"

• • •

The next evening, we pulled into the driveway, and the kids ran out to greet us. Surrounding our car with smiles, they were eager to see the three of us—but their smiles faded when they saw Life's pale face and the awful black brace that encompassed his whole lower body. They stood speechless as they watched the painful transfer process from the car to the house. They heard Life's fearful moans of anticipation as Andrew counted out loud before lifting him; they saw the tears pouring from Life's eyes and the sweat forming on his brow; they saw his fingernails digging into Andrew's shoulder; and they watched their dad carry their screaming brother into the house. It didn't seem right.

I offered them all a weak smile and told them how much I had missed them, but I couldn't hold back the tears as I followed right behind Andrew and Life. It was all too much. Earlier in the week, friends had shown up and moved Life's room downstairs to our office. Andrew lowered Life to the bed and the sound of pain filled the entire house. The kids peeked in, scared. I turned my wet face to them and said nothing.

As I gave Life more pain medication and tried to get him comfortable, I noticed all the things people had brought for him: a welcome home sign, a brand-new iPad, a piano keyboard, books on CDs, and coloring books with fancy marker sets.

Somehow, we functioned enough in the next two days. Thankfully, a week of meals had been arranged for us as I was full-time caring for Life: emptying the pee bottle, changing him and the blue pad, administering and keeping track of pain meds, reading stories, and bringing food and drinks. He could not get comfortable. In the rare moments when Life slept, Andrew and I tried to catch up with the rest of the kids and their lives and what was happening on the ranch.

"I've got some bad news, Dad," Abe said. "I kept baling once you took Life to the hospital, and I think I must have turned too tight and bent the PTO shaft, 'cause as I was going along, the thing just busted right in two."

Seth had dealt with the broken PTO, and he and Susie and Grammy and Papa had kept the ranch—and the rest of our life—rolling along in our absence. Seth took all of Andrew's irrigating on, as well as the remainder of the hay harvest. Susie took over the hay sales, and between them all, our kids were cared for. It's never easy to just step out of life.

• • •

Sunday came, and Andrew took the kids to church. I stayed home with Life. He kept complaining that his knee hurt and didn't feel right. I kept telling him that nothing was going to feel right—his leg was in pieces—and the rods had been inserted through two new holes on the sides of his knee. He was insistent. I figured I had better take a look, mostly to appease his fears.

I unbuckled the brace, laying it open on the bed. As I unwrapped layer upon layer of gauze—as his whole leg was wrapped to his waist—I couldn't believe what I saw. It wasn't the barbaric row of shiny steel staples running along the side of his femur like a railroad track that horrified me—no, it was the tip of what looked like a knitting needle poking from beneath the skin of his knee. My stomach tightened as I thought about what it must feel like for him. I wanted to sob for the pain he had been through—it all felt like such a waste. Wasted pain. I wanted to scream for him, but I tried to be calm.

"Oh no," I said, trying to blink away my gathering tears.

"What? What happened?"

"It's one of your rods, I think. I think it's sticking out of your knee. Geesh, I thought they were thicker than that."

He closed his eyes and laid his head back on his pillow and cried.

"I'll call the doctor."

• • •

I was given strict instructions to drive Life back to Colorado Springs, immediately. Andrew and I stepped away from our lives, our other kids, and the ranch, once again.

The next weeks involved a second opinion, another failed surgery, a huge ankle-to-waist cast, a third opinion, and eventually a third surgery at Children's Hospital in Denver.

The main campus of Children's Hospital in Denver, where we eventually ended up, is incredible. Enormous—full of colorful artwork, sculptures, and murals—the entire building is created for kids. Even the elevator was made so kids could see its inner workings through glass walls. I caught myself staring at other families as I followed behind Andrew, who carefully wheeled Life in his chair to the orthopedic floor. I watched them pushing their children in wheelchairs or pulling them in the hospital's red wagons. Some of the other children's conditions were obvious and heart-wrenching, while others were hidden, seen only by the agony on their faces. I can't believe the atrocities that many children face, daily. We checked in and were taken to a room where an assistant helped Andrew lift Life onto the examination table. She was horrified at the process.

"I can't believe this," she said, standing back and looking at Life who was sweating and crying on the blue vinyl table. "Buddy, I don't know how you've been enduring this, but we're going to fix you right up." I teared up in relief, as if she were talking to me. She had acknowledged in one sentence all of the pain he had been through in the past weeks . . . all that we had been through.

She cut the enormous orange cast from Life's body. Fear and relief mingled on his face. She unwrapped his bandages and was horrified, again.

"What? What is it?" I asked, looking at her face.

"It's just that I'm not used to seeing staples . . . we don't *staple* children."

We met Life's new surgeon, Dr. Heare, and he explained the procedure, step by step. It sounded so simple—no rods—no glorified knitting needles floating next to jumbled bones. He would pack Life's femur with cadaver bone and then screw a steel plate to the outside, acting like bone until Life's bone healed. Brilliant. And Life would be able to walk with a walker the moment he felt ready. Incredible.

And, Dr. Heare, he never used the word *tumor* once. He used what we learned was the real term—unicameral bone cyst (UBC). More common in males than females, UBCs are pockets of fluid inside children's bones. Adults don't have UBCs since the cysts are fed by active growth plates. Found usually in the long bones of the body (like the femur or humerus bones), UBCs are often not noticed until seen in an X-ray for another reason, or until the bone thins enough and breaks. The cysts come back twenty-five to fifty percent of the time until the child's growth plates close.

We learned that the large bones in our bodies have a hard, outer shell that protects the spongy bone marrow inside. That spongy bone marrow houses our stem cells. Stem cells constantly replace the different cells in our organs, bones, and blood. Our red blood cells, which deliver oxygen throughout the body, only last about 100 days and are replaced by our bone marrow at the rate of 200 billion new red blood cells every day. It takes about twelve weeks for a broken bone to heal, and our skeletons are completely regenerated every seven to ten years. Dr. Heare was confident Life's femur would heal.

Life's third surgery was a success, and soon he was back home walking with a walker—the wheelchair gone from the table. Knowing that a calcium-rich diet would help Life's femur heal faster, I fed him every healthy thing I could think of. I gave him spinach, steak, smoothies, soup made with homemade bone broth, and as many fruits and vegetables I could get him to eat. Eventually the bone graft was absorbed by his body and replaced with new bone and new bone marrow.

His leg was as good as new. Though we had new routines of homeschooling, since Life's months of surgery were prohibitive as far as public school went, we finally began to settle into our new life.

Trauma, with its unexpected interruptions into our routines, has taught me not to take myself or others too seriously. I am learning to find joy in the lists and routines, realizing that these things are my *life*. I'm learning to appreciate things like grocery trips, paying bills, and making sandwiches because I've been in a hospital room, in the early hours of dawn, listening to the sounds of pain. I am learning to pay attention, looking the tools of trauma, pain, and disappointment straight in the eyes as they sand away my rough edges.

Chapter 14

It was a sweet summer night, and almost a year had passed since Life broke his leg. The first hay harvest was cut, baled, and in the barn, and the second, like Life, was growing taller each day. Ruthie had called just after breakfast that morning to invite us to a six o'clock Family Dinner at her house—Chinese take-out—as Andrew's youngest brother, David, and his family were in town for a visit.

I was so excited. For years, Ruthie had invited us all over for family dinners, but since her lung cancer diagnosis following Life's third surgery, the roles had reversed—she and Ted more frequently came over to our house, and to Seth and Susie's, for dinners. But lately, Ruthie had no appetite as she sat at the table. I tried to make things she was craving, like mashed potatoes and pot roast, but eventually she grew so tired in the evenings that she and Ted came over less and less. For her to stay up with everyone after six was rare.

Six o'clock neared, and the sun was still hot as it filled the western sky. Irrigation shovels set their last tarps, wrenches turned their last bolts, and clothes lines let loose the last load of clothes to fold for the day. As we drove the mile and a half down the dirt road to Ted and Ruthie's, we waved at our neighbors as they gathered vegetables for dinner from their garden. We passed bikers, walkers, and runners—all out on the scenic country loop after work. Trucks pulling trailers loaded full of rafts and kayaks were headed for an evening float.

As we drove along the river, we watched a fly fisherman standing in the current in his waders. He swished his rod back and forth, back and forth, back and forth through the air, ending with a cast of his thin line at an eddy swirling with late sunlight, road dust, and real caddis flies.

We turned into the dirt driveway and parked at the log fence where various mountain bikes, four-wheelers, cars, and trucks were parked in the first-come-first-served disorderly fashion of hunger. We walked across the yard to the front door. The screen door snapped closed behind us as we walked into a pile of rubber irrigating and cowboy boots, all with varying degrees of mud and manure caked to the soles. We added ours to the pile and walked across the wood floor in our socks to the kitchen where everyone gathered.

"Hello, Lara," Ruthie said, in her ever-cheerful voice, though she sounded tired. A kiss on the cheek and a hug. Her jeans hung on her hips, and her sweater sagged from her shoulders.

"Hey, hey!" David's happy voice followed Ruthie's as he gave us all big hugs.

"Hi, guys!" David's wife, Anne, said, greeting us with more hugs. She hugged Life and then held him at arm's distance: "Oh Lifey! Look at you! So good to see you healthy and walking!"

So went all the greetings and hugs throughout the family. Only Andrew's sister, Nancy, and her family were missing—but they we scheduled to arrive in a day or two as they were driving out from California.

The kids made it through the gauntlet of hellos and quickly joined their cousins who were running all through the house. Ted intercepted the taller ones, one at a time, measuring them against the wood door filled with decades of dates, feet, inches, and names—marking the latest growth with a ruler and pencil: "Stand tall, chin up, hold still." Comparisons rang through the house and wrestling competitions began on the wool rug in the living room.

Talk of tractor repairs filled the kitchen as dirty Levi's and Wranglers leaned against the counters. Grease was washed, and washed again, from grimy fingers and dried with paper towels. Anne filled the silver water pitcher, I set out a pile of napkins, and Susie grabbed forks. We called everyone in, and eventually the family gathered around the island full of white rice, fried rice, Kung Pao chicken, sweet and sour chicken, beef and broccoli, Mongolian beef, and so on.

With tousled hair, sweaty hat lines on foreheads, and arms over shoulders, we sang "Johnny Appleseed":

> *Oh, the Lord is good to me,*
> *and so, I thank the Lord,*
> *for giving me, the things I need,*
> *the sun and the rain and the apple seed!*
> *Oh, the Lord is good to me . . .*
> *A-men, A-men, A-men, A-men, A-men,*
> *A-men, A-men, A-men, A-men, A-men,*
> *A . . . MEN!*

Everyone grabbed paper plates and dug in. We congregated in the big dining room at the long table where the piano bench was pulled up and the littler cousins shared chairs, sitting half-cheeked. The water pitcher was passed and refilled.

When asked, Ruthie updated us all on the next steps in her treatment: she was headed to Denver for one more session in the hyperbaric chamber, and then she would have a break. She and Ted were so encouraged. After months of chemotherapy and radiation treatments, they were finally making plans for future trips.

David and Anne shared the latest happenings with their family, and a speaker call was made to our niece in California as we all sang *Happy Bithday,* on Nancy's voicemail, as a family.

Susie and Anne dished out vanilla ice cream topped with fresh berries—something Ruthie normally would have loved.

But she didn't touch her dish.

Dinner ended, the kids ran off, and the guys went back out to the shop to try the tractor fix they had discussed over dinner. Susie, Anne, and I helped Ruthie tidy the kitchen, chatting away as we worked. Eventually, as the sun settled lower in the sky, Susie left to move one more irrigation tarp. Anne gathered up her kids for bathtime and hesed upstairs.

I lingered in the kitchen as Ruthie was still wide awake. She surveyed her forest-green countertops, arranging things as she went along—the pile of unused napkins, the folded dish towel, the soap next to the sink.

"There," she said, "now we're ready."

Over and over, she kept saying those words. I wondered what it was she was getting ready for? Bedtime? The morning? I, too, appreciate an orderly kitchen when the day ends, as I do not like waking up to a messy kitchen.

But then, when I was ready to gather sleepy kids and my even sleepier rancher from the shop and head home, Ruthie started going through her fridge and giving me old leftovers. She went through every shelf and drawer, sending me home with a large grocery bag full of wilted lettuce and other discards for my chickens.

"There," she said, adding a blackening bunch of cilantro to the bag.

Nine o'clock came, and the guys returned from the shop. Andrew and I gathered up our kids. Wide awake, Ruthie stood in her doorway near the waning pile of boots and kissed and hugged each one of us before we walked out the door.

"Goodnight, Lara, love you," she said. A kiss on the cheek and a hug.

We drove home along the river with the windows down, feeling the warm air currents from the day mixing with the evening cool as it settled throughout the valley.

• • •

In the quiet dark, just before dawn, Andrew's cell phone vibrated in the pocket of his Levi's crumpled on the floor beside our bed. I nudged him, "Hey Darlin', your phone's buzzing." He rolled over, and the phone quit. The sky was turning a light gray. His phone buzzed again.

"Darlin, your phone," I said, nudging him again. "Who's calling this early?"

He leaned for his jeans and found his phone.

"Hello?" He listened for a moment, and then sat straight up. "We'll be right there." He set the phone in his lap and looked at me and said, "Mom's gone."

"What? What happened?"

"I don't know." He shook his head in the gentle morning light. "Dad found her on the bathroom floor."

We dressed in silence and walked down the stairs, careful not to wake the kids. We would come back for them later. As my feet hit each step, I choked on the sound coming from deep within. It wasn't crying—it was the moan of my soul. *She must have known*, was all I could think of. She had one last Family Dinner at her house, one last kiss on the cheek, one last hug. *It can't be*, I thought. Without even knowing, I spoke a long, quiet, "Noooo," the sound of my own voice surprising me.

In the car, we watched the valley fill with soft sunlight—that golden hue that warms and wakes the doe and her fawn, bedded down in the tall grass. We were silent except for the sound of my sobs. Andrew slowed our truck on the dirt road as we came upon a quiet fire engine, Number 15. No hurry, no siren, just black tires rolling along the gravel road beside the river. We passed a blue heron standing tall on a sandbar, water flowing around both sides.

We followed the long red truck into the driveway and parked at the log fence. Walking to the front door, everything felt magnified—the mountains, taller; the dew, earthier; and the sun's first rays, softer.

The adult family sat at the oval kitchen table, steeped in grief. The same bewildered look was on each face as we hugged in silence, until my tears found their voice again, and I wept. I will never forget Ted's face that morning . . . the day his life changed forever.

We sat around the table, holding hands, weeping. No "Johnny Appleseed" song this morning. Instead, we prayed a prayer asking for strength and wisdom—a prayer of thanks for a merciful passing and for the chance to be loved by Ruthie. We lifted our heads and opened our wet, red eyes to see a police officer standing in our midst, hat in hand.

He took a step toward us and said, "I know I don't know you all very well, but I just want you to know that the strong faith I just saw, that's what's going to get you through this." He looked at each of us, and we all thanked him with our nods. "I am sorry to interrupt you, but we are preparing to take Ruth's body to the funeral home now. Does anyone want to come back before we move her?"

Andrew and I looked at each other and nodded. "Okay, please come with me," he said.

We followed him to the back of the house. At the bathroom door, he turned and stopped. "Just to warn you, she's lying in quite a bit of blood, just as your dad found her." We nodded, and he motioned for us to go in.

I saw her bare feet first, then her black pajamas with the tiny white dots. She was lying on her side in front of the toilet. We walked a little closer and stood. "Oh, Grammy," I said. I took Andrew's hand. He squeezed mine.

The image of her lying there, in her own blood on the cold tile floor, has stayed in my mind. I didn't think her life would end that way. We didn't even get to say goodbye; but then I remembered, that we did, in a way—with a kiss on the cheek and a hug. And then I thought of Nancy and her family, and my heart ached even more.

I didn't know what to do and I didn't know what to say.

A while later, we all stood on the porch, watching the coroner and the officer push the gurney carrying the black body bag across the dewy grass. When it neared us, they stopped. The officer asked, "Would you like to see her again, before we go?"

Standing in the gentle morning sun, we watched him unzip the bag to her shoulders. He held it back. She looked beautiful. Peaceful. The moment seemed otherworldly. Holy. I'd lived a life mostly insulated from death; but on that day, death felt tangible. Its weight filled my chest.

Looking at Ruthie's face, it was clear to me that she wasn't there. Though her spirit was no longer in her body, it was just as clear to me that she still existed—that she still lived. Just not here, and just not with us. Though I could sense her all around, I couldn't bring myself to touch her. I wanted to smooth her red hair along her forehead and give her one last kiss on the cheek. But I couldn't. I just stood there, with death right in front of me.

Death felt like the final word spoken by God, silencing all others. Like looking up at a moonless night sky in the wilderness, I was speechless. It seemed, in that moment, that a veil had been lifted from my eyes and I was given a glimpse of a world I had never seen before. I was surprised that Ruthie's death reminded me of birth—the miraculous moment a new life enters a new world. Though Ruthie had left ours, I knew she had entered a place she could not explain to us—like trying to describe a color we have never seen before.

In Ruthie's death, God felt very close. I felt one step closer to eternity—like part of me was already there. Death was the rarest reminder that God is very active in our comings and goings, whether we choose to see it, or not.

. . .

Family Dinners, along with the rest of our lives, have never been the same since Ruthie's passing. The matriarch of her family, she left a void that is noticeable on every hike, every cross-country ski, every holiday, every river trip, every birthday, and at every family prayer when we gather and hold hands. And yet, in some way, a part of her is still at each one. Though Ruthie is gone from my sight, I can still hear her welcoming voice when I walk in the door to say hello to Papa.

Ruthie's mother, Gammy, died less than a year later at breakfast one morning. She died, not flipping pancakes as Gan read scripture at their table, but while working a word problem to keep her mind sharp. She was 96. Matriarchs are often the connective tissue of a family. They bring everyone together and keep traditions going—like a Yule log on Christmas Eve or chili on branding day.

Yet no matter our importance or role on this earth, none are exempt from a chair at the table in the house of mourning, and eventually, death. It is one of the guarantees of life. But how often do we live as if we are dying? Observing death is a gift to the living in that it moves us past complacency into gratitude for another day. When grieving fingers touch the grain of the table, the linen of a napkin, the weight of a spoon—everything feels different—everything is forever different when you lose someone you love. It is in this loss that we are sanded and refined. Death forces us to ponder our own mortality; and like our reflection in the shine of a spoon, it changes us and turns our world upside down. And just as darkness and light need each other to exist, so it is with sorrow and joy. Death adds a new weight to the natural things as it bids us to wake for every sunrise and linger at every sunset.

When confronted with death, we become more alive.

Chapter 15

One summer morning, a few years later, I went for a walk. Andrew asked me to irrigate for him, and I was glad to help while he stayed with our sleeping summer kids, giving me the freedom to go. My going gave him space to do yoga on the porch. It gave him opportunity to sit in the sun and linger with a cup of coffee—to read his Bible and journal a bit about life and the ranch. He would savor it all, especially the warm sun that rarely sees his farmer-white legs.

My going allowed him to stay. Soon enough his day would be filled with flood irrigating, checking cows pastured in the high country, and getting machinery lubed and ready to harvest hay. My going gave me space and quiet—time to think and breathe. Eventually, the list that existed in my mind would surface, and I would cross off and add, as Andrew did the same on the pages of his journal.

He would stretch, write, sip, read, and reflect until chubby little fingers unlatched the front door. The little girl with the sleepy black hair would wander onto the porch with her froggy blanket trailing, while the others, 14, 16, 18, and 20, slept upstairs. Essie, wearing only a diaper, would climb up and get comfortable in her favorite place in the entire world. Her brown legs would fall across his. Andrew's time alone would end, but he would be happy to see her. There is a place in Andrew's heart reserved only for this tender little Navajo soul.

As I trotted down the stairs of the porch and into the grassy yard, I called Molly and our cattle dog, Boots, who both appeared from their dog houses under the porch. They poked their heads through the tall hollyhock stems and adjusted their eyes to the light. They snapped awake and squealed as they realized it was time for a walk.

I crossed the yard and started south down the dirt road with liberated legs—stretching and feeling a strong forty-five years old. Without a stroller, I could go anywhere. I teetered over the cattle guard, and the dogs ran ahead, pulling at each other's manes, peeing here and there. The sunflowers—whose roots grew deep into the banks of the ditch that flowed beside an old barbed-wire fence—looked east to greet the morning sun. Tall grasses and flowering weeds all but covered the fence with a beauty of their own. Bushy asparagus plants grew at the aging fence posts, round seed heads starting to hang as their brief harvest had come and gone. I already felt invigorated as I breathed the new air.

Texture was on full display all around: fluffy explosions of seeds, mature thistle, gray and wrinkled wood posts, and flat leaves of tall grass. I couldn't see the ditch for the overgrowth, but I heard it bubbling next to the road, free and happy, joyful in its journey. The line of peaks to my right, as well as an entire time zone, divided me from the Pacific coast where I was born.

I thought of sun, sand, and waves—and I thought of Grace, asleep in the attic upstairs. Back from her California college for the summer, living and working as a river guide just upstream, she came home for the night to eat and shower and sleep. Normally in a room full of girls and bunk beds and damp river gear strewn about, she needed home for a night. I thought back to how I had once slept in that exact bunk bed—working as a raft guide when Andrew and I met almost thirty summers ago. Same bunk, same blonde hair and blue eyes, same love for anything outdoors. She would return to school that fall and live off-campus, with no meal plan.

How had I not taught her to cook? I loved to cook, but we'd rarely engaged while making a meal in the kitchen. I remembered back to one Christmas when the four kids were younger and I tried to teach them how to make pot roast. I split them into two teams: Abe and Life were on the boys' team and Grace and Naomi were on the girls' team. Not only was it the Christmas season, but it was also a season full of ideals when I was attempting to rid the kids' minds and vocabularies of the word "crap." A couple weeks earlier, after a guest preacher at church had used the word in a sermon, the kids argued in its defense.

"It's not a bad word, Mom," Grace said. "Everyone uses it."

"Well, we aren't *everyone*, are we?"

That Christmas day, as the pot roast teams seared their respective hunks of beef in pots crackling with hot olive oil, Grace had had it. She wanted to be up making first tracks at Monarch instead of first helping to prepare the perfect Christmas dinner.

After attempting to flip the heavy, sizzling roast with a pair of tongs, only to have it flop back into the oil and splatter her face, she rolled her eyes, handed the tongs to Naomi and said, "Your turn."

My expectations sizzled away and my anger got the best of me. "Gracie, if you're gonna act like that, you can take your crappy attitude and head out."

I immediately realized I had just used the word I had so vehemently been attacking as Grace stormed out—our Christmas and my cooking class burned by my words. The other three just kept their heads down and giggled over the cutting boards where they started cutting onions and carrots into chunks for the pot.

Not my best mothering moment.

Thankfully, Grace and I have the outdoors and love adventuring together. As I walked along, I reconciled that there were millions of recipes online—and I was glad that we could raft and rappel together. However, I at least wanted to teach her how to make Chicken Piccata before she drove west to school. As I walked, I began another list in my mind:

1. *Make Chicken Piccata with Grace*

I made my way down the road and glanced eastward across the field to the old house, looking to see if my dad was out that morning. Just shy of eighty that summer, he walked or rode his bike almost every day with my Uncle Dan. Their walk paralleled mine—a large hay field in between us—but they weren't out yet. If they had been, I could have easily spotted the two old bearded cowboys in their Wranglers and weathered cowboy hats. Uncle Dan even wore his Wranglers and hat on their bike rides. Not Dad—he was practical and wore sweatpants and a neon yellow shirt—the tubes of his oxygen cannula traveling from his little backpack through the straps of his helmet to his nose, just like Ron Jones. Oxygen was the little boost needed since his open heart surgery a few years earlier. Uncle Dan used to have a cigarette hanging from his lips on their bike rides, but they had both quit after decades of smoking. They are famous on these county roads. If they were out walking, we would have waved across the field, too far to shout a good morning. I needed to stop by and say hello.

2. *Stop by Dad and Uncle Dan's*

I tried to leave the list behind as I walked, though it seemed to follow me. At the time, Dad and Uncle Dan still lived in the old farmhouse where Andrew and I had started our family—and where Joseph Sage and his wife had raised twelve children one century earlier. Before Andrew renovated it, every room in the house had two doors. In their very rocky marriage, if Joseph walked in one door, his wife wanted a separate door to leave the room; likewise, if she walked in the room, Joseph needed his way out. Somehow, they raised a large family together before their marriage ended in separation and their land was lost after the Depression.

I thought of my marriage without doors and I was grateful. I shook my head at the thought of twelve children. Five seemed more than enough. Sometimes it was overwhelming, the desire to connect with each of my kids. Naomi, who had just graduated from high school that May, was leaving in a few weeks for a medical gap year in Australia and the jungles of Papua New Guinea. I was proud of her desire to live outside the norm and seek extraordinary adventure, but I would miss her joy and laughter that filled our home. Searching for meaningful time with Naomi before she left was like grasping for water with my fingers. My chest heaved, and I walked on to sort out the things of life.

3.   *Spend quality time with Naomi*

I made my way down a steep dirt bank to the left and planted my boot on a river rock hidden in the weeds at one side of the small ditch. I hopped across to land on another rock, shallow water running over its gray and white speckles. I scrambled up the other side of the bank, past the sunflowers and puffy seeds that teetered in the air, to the base of a wooden ladder that led up and over the barbed-wire fence. Andrew had built the stile for us, an upside-down V. I climbed up one side and grabbed the rusty wire in between the ancient barbs, swung my leg over, and climbed down the other side, careful not to snag my skin. I wondered if Joseph Sage had strung the wire on the old fence.

Stretching across the big ditch was a thick railroad tie. I balanced across and then up to the edge of the hay field where the wild grasses and weeds of the ditch cease to grow—where the view opens to the hay fields and what we endearingly call "The Sage Place." Quietly adding one deep green alfalfa leaf after another, the plants would soon display their buds, and the purple blossoms would open to the bees. I walked the dusty perimeter of the 160-acre hay field watered with a center-pivot sprinkler—a large arm that pivots from the center of the circular field and travels in a constant circle, with nozzles that hang low over the plants every few feet. Gravity-fed from a pond nearby, and filled since 1875 by the Hills-Sprague Ditch that carries snowmelt, the irrigation system is a mastery of hydro-engineering.

After a long summer of irrigating and two cuttings of hay, the fields will rest. We all will rest. The cattle will eventually be brought home in semi-trucks from their pastures in the high country. They will be unloaded into the corrals at the old house. Their hips will sway and their hooves will clack down the steep metal ramp off the semi until they reach the soft dirt of home. The cows and calves, separated for safety during transport, will find each other as they call out across the green pastures where the calves were born just five months before in the February snow. Paired up, some cows will rush to eat the first sprig of green they see, while others will kick up their heels and run—calves sprinting to keep up.

The dirt path I followed was a no-man's land, where the cultivated fields met the wild rabbit brush and badger holes. It wound through the stubble of dry weeds along the edge of the lush fields. The no-man's land was like the teenage years. Abe had just turned sixteen and finally had his driver's license, though he had been driving on the ranch for years. He was saving for a pickup truck—living in the world between boys and men. With a squeaky voice, long blonde bangs, and constantly too-short pants, his capability and joy in working far outweighed his age. As I walked, I pictured his big smile that I could see from a distance each time I brought him lunch or an afternoon milkshake while he was on either a swather, a tractor, or a stack wagon—cutting, baling, or stacking hay. I ached to know what he thought about, what his fears were, and what girl had caught his eye, if any. Connection requires intention. And time.

4. *Slow down and listen to Abe*

As I rounded to the east, my eyes left the fields and found the line of tall cottonwood trees that grow in a ravine that runs up to the mesa, a short walk away. I found the one leafless, dead cottonwood that holds the artful mass of twigs and sticks lodged high in the naked gray branches. There, perched on one lonely branch above the nest, sat the feathered child left at home, nervous. Then, I realized, I must have missed him. I turned back to look west and saw the noble father, tail and head of the purest white, with the most impressive backdrop of mountains stretched out behind him. He hadn't missed me. With his famous eagle eyes, he could spot a rabbit more than three miles away. I was confident that he had seen me descend my porch steps, call my dogs, and walk over the cattle guard and down the road toward him. He had seen me hop the small ditch, climb up and down the ladder and cross the rugged, oily black tie. His eyes had followed me as I moseyed along the dry trail toward his family. He hadn't flinched or chirped.

I looked again at the eaglet above me, perched with all its dark feathers—no white at all. Recently hatched from its thirty-five-day incubation, it had finally ventured past the walls of its home to sit on a branch just above the nest. For now, the parents delivered torn tidbits of food in their beaks; but soon, the fledgling would practice hopping from branch to branch and then, on one glorious day, it would fly. It would practice swooping and diving; practice catching with its talons and tearing with its beak; and would, after three months, leave to make its own life somewhere else. The white of the head and tail would appear in four to five years.

Essie had just turned four, and I wondered what growth would happen in her that year. Maybe I would teach her how to read?

5.　*Teach Essie the alphabet*

If the eagles had adequate water and food supply, they would stay; however, if water and food ran short, or if they felt threatened or if the winters were just too much, they would migrate further south.

A bald eagle is not always a welcomed sight: standing like a huge dinosaur with wings over a dead baby calf in the snow sprinkled with blood, they are aggressive scavengers. Eagles often steal the kill of another animal for their own. For this very reason, finding the eagle "a bird of bad moral character," Benjamin Franklin thought the turkey to be a better choice for our nation's bird. The committee that eventually selected the bald eagle praised its strength, long life, and majestic nature—as an eagle in flight was a clear representation of freedom. Therefore, since 1782, the bald eagle has been the national bird of the US. It appears on the Great Seal, wings outstretched, with a real-life wingspan up to seven feet.

I thought back to the time when Abe was up checking the trees for new calves one spring and he came across a dead eagle. We knew eagles were a big deal, so Andrew called CPW (Colorado Parks and Wildlife) and they sent an officer out. We learned that eagles are federally protected under the Bald and Golden Eagle Protection Act and that dead eagles are actually federal property. There are big fines and jail time for even having an eagle feather in your possession—and more for the whole bird.

"One of their tail feathers goes for around $1,200 on the black market," the officer said, bending over and snapping a few pictures of the huge bird who had died in a bed of old leaves beneath a circle of cottonwood trees. "I'll take him back to the office and send these pictures up to CSU. They'll give me their best guess as to the cause of death. Then I'll freeze him."

"Freeze him?" I asked.

"Yeah, we freeze them and eventually drive them to Denver to the National Eagle Repository where they'll be used for education and for Native American tribes who request eagles and their feathers for religious ceremonies and graduations and stuff—they are really the only people who are legally allowed to possess the feathers—or any eagle parts, actually."

I remembered watching the officer examine the bird—the bumpy, yellow, dinosaur-like feet with black talons; the pure white feathers so bright next to the quilted brown; and the eyes—those eagle eyes that had scanned mountains and fields and that had searched the river's eddies for trout. Upon examination, the officer found puncture wounds under the eagle's wings and told us that the eagle had most likely been trying to occupy the established nest and that the wounds had probably come from the other eagles who were trying to protect their home up high.

Walking to see the eagles is one of my favorite things to do on the ranch, and as I continued my journey along the line of trees, I was quiet, not wanting to scare the eaglet above me. And that's when I finally saw her: perched in the quiet shade of the leaves, her dark body and white head and tail looked regal. Like all female eagles, she was noticeably larger than the male by twenty-five percent. Her knobby yellow feet and sharp black talons gripped a sturdy branch, strong enough to hold her ten to fifteen pounds—a sack of potatoes or a bag of flour that can perch, fly, and soar. She kept watch, like a guard at a gate, not quite welcoming me.

Just beyond her, the sun filtered through the trees, illuminating the circle of mown grass surrounded by the tall grasses. Long heads, heavy with soft and tawny seed, moved with the gentle morning air. Her abrupt and high-pitched peal, like a seagull, startled me, and I barely caught sight of her eyes darting side to side as she left her perch and circled back to her nest. I wondered if she was wishing me a nice morning alone, or if she was annoyed that I had interrupted hers? Had she also gotten away for some solitude, having left her toddler at the nest as I had done? Maybe she, too, needed time to gather her thoughts, make her list, and savor the quiet.

In the middle of the grass circle sat a thick gray cottonwood resting on its side, smooth and weathered. My heart quickened and my eyes widened when I saw, like a quill resting in an ink jar, a long white feather balancing in a crack of the log. An eagle's tail feather.

It felt like a gift.

I left the feather as a reminder for those days when I feel lost and off-balance—a reminder that I am seen and known by the One who holds this beautiful, yet complicated, ball of green and blue and white—this ball of pain, beauty, and sorrow. He sees me in the places where I walk, where I write, and where I pray.

I looked at the feather, and my soul was quieted.

A gathering of tall cottonwoods guards the edge of the sanctuary, and the sun peeked through their east leaves. I looked to the treetops where a brilliant circle of blue morning sky hovered. A green leaf fell and floated down to the century-and-a-half-old ditch that trickled past. The leaf meandered, paused on a twig, then let loose to rest for a moment on a rock. It released and continued downstream.

I wondered if Joseph Sage dug this ditch.

6. *Research the history of this land, one day, when I have time*

I looked up to the tree that held the vacant owl's nest from years ago. I thought of the last walk I took here with Ruthie. With her diagnosis of lung cancer, she and I didn't know then that it was our last walk up here together. I didn't know it would be the last time she would balance along the railroad tie, the last time her walking poles would tap her rhythm into the dusty trail through no-man's land. I didn't know it would be the last time we would climb to the top of the mesa to look out at the whole valley. She grew tired and eventually decided to take her daily walks through the fields near her house instead of driving over and making the climb.

I remembered the mother owl sitting still and quiet in her nest, yellow eyes blinking from a mottled coat of brown, gray, and white feathers. Ruthie was elated to see that the owl had finally had her chicks. Smaller and fluffier than a great horned owl, the feathered mother sat next to the three little downy gray heads that barely peeked over the edge. Together we watched them—their new eyes opening and closing—as Ruthie leaned her tall thin frame over her poles.

I remembered how, as we walked, she listened while I spilled the contents of my mind; and I remembered how she prayed out loud. Walking and praying were two of her favorite things. With her kind and energetic voice, she prayed for the kids' futures, for their education, for the ranch, for her son. And she prayed for me—for me to be able to handle being a mother of four and a rancher's wife.

She never got to meet Essie, who would have loved her, because Ruthie loved children. Red-headed and Irish—she always had an opinion—just like her parents, Gammy and Gan. Ruthie cautioned me not to get too busy, but instead to do my job well. She told me not to worry too much about what everyone else thought, or what everyone else was doing.

I sat in the grass and leaned against the old log, the feather balancing behind me. I wore one of Ruthie's faded cotton shirts that morning, but it no longer smelled like her. It no longer smelled like she had just showered the ranch off in time to start dinner. Lavender lotion. I smiled at her memory, missing her.

7.   *Love like Ruthie loved*
8.   *Research the owls*

Molly, my old golden who panted all the time, blended into the tops of the grass. Like Andrew and me, Molly and I were beginning to gray together. She explored the trickle of water in the ditch and then came and nudged me with her wet muzzle. Boots, who constantly needed something to herd, was sitting at attention and watching. His black pointy ears mixed with the brown seedheads and green stems. He watched Molly as she sniffed around—then popped up to see what she had found. The warm morning sun shone on their coats as they scurried together through the tall grasses.

There was a steady and quiet hum as the flies and insects started their day. A distant airplane buzzed—an enormous fly about its business. Reminded of the world beyond and my world at home, I wondered if I had been gone too long?

The morning warmed, letting go of the cool night. Molly settled in the shade near the log. She licked her wet paws and lowered her chin to rest. Boots sat again, ears on alert, eyes scanning. He moved one ear to twitch away a biting fly, then deflated and relaxed, looking at me with a panting smile. Hearing something, he closed his mouth to listen—radaring his ears from front to back. I then heard the center pivot sprinkler and its end-gun watering the grass and alfalfa growing in the hay field.

Just a few moments more, and I would go.

The bees added to the morning music. On the east side of Eagles' Nest, on the way to the forty acres watered by the side roll sprinkler, dozens of white wooden boxes sit in stacks all summer. Waist-high, the stacked boxes are surrounded by an electric fence, discouraging the bear from ripping them open and clawing through sticky mounds of angry bees to devour the sweet filled frames inside.

The bear, I'd seen its wet paw prints before up the old road to the top of the mesa, squished in the mud under the mist after rain. It was the bear who had scratched and climbed the two old apple trees growing in the shelter of the mesa. I wondered if they were planted by the family who first homesteaded the land on paper—the parents who had moved away the year their daughter died of cholera. I imagined the mother picking one last bouquet of wildflowers and setting it at the child-sized oval of rocks that still marks their daughter's grave on a knoll near the apple trees.

I thought of Life and his six surgeries: the first two gone bad; the third when Dr. Heare put the plate in; the fourth when it was taken out; the fifth when the tumor came back and the plate was put back in; and the sixth, when the plate was taken out for the last time. I remembered the times we thought we'd lost him—when the pain medications were too much—and when his hand went limp in mine. I thought of how he could now run and play soccer, once again.

Knowing I should be going, I looked to the day ahead: Life, Essie, and I would walk Life's 4H pigs, Wilbur and Uncle, both over 250 pounds each. We would walk them down the road to a pasture where a shallow ditch opened up. In our rubber boots, we three would follow behind, each of us carrying a long, woven stick with a little leather flap on the end to encourage a stray pig to get back on the road. We would laugh as the fat hogs saw the water and ran, squatty and awkward, their little legs kicking up and out behind them. They would roll, snort, wallow, and dig in the mud. Back home, we would spray the pigs, and each other, with a hose; and then Life would spend the day working at Andrew's side. I was astounded that he would start high school that fall. My heart felt the tug of time.

9. *Pick a bouquet*
10. *Walk and wash pigs with Life and Essie*

Two stealthy mosquitoes visited me. The first, I shooed away. The second, I clapped between my hands, disrupting the sanctuary. The trees shushed me with the tiny breeze that filtered through their leaves. The dogs, startled by my clap, hopped up and rushed to me, panting in my face, then quieted at my feet. A monarch butterfly, with her fragile wings, floated and waved, a stained-glass masterpiece in the outdoor cathedral. A quick showing and she was off.

There was a constant chatter between the birds hidden in the leaves up high. One darted—wings popping out to rise—then tucking in again to land at a new branch. A flock of geese sailed over me . . . one solitary voice speaking for them all. A new hum broke through as the highway to the west filled for the day. The busyness had begun.

Sitting against the log, in the place where my soul filled and settled, there was no stress, no worry—just beauty. However, there is always movement amidst any stillness. The trees, the earth, the eagles—along with you and me—we are all travelers passing by the sun's fiery face. Spinning a thousand miles an hour and orbiting nineteen miles each second, we are all undoubtedly moving. Yet we remain unscathed.

Somehow, a part of all the miraculous movement—I sat unmoved—on one little piece of earth. It was all too much, the glory, grace, and gravity.

The day was set in motion, and I had my list.

11. *Move the side roll for Andrew*
12. *Laundry*
13. *Ranch bookkeeping*
14. *Weed garden*

As I stood, I was energized by the perspective I gained from linger-ing in that place. By observing design, beauty, and order, I was remind-ed that my often overwhelming world need not be out of control. The things on my list, they each fit together to make my life.

15. *Pay bills*
16. *Get groceries (Chicken Piccata)*
17. *Read to Essie*
18. *Porch time*

I thought of Andrew's hand I get to hold as we often sit on the porch at the close of the day—when he tilts his head back and takes a swish of beer—when he smiles as the evening cool trades with the tired heat. *Andrew's hand I get to hold.* I was not holding a bouquet for my daughter's grave and leaving the apple trees and the valley I love. I was not searching for the other door whenever Andrew entered a room. And I was not sitting under sterile hospital lights waiting for news of my son's bone biopsy.

I had my day, my life—as far as I could see—in front of me.

The sun was hot on my neck as I headed for home, almost stepping on a daddy long-legs as it poked across my shadow. I looked ahead at Mt. Shavano—whose majestic presence was always so steady. In the fore-ground, I noticed that both eagles were now perched in the cottonwood overlooking the ladder that crosses the fence. The female ruffled her wings and tail and dipped her beak under her feathers. He was a statue. I smiled and thought that maybe they were having their porch time.

Across the ditch and over the fence, back at the dirt road, I grabbed a few long stems of alfalfa from the side of the field, choosing both pale and deep purple blooms. I added yellow clover, white yarrow, and a sunflower. Essie would be delighted. I continued on down the road back home.

19. *Polish Mom's silver pitcher for bouquet*
20. *Call Mom*

Boots picked up his pace, heading home to the shade beneath the front porch. Molly trailed behind me, stopping once in a while to play in the ditch. She panted and smiled, throwing water drops from her shaggy tail onto the dusty road.

21. *Brush Molly*

I crossed the cattle guard and my boots soon found the lush grass of our yard. I turned and looked back at the eagles. Though I couldn't see them anymore, I knew they were there, watching. I walked across the lawn where Boots joined Molly and they rolled, rested, and panted. I was greeted by the hollyhocks, in full bloom of all shades of pink, as I made my way up the stairs to the porch where Andrew and Essie sat together, watercoloring.

I leaned against the railing and watched them with a smile, as I knew watercoloring was probably not on Andrew's list.

Chapter 16

"When it is dark enough, you can see the stars."

— Ralph Waldo Emerson

Amidst the pandemic, I woke one summer night to the dogs and the coyotes threatening each other—back and forth between the hay fields and our yard. Beside me in bed, Andrew coughed again from deep down in his lungs and rolled over. I got up and yelled out the open window to *quiet*. I lay back down, knowing that getting back to sleep was not going to be easy.

Then I heard them from across the field—the low moans, deep and throaty, followed by the long squeals. Nine bulls, in the corrals near the old house, were on vacation after their two busy months of siring and servicing their harems.

I lay there, the night air coming in through the window. As I listened to the raucous ranting, I realized I was scared—scared because of a bad dream from just moments before. I held still in the dark, as if it would help me remember better. I searched my mind for the dream and why it was so scary. The details came in bits and pieces—floating to me like the braying of the bulls—quiet and dull, then sharp and shrill and frightening. I then remembered it very clearly: Suzanne, my friend who had been missing since Mother's Day, had called out to me for help. In my dream, I tried to find her, but I couldn't.

Andrew sniffed next to me, plagued by a mid-summer cold.

"Do you hear the bulls?" I asked. We held still, and the deep calls came through the window.

"I forgot to feed them today," he said, grabbing a tissue and blowing his nose.

We both knew that the massive bulls must be fed. If not, they would eventually break out and find food on their own. I've seen those testosterone tanks, made of pure muscle, jump corrals or bust through thick, rough-sawn boards as if they were toothpicks. Neither of us wanted to leave our cozy bed and go out into the night. Especially me. Especially tonight . . . my dream and my fear both lingering in my mind.

He moved first, sitting up at the edge of the bed to cough and blow again. I popped out of bed.

"I've got it—you go back to sleep. How many bales?"

"Nine," he said, lying back down with a sigh.

I fumbled and found my glasses, jeans, and a shirt. Normally midnight things on the ranch were his deal—checking a heifer in labor or putting renegade cows back in their pasture—but that night he was so sick, so tired. That night, the bulls were my deal.

Downstairs, I grabbed a pair of leather gloves, a vest, and rubber boots. I walked out into the dark night to the old gray pickup and drove the three minutes, only my solitary headlights on the road. The night air against my face woke me as the handle to the window had been gone for years.

I could think only of the dream—so compartmental . . . evasive . . . scary. Suzanne, she had begged me for help from different places all over town—all over the country. I would rush to a place to find her, but when I arrived, she was gone. Then she'd appear somewhere else, screaming for help, and I would rush there. Gone. On and on I followed, listening, looking, and failing to help my friend. All the while, I felt an evil following me—a muscular presence in the shadows that I could not clarify.

It was frightening.

There were countless ideas as to who had taken her. Had she left? Had she been kidnapped? Murdered? The theory that haunted me the most revolved around her own husband. After several interviews with the FBI, they assured me they were working overtime to find her.

I could still hear the discontented din as I passed the mailbox and drove the county road, curving around the perimeter of a hay field to the old house. As the tires rolled along the dirt driveway, I stared ahead to where the mountains kept watch. It was too dark to see them, but I knew they were there. I parked near the corrals, turned off the engine, and stuck my hand through the open window to let myself out. The warm night smelled of manure as I walked through the darkness toward the bull pen.

The intensity of their rancor increased when they sensed my presence. Their loud, low moans, followed by eerie high-pitched squeaks, terrified me in the night. Usually brave enough, I wanted to turn back. *I'll just feed them tomorrow.* But I knew they would eventually break out—and then my deal would change to chasing the dangerous monstrosities through dark hay fields. I persisted. Between the bellowing beasts and me was a long section of diagonal steel bars with just enough space between them for the bulls to squeeze their wide skulls through to reach the hay. Though the sturdy steel is grounded in concrete, I never turned my back.

I grabbed a bale of hay from the stack and lumbered with its sixty pounds over to the loudest voice. The volume was shocking, and I had to brace myself. It was scary to be near the huge beasts as their booming voices collected and came closer. I knew they could smell both the hay and me. I wondered if they could smell my fear. I knew they wouldn't get to me (it was the hay they really wanted anyways), but their mere presence was terrifying. I thought of the intimidating presence in my dream—how it couldn't get to me—but, still, it haunted me.

I dropped the bale beneath the huffing wet nose of a huge, loud bull who honked and brayed and yelled. I could barely see his black form in the night, but his voice defined him. I pulled the first piece of orange twine from one corner, and then the second, splaying the hay like a deck of cards. I went to scatter the hay with my boot, but the bull's massive head tore right in, thrashing left and right, up and down, like a shark attacking its prey. I yanked my boot back.

I thought of the story a hay customer once told Andrew. The man's father was transporting a 1,000-pound three-by-four-foot hay bale high up in the bucket of his open-air tractor, the kind without a cab. He hit a pothole, and the bale toppled backwards onto him, paralyzing him from the neck down. Sometime later, he was sitting outside in his wheelchair near his bull pen, watching his wife fork hay to an enormous bull they had raised from a calf. She scratched the bull's hairy head as he lifted it up and down—up and down—against her fingers.

The man watched as the bull began to play with his wife, nudging her here and there. The nudges turned into knocks—and eventually ended with the bull repeatedly tossing and flipping her body into the air. From his wheelchair, the man screamed and screamed in helpless horror. His son, who lived just down the road, heard the screaming from across the field and came as quickly as he could. But it was too late. The bull that the man and his wife had cared for since birth had killed her right before his own eyes.

As I grabbed and fed each bale under the dark night sky, I was reminded of the power of the beasts as I faced them and fed them. I reached out to touch one of the black foreheads, but it knocked my hand away. I moved down the row to a quiet space and dropped the last bale on my side of the steel bars. As I bent and pulled the twine, I looked straight ahead into the dark corral and into two silent black eyes, inches from my forehead. I screamed in the night at the motionless face caked with dried mud and blood, probably from a fight. He didn't flinch as my scream absorbed into the darkness. The starlight shone in his eyes and on his nose as he stood still for one moment more, before snorting and tearing into the hay.

I gathered my wits and then all the twine, careful not to leave any for the bulls to digest and tie up their guts. I watched and listened as they chomped and chewed contentedly. They had bad manners, shoving each other this way and that, like teenage boys. But at least they had quieted.

My heartbeat slowed.

"Goodnight, guys."

◆ ◆ ◆

On my way back to the truck, I stopped in the moonless night and looked up at the stars.

I all but gasped at the umbrella of glitter that covered the valley and gave shape to the mountains lost in the night. As I stared up at the brilliant night sky, I realized that the stars, with a light of their own, shined brighter and more numerous because of the deep darkness. There are certain treasures that can only be found in the blackest of times, and I needed to have the eyes to see them. The quiet sky stirred the depths of my being and loosened the hidden places in my soul, offering me the freedom, space, and time to let my fears, doubts, and questions rise to the surface.

I realized that, lately, I had been feeling lost and forgotten by God—unseen like a new moon. I felt as if my prayers for Suzanne had fallen on deaf ears. Where was the One who was normally the Light and Hope of my life? How was I to reconcile the promise of protection with the presence of pain?

The vastness and beauty of that dazzling night sky absorbed my words as they spilled out. As the Milky Way sparkled above me, I focused on the light in the night, understanding that without the darkness, there would be no light at all. There are beauties that can be seen only in the dark—strength that only appears in hardship—and it is the contrasts in our lives that bring us meaning.

I realized that my trust in protection and my hope for a life void of trouble and pain were misplaced—how the promise left with us was for peace. Peace in pain. Peace in death. Peace not as the world gives. Though my circumstances did not change in that moment, my perspective did. I traded my temporal lens for one eternal. The night sky pointed to a place beyond this world, reminding me that my time here on earth is not the end. No longer was the dark terrifying and evil; instead, it extended a gift.

• • •

As I drove home, the cab filled with the sweet smell of hay growing in the fields. Though still in my mind, the dream with its evil presence no longer plagued me.

At home, I kicked off my boots, put my gloves away, and hung up my vest. I climbed the plush stairs and opened the door to the quiet room. A gentle breeze billowed the white curtains as if they were on a clothesline. Andrew was deep asleep, his breathing rhythmic and peaceful. I dropped my clothes by the bed and climbed into the crisp white sheets next to his warm body, where his hand found mine.

"Thanks," he said.

"You need anything?"

He gave a sleepy laugh and said, "You wanna go irrigate for me?"

"Tomorrow," I said, getting cozy by his side.

I listened as he fell back to sleep. I laid there, watching the curtain fill and settle with the breeze. I thought about how to best live days that are steeped in tragedy and sorrow, how to continue, how to function, how to be helpful—and how to still find joy. I realized that I can let fear and grief paralyze me and keep me from living, or I can choose to allow sorrow to do its work of sanding and shaping, ridding me of rough surfaces and revealing the deep grains of who I really am.

Chapter 17

"There's something about the outside of a horse
that is good for the inside of a man."

— Winston Churchill

Halfway through that first summer of the pandemic, we had received only an inch of rain. On a normal year, at least twelve inches of moisture soak into the soil on the ranch. Not only was the ground brittle and cracked, but there was a hint of smoke in the air from distant forest fires.

The drought the earth felt, I was feeling it, too. Mid-summer was withering and exhausting. I was thirsty to get out and fill my cup. And I could see it in Andrew's face—he needed a day away.

It wasn't just the ranch that was draining us. We were tense and wound up like much of the world amidst the pandemic. So, we arranged to take the day—just the two of us—to get out and ride horses.

We would drive for two hours, pulling the horses in a trailer, to a 3,000-acre summer pasture we leased in one of South Park's high mountain valleys. The cows needed to be moved from one side of the pasture to the other—separated by an old barbed-wire fence. The move came a little earlier than normal as Andrew was worried the water at the other side might dry up since the little ponds were spring-fed. He didn't want the cattle to miss the grass before the water was gone.

Though we needed the day of restoration and rejuvenation, even the getting away was stressful. The day's to-do list seemed to grow longer with each minute.

That morning, I walked by Abe, who was strewn over the *La-Z-Boy* chair—and I thought it was aptly named. He was engrossed in his phone. Worried he was watching some cute girl do the latest saucy dance on TikTok, I tore into him, telling him how much I hated those phones and how they were the demise of society (though I still can't seem to function long without mine). He turned his phone toward me and showed me he was logging his summer work hours he had just started keeping track of on a new app on his phone. It was then that I noticed his old paper logbook and pencil in his lap. I wanted to cry.

"Sorry," I said. I moved on to the office where I needed to write a check for an overdue equipment payment, but Essie followed me in, asking me questions.

"Mama, can cows swim?" she asked, standing beside the desk where I sat, writing the check.

"Uh, well sure, but not very far and not very well," I said, not looking up. I looked at the amount I wrote, and it was wrong. I tore up the check and started again.

"Mama, what if they have floaties? Could they swim better then?"

The thought of cows wearing floaties made me smile. I stopped and looked into her beautiful brown eyes—so sincere, so full of wonder.

"Well, *that's* a funny thought, cows wearing floaties. Can you imagine how big a floatie that'd take?" Her eyes and smile widened as she giggled. I got the check written and the envelope addressed, stamped, and into my purse.

Next on my list was feeding the overfull bucket of smelly kitchen scraps to the chickens. Heavy load in hand, I headed outside and saw Andrew walking by the garden on his way to load up our saddles. With a big grin on his face, he stopped to let me know that he was in charge of the picnic. *Picnic?* I hadn't even thought that far into the day.

"Any special requests?" he asked. I had no mental space to think past the next item on my list and told him no. My lame response didn't seem to discourage him. His excitement for the day ahead trumped all.

We often do this for each other.

We hold each other up when one of us is faltering.

I knew he was just as exhausted as I was, or more—and his list was just as long—if not longer than mine. He reminded me that the day was designed for fun. No time schedule, no pressure. He left me with a smile and was off to the tack room, whistling a little tune.

Though the day was all about getting away and having fun together, the work part was important to me. I wanted to be helpful. I often get left behind on cattle drives because of our little one. I know it's just a season and soon she'll be saddling up her own horse to help, but I didn't want the day to just be my token day on a horse because I missed out on all the real rides, the needed rides. No, I wanted the day to count for something. I wanted something legit to write in the log book of my mind. Andrew's goal was to have a special day away together, and if we got the cows moved, just the two of us, well, that would only make a great day even better.

With lists crossed off, a picnic in the cooler, Essie at Susie's, saddles in the back of the truck, and horses in the trailer—we pulled out of the driveway. It felt like we were playing hooky as we left the ranch behind for the day. The rest of the crew had been going since early that morning, raking, baling, and stacking hay, and I could tell it was hard for Andrew to leave them.

"Well, hopefully everything goes okay today," he said, scanning the fields as we drove past, the tires on the truck and trailer all rumbling on the dusty washboards.

But our work that day was different—it was a treat. Our job was to find forty-two cows and their forty-two calves and try to move them all to the other pasture by ourselves. But the day—it was mostly about getting away together. For once, the work started to feel secondary.

• • •

Our lists had gotten the best of our morning, and it was already afternoon when Andrew parked and turned off the truck, hot from the long drive. The horses stomped in the trailer.

"First, we picnic," he said.

"Oh, good. I'm starving."

He grabbed the cooler, set it down in the grass, and we sat beside it.

"Just like Ma and Pa," he said.

I thought of all the *Little House* stories we'd read to the kids over the years. How Ma and Pa had loaded their covered wagon with their family and their most essential and treasured possessions and had traveled across the wide open prairies. With no table on their journey, their family still gathered together in the tall grasses to share a meal and gain sustenance for their bodies.

I thought of the families who had joined together in these meadows long before wagons had made their ruts in the grass—before cattle replaced buffalo—a people who called this place their home before barbed wire sectioned off the land, once undivided like the sky. I looked down the valley at how the mountains rose along both sides. The air was still and hot. The ground was thirsty. I thought of the hay crew and the lunches Susie and Essie would make and deliver to each tractor.

"Thanks for getting us away," I said.

He opened the cooler and pulled out a fat loaf of French bread, spicy salami, a thin slab of smoked salmon, and a block of pepper jack cheese. And to top it off, two plastic wine glasses and a miniature box of my favorite red wine.

"Wow," I said, picking up the little box, "this is fun."

Not usually day-drinkers, the wine added a special touch. We toasted each other and dug into the bread, cheese, and meat. He leaned back on his elbow in the grass, crossing one worn cowboy boot over the other. Tearing a bite from the hunk of bread in his hand, he looked happy and relaxed—so handsome in his hat, striped Wrangler shirt with pearled buttons, and old Levi's. We devoured the lunch.

"Save room for dessert," he said, pulling out a clear plastic container that held a huge piece of cherry cheesecake. He opened the lid, dug in his thick, weathered finger (careful to scoop up a cherry), and offered it to me. "I forgot forks."

I licked his finger and savored the sweet treat. We took turns feeding each other.

The day, if it ended right then and there, was already sweet; but then, licking the last of the cheesecake from his fingers and wiping them on his jeans, he said, "Well, should we try moving the whole herd by ourselves?"

"Yes!" I said from beneath the brim of my hat. The idea of riding horseback side-by-side through the forest and helping him check something off his list—it was the cherry on top.

• • •

As we rode our horses, Gem and Kelly, along an old dirt road in the high country, my tight shoulders loosened. The simple back and forth motion of riding through a forest of aspen and spruce trees was therapeutic and worked away at the stress that had taken a toll on my body. We guided the red cows and their black calves over a ridge from the grazed valley to one that would be long and lush. I realized that I, too, had been living in a tired pasture whose grass was short. The getting away—even just for the day—was so necessary, so life-giving.

I loved the way Gem moved as we made our way through the forest together. She calculated the path of least resistance—sometimes backing up to choose another way. She was not afraid of the cows. I thought she liked them as much as I did, liked getting out as much as I did.

I inhaled the summer air filled with the familiar scents of pine, horse dander, wildflowers, dirt, and manure. Like smelling salts, the combination brought me to life. With each step Gem took, all the things in my mind that had tied me in knots for months unraveled and traveled down my spine to the saddle and dropped to the ground, left behind in the dust. Gem whinnied, and Kelly replied from the trees where she and Andrew were moving along a slow calf.

"Shhh, shhh, come on little one, come on," he said to the calf. Andrew was gentle with the cattle—and gentle with me. The three of them emerged from the trees and we met at the back of the herd where we trotted together. I was thrilled that it was working—we were keeping the herd together while moving them where they needed to be.

Gem picked her way through the forest as we pursued a stray cow. She didn't cringe at the crack of sticks beneath her hooves or the ping of her steel shoe on a rock. She was steady and strong, and I trusted her. We guided the cow back to the herd that rambled up the dusty road. Along the edges, grass grew in the sunlight. We rode past outcroppings of steely granite patterned with lichen and neighbored by crisp blue and white columbines and bright yellow yarrow. I loved how the mountains were so calming, uncultivated, and free.

Being outside seemed to heighten every one of my senses. I thought to myself how incredible it is that we have been given the ability to see in color and that we have smell, sound, touch, and taste; how amazing it is that we live in a world in which we find things beautiful; how each day begins new with a sunrise and ends with a sunset. As I rode along, I was thankful for the unending gifts that I so often take for granted in all my hurry and worry.

We crested the hill where the terrain flattened out before tilting down the other side. The cows spread out and picked up their pace as if they knew fresh pasture was ahead. And they did—they had done the same drive for years. They began to hustle, looking for the water they could smell but not yet see. I thought of cows, water, and floaties. I pictured everyone back home and felt so grateful for my life there, though I was enjoying every moment of the time away.

Side by side, on Gem and Kelly, we were getting it done. Not only was my empty cup being filled, but we were accomplishing something important, something needed, together. Andrew urged Kelly ahead and dismounted in a fluid motion to open the stiff barbed-wire fence. I was worried the cows would divide and scatter with only Gem and me following behind them, but they moseyed right along. Then one cow spied the opening in the fence—and the tall grass beyond—and she quickened, her calf running to keep up next to her big swinging belly. The rest of the herd followed, flowing into the meadow like water.

"We did it," I said, when Gem and I caught up.

"We sure did," he said, slipping the gate's wired loop over the weathered post.

I watched him place one boot in its stirrup and swing the other over to sit again in his saddle. He counted the herd from beneath the brim of his straw hat, wide as his smile. The whole scene felt perfect: the high mountain valley, the vibrant grassy meadow, the successful cattle drive, the happy herd, the wildflowers that welcomed us to the other side, and my handsome cowboy on horseback.

"Let's walk them down a bit just to make sure there's water," he said.

Gem and Kelly took us through the thick grass. It was slow going as they stopped every few feet to grab a mouthful. We watched as the herd gathered down the valley at the water. Andrew stopped, swung down to the ground, and draped his reins over the saddle horn.

"Let's rest here a while," he said, taking off his hat and lying down in the grass. Kelly walked over and sniffed his hair. When my feet met the ground, my knees ached, but it felt good to stand. I joined Andrew and laid my head on his chest, our bodies making a T in the tall grass.

The horses looked enormous as their heads hung over ours. I reached up and touched Gem's brown velvet nose. She sniffed my hand and her long whiskers tickled my palm. She turned to graze, and Kelly followed. We drank in the quiet, listening only to the horses pulling and chomping the sweet grass. Tall, healthy spruce trees grew along the edges of the lush meadow where we rested. Aspen leaves hung green and peaceful from their white trunks speckled with elk nibbles and bear scratches. The world smelled fresh and clean. The sun had started its descent in the west and shone hot on my jeans. We tilted our hats over our eyes. Buzzing flies came and then went with the long swish of a horse's tail.

All the things that had me feeling withered and worn now seemed far away, less important, and not so urgent anymore. I wanted to bring a cup of this day home with me and let it forever permeate my comings and goings—let it soften the edges of me as I worked to check off my list each day. I wanted to do a better job of enjoying the busy days, the ones full of messy teenagers and toddler questions, days that I rushed through only to miss their humor, wonder, and beauty.

I didn't want to miss my life while I was so busy living it.

Eventually, we said goodbye to the herd and made our way back up the ridge and down the other side to the truck. Andrew loaded the horses into the trailer. It was six p.m. as we climbed into the stuffy cab, stirring dust from the seats. We rolled down the windows, took off our sweaty hats and set them on the dash. The cushioned seat felt nice. I kicked off my hot boots and extended my legs to the windshield, wiggling my stiff toes. Andrew looked over at me and said, "Well, hard to beat that day."

I couldn't have agreed more.

• • •

The hay crew was still out in the field when we pulled into the driveway. The three balers were on their last rows as Seth and Abe picked up the bales in the stack wagons. Susie sent out a group text inviting everyone over for burgers.

Exhausted, filthy, and happy, we all gathered around their table as it neared nine o'clock. We heard the stories from the hay day and shared ours, too, as the sun finally went down behind Mt. Shavano, closing another day on the ranch.

FALL

Chapter 18

Every fall, faithful as always, the leaves begin to turn, the days grow shorter, and the herd comes home to graze the hay fields until the first snow. I find joy and comfort in the change of seasons, in the rhythms it gives the ranch. When life feels overgrown and beyond my control—the earth's continued orbit around the sun helps reset my harried summer pace.

Just when we all think we cannot set one more irrigation tarp, fix one more tractor, look for one more lost cow, bale one more bale, stack one more load, sell one more trailer full, or work one more seventeen-hour day—the clocks fall back an hour, the fields rest from growing, and the ditches slow to a trickle.

The year we made the table, when fall arrived and the morning air changed from warm to crisp overnight, I made soup. Once the kids were off at school, I went to the cold morning garden and picked a few carrots. I cut kale from its crisp stalk. I sautéed garlic, onions, celery, and carrots in a swirl of warm butter as a pot simmered bone broth from the remnants of a roasted chicken the night before. The kitchen filled the house with the cozy smell of fall, and I added pumpkin muffins to the menu for dinner—the ultimate comfort food.

I combined the shiny, tender vegetables with the chicken and broth and dropped in another bay leaf. I added a cup of barley and pictured the faces of my family that evening when they would sit down to one of their favorite fall meals. To make the change of seasons even more special, I wanted to decorate the table. I wanted to celebrate fall before winter appeared, when summer's pumpkins would be baked into pies. I wanted to celebrate the new season in which we would gather as family to give thanks—to remember to be grateful in a world that often revolves around ourselves—as if we were the sun.

From the table, I cleared the tarnished silver pitcher with its sagging sunflowers. I looked out the window and saw how most of the leaves bordering the hay fields had changed from summer's green to the gold of fall, and I was ready for a change, too. It had been a long summer of work on the ranch with days that began before sunrise and often ended long after sunset.

Fall was the season when I understood, once again, why I craved the idea of reading a book by the fire and longed for things to cease growing for a season. I had an entire garden—the size of our living room and dining room—to harvest. Though I had rows of carrots to pull and vines of pumpkins to pick, I wanted to decorate the table before I got to work.

I rolled up summer's table runner and shook it from the back porch—sending flower petals, hay dust, and bits of birthday candle wax flying off to the weary lawn. The crisp air made me stop and breathe in the newness of the season. Back at the table, I unrolled a linen runner from the north end to the south.

Then I went to the garden.

• • •

Like an autumn treasure hunt, I looked under the wide leaves growing along the pumpkin vines. The nights were getting frostier, and the
prickly leaves, big as dinner plates, were waning and darkening from
verdant green to black. I lifted and looked beneath them, finding all
sizes of pie pumpkins in varying degrees of color. Some were still deep
green, while others had begun to change on one side, waxing like the
moon, to the robust orange of fall. I loved how the colors of September
came in slow waves, like a gentle warning that winter is nearing—time
to cut firewood, time to bring the cows home, time to harvest the garden—time to prepare for cold. I twisted the poky stems so they wouldn't
snap short and protected the fragile little curlicues that wound translucent green, around and around, like a ribbon on a gift.

With an apron full of pie pumpkins, I climbed the porch steps back
inside and unloaded the bumpy green and orange bounty onto the deep
chestnut table. I arranged a cornucopia of pumpkins along the linen,
then filled the oil lamp and polished its glass shade. I was ready for fall.

• • •

Fireside

It's the quiet of an evening
the sun having set on a full fall day
the last of the carrots harvested
some checks on my list
enough left for tomorrow.
The temperature lowers outside
and Molly
she claws the cold side of the door
both a thermometer and a clock.

• • •

We welcome the crisp mornings that come when the fall winds blow over the mountains and settle in the valley. When the first fire of the season crackles in the wood stove, we unwind a bit and breathe a little deeper.

Though we are grateful for the change of season and the change of pace, fall is also a reminder that the warm days of summer are about over. There is a scramble to finish projects and take one more hike up to a high lake before the snow flies. When fall arrives, we often realize that the entire summer flew by and our pre-summer plans for fun things never happened—or, as our kids are quick to remind us—were never even planned in the first place like "normal" families do. Work seems to always take precedence over fun.

One fall morning, when the four kids, then ages 10, 12, 14, and 16, were back in school, Andrew and I were lingering with a second cup of coffee on the porch. In our attempt to slow things down a bit after the summer, we reflected on the year so far and soon realized that he was getting closer to fifty. We were both starting to feel the speed of life.

The arrival of fall had turned another year on the school calendar, and time seemed to be blowing by faster and faster. Creating meaningful time as a family felt like trying to capture the wind. Not wanting to waste the years we had with the kids before they left home, it was frustrating to feel like so much of our time with them was spent managing their time and complaining about what we needed them to do better—instead of just enjoying them. Though life faithfully offers consistent and painful reminders, it's easy to forget to treasure those we love in the day to day.

Andrew and I do not know the intense grief of losing each other, or a child. We also do not know how many days we, or our loved ones, have left. A marked desire to live a more meaningful life became stronger when we lost Ruthie, and we wanted to do our best to live each day well by trying not to fill it with busyness.

Though life on the ranch breeds busy days, we realized that we were cultivating a world heavy on the side of work, and our kids needed to play. Sure, we had spent amazing days riding horses, hiking in the mountains, and camping at the summer pasture—but we wanted a new family adventure. Agreeing that they were finally ready, Andrew and I wanted to show our kids a little more about a place where their family roots run deep.

So, we took our family on their first week-long river trip.

The kids were plain giddy about the trip, and so were we. After weeks of planning and packing, we headed west. Soda cans cracked open and spicy Cheetos and Doritos were passed around the Suburban as we all wallowed in junk food—almost as foreign as a vacation itself. The temperature climbed as we made our way to Utah's San Juan River, with Papa following behind in his truck.

Hundreds of miles later, at the Sand Island river put-in, the sunset was warm and still. The sky was big above the tan desert and faraway buttes. Though different from the Rocky Mountains back home, the wide spaces and soft colors caused me to slow down and watch the last moments of light. The evening cool of the desert settled in as we set up camp and turned in for the night.

We woke to a cold, foggy morning—not so ideal for the start of a river trip.

We cracked open a cooler and ate a breakfast of orange juice, granola, yogurt, and berries before unloading all the river gear from the trailer. Two blue rafts were pumped up at the river's edge and loaded with their frames and oars; drink bags were filled with more soda than we saw all year; and sunscreen was applied in hopes that the day would warm up.

In his stiff green hat, the river ranger arrived and gave us a very thorough safety talk. He checked our permit and Andrew's ID as our trip leader. He checked our life jackets, making sure they were not too worn; and he sorted through every other single required piece of gear—making sure that every kit was complete and every oar was accounted for. Finally, we passed the test, and we were free to put on the water.

A hint of morning sun gradually appeared through the October fog, a promise that the day would soon be warm. We all stepped into the chilly, muddy water. Abe and Life each sat in a ducky—the inflatable kayaks we'd bought especially for the trip, and Papa sat at the oars on his boat with Gracie and Naomi as passengers. Andrew and I were on our boat, the Pinche Milagro; bought used, and named before we were married, it means f---ing miracle. The moment we finally pushed off and began floating on the water's surface—it felt like a pinche milagro.

The river started wide and slow. We made our way around the first bend and found it hard to see any current. The beginnings of canyon walls grew from the sandy banks, stretching taller with each calm mile. The sun finally made its appearance and flowed bright as lightning on the water. We shed long-sleeved shirts, donned sun hats and sunglasses, and dug for cold drinks in the bags that floated at the back of the boats. We eased into life on the water.

I thought of how a change in scenery—a change in routine—was so important. I thought of our niece, who had just welcomed her new baby girl into the world. I wondered how they would fare while I was gone. I worried our niece would stay inside and forget to get outside for a walk, discouraged with her new life of motherhood. But as I watched my kids laughing and smiling, watched Andrew make his white legs whiter with another layer of sunscreen, and saw his big smile from beneath the river hat that would replace his cowboy hat for the week, my worries floated away.

Without warning, the boats slid to a smooth stop—lurching everyone forward and spilling our drinks. Like an alligator surfacing from under the water, a huge sandbar had emerged, catching us all off guard. I took the oars while Andrew jumped out to move us off and back into the weak current. In ankle-deep water, Abe and Life walked duckies to deeper water and hopped back in, splashing and playing as the day heated up. I thought only one thing: *there's not enough water to run this river.*

But we were committed—there was no going back.

The San Juan River flow is controlled upstream by the Navajo Dam in New Mexico and its peak flows are in May and June. River flow, like an irrigation ditch, is measured in Cubic Feet per Second (CFS)—how many cubic feet of water (one foot deep by one foot wide) flows the distance of one foot in one second. Each cubic foot of water is equal to about 7.5 gallons of water flowing each second, or 449 gallons per minute. The San Juan needed at least 300 CFS in order to be boated, and the ranger that morning had claimed the current flow was around 350 CFS. Our irrigation ditches at the ranch each flow around six CFS all summer long.

We managed to float a few miles and made it to our first camp. I love exploring new river camps—it's like opening a Christmas gift you've been waiting for all year. We pulled each boat up on the sandy shore and tied them off to two big boulders in the sand near tall, skinny clumps of willows. We buckled life jackets to the bow lines and the kids all made the mad dash to find the best tent sites. Papa, Andrew, and I lagged behind, just hoping for somewhere flat to sleep. Past the willows, the camp opened up as the rock walls had scooted back considerably—creating a sandy expanse with a few cottonwood trees—the last wide spot before the walls narrowed completely.

Everyone spread out through camp, setting up tents between the well-worn pathways. Andrew and I dropped our dry bags, tent, and sleeping pads beneath a cottonwood tree on a flat sandy spot away from the main camp. As everyone delivered all the gear to its correct location, I set up the kitchen area—a job I look forward to. I like arranging the prep tables, lanterns, and stoves in just the right way to make things functional and welcoming, as a river kitchen is where everyone gathers.

Abe made a campfire, and I lit the camp stove to heat the beef stew I had made at home. I set water to boil for rice and organized hummus, snap peas, carrots, cheese, and crackers for appetizers. I poured a camp cup of box wine and hummed a little tune as I looked around at the peaceful desert that would be our home for the night.

It didn't take long for everyone to hover like bugs around a porch light. A table with food on it—no matter the location—is a magnet that brings everyone together in our common needs for nourishment and community. We chatted and snacked while the stew simmered on the stove and Abe's fire sent sparks crackling into the desert sky. I couldn't believe it had taken us so long to finally get our family on a river trip.

After dinner, we sat in camp chairs around the fire and sipped hot drinks. We watched the coals in the fire turn brighter as the sky above the red walls grew darker. Andrew took my hand and held it in his lap as we listened to the kids as they shared the highs of their day, the warmth of the fire reflecting in their smiles.

It was the trip we'd hoped for.

Papa sat smiling and listening, his toes buried in the warm sand. I knew thoughts of Ruthie, who had been gone for over a year, were close in his mind. She would have adored the memories we were making.

Dishes were done by lantern light, teeth were brushed at the river's edge, and goodnights were said. A few fall bugs swarmed around our headlamps as Andrew and I walked along the sandy trail to our tent site. We stopped to stare up at the dark sky. As we turned off our headlamps, the darkness absorbed us. There was no moon, and the black was so black. The flawless canvas of stars above was even more clear and intricate than the night sky on the ranch. It seemed out of place to utter a word as we looked up at the Sistine Chapel in the desert.

I felt small, but I felt known.

As we set up our tent, Andrew told me that when he was growing up, his younger brother, David, was stung by a scorpion while on a San Juan river trip. Having already passed the tiny town of Mexican Hat (population: 23), which was still downstream from our camp, Ted and Ruthie had to hike David back upstream for help. I hoped our trip would be free from any dangerous disruptions like that.

We unzipped the tent and got cozy in our sleeping bags. Exhausted, yet content, we talked only for a minute and fell fast asleep to the soothing sound of the river.

• • •

Around midnight, we woke to the soothing sound of rain.

I was thankful for our rainfly as the gentle drops traveled down its sides to the thirsty sand. I thought of the pink and white cactus flowers collecting rain in their soft petals as the scent of the hydrating desert filled my soul. We fell back to sleep.

Two hours later, the rain was not so gentle, and the sound was definitely not soothing. We woke to a powerful torrent that pelted our tent like hail. The branches of the big cottonwood that hung over our heads twisted and turned in the violent waves of rain. We tried to remember if all the kids had actually set up tents—we hoped they did—as we did not even entertain the idea of leaving ours. We stayed, but we did not sleep.

The gray morning finally appeared—but it was dim—as if the sun was taking shelter in a tent, too. There was no change in the storm. The intensity had not let up. The noise of water hitting the earth filled every single space. We peeked under the rainfly only to see stippled streams of water flowing everywhere. No one was up and about, not even Papa.

This was *not* the morning I wanted. We waited. We hoped that maybe the storm would exhaust itself, but it endured.

Two bare feet appeared at our tent as it zipped open. It was Life, looking like a wet rat. He sloshed in, bringing what seemed like gallons of water into our dry and cozy nest.

"Close the zipper!" Andrew and I both said. Life's cold fingers fumbled as water pooled on the tent floor. We scooted our dry sleeping bags away.

"You won't believe it," Life said, "our tent is literally floating! We picked the worst-ever spot, and our sleeping bags are soaked." He sat down in his own puddle, pulling his bare legs to his chest. Water dripped from his hair, down his forehead to his nose, and off his lips. "Can we make some hot cocoa, *right now*? We've been soaked and frozen all night long."

Andrew and I groaned, looking at each other with the "time to be responsible" look. It was no longer the trip we'd hoped for.

We sent Life back out in the rain to rig the big gray tarp over the kitchen. I wanted to stay in my warm, dry sleeping bag and wait out the storm, but I knew the rest of the kids were probably soaked, too. We put on long underwear, fleece hats, rain jackets, and rain pants.

It was *freezing*.

Hoods on, we ventured out into the deluge. Heavy rain penetrated my raincoat in seconds, and I could not believe what I saw: enormous puddles everywhere that filled fuller with each second. Scanning the drenched camp, I saw more water than land. I wanted to cry. I hated that everything was completely soaked, and I wanted to go home. I found Abe, still in his tent, wide awake, and so wet.

"This is crazy, Mom!" he said, his bright blue eyes looking out the hole at the top of his red sleeping bag. "Can you bring me some hot chocolate?"

"You'd better get up," I said through the rain. "We're gonna need your help." I wasn't sure what any of us were going to *do*, but I certainly knew I was *not* going to deliver hot chocolate in the pouring rain. I felt bad, for a second, and wondered if a good mom would bring cocoa to her son. *It doesn't matter*, I told myself, *I'm not doing it*.

I walked through curtain after curtain of rain on my way to the kitchen where Andrew and Life had strung up the big gray tarp and were getting stoves started and water set to boil. The soft hiss of the stove gave me hope . . . something dry! We stood hooded and shivering—crowded close together in our bright-colored raincoats. We waited for the water to heat and for the rain to stop.

I put my head down to shield my face as I left the tarp and ran to the girls' tent. My hiking boots and socks were soaked, and rain poured off me in all directions. I opened the girls' tent zipper an inch and saw that they were wide awake—and *dry*. Not wanting to leave their little haven, they propped up on their elbows, blonde halos encircling their sleepy faces.

"We aren't going to *raft* in this, are we, Mom?" Grace asked.

"What's it like out there? Is anyone else up?" Naomi asked from her cozy cocoon.

"I'm not sure exactly *what* we're gonna do," I said, as rain waterfalled from my hood. "Everyone's up, except for you guys." I zipped the zipper with freezing fingers. "Love you!" I yelled, and I ran back to the shelter of the tarp.

No one was there. From under my hood, I looked all around. Through the willows and falling rain, I saw a rainbow of jackets standing at the river. I hustled and splashed through puddle after puddle to join them. The boys were wide-eyed, whooping and hollering.

"Mom! Look at those waves!" Life said, pointing to the pocked and flooded river, rain pouring from his yellow hood. "Isn't this *awesome*?"

Our boats were rocking and bobbing, testing their bowlines and the boulders to which they were thankfully still tied. Papa hovered over each knot, retying each one as the rain poured off his stiff fingers.

In the middle of the river, there was now a very fast current in which an impressive row of waves had formed overnight by the sheer increase of water.

It was a whole new river.

And it was a whole new trip.

Andrew and I stood together and watched strange debris floating by . . . huge logs . . . a propane tank . . . a basketball. Collections of pine needles, like chocolate sprinkles, rode each swirl in the dirty brown current. I didn't know what the next step was—but whatever it was—I didn't want to take it. I wanted to be in the warm, dry desert, *not* in the soaking, miserable cold. But I knew I had to be an adult. I had to be strong and brave. But I didn't feel strong, or brave. I was cold, wet, and scared.

This was *not* the change of scenery—or the family adventure—I had been looking for.

"Looks like we're gonna have plenty of water for the trip," Andrew said, taking a sip of his hot tea. "This is gonna be fun." I turned and looked at him from under my dripping hood—his blue eyes were smiling in delight.

He handed me his mug. I took a long, slow sip and thought to myself, *He's not even fazed by this.*

I looked at the wild river and shivered. All I could say was, "This is crazy."

Content that the boats would stay put a while longer, Papa joined us and said with a smile, "That's a lot of water."

Everyone made guesses as to what the water level was. Maybe 3,000 CFS? We didn't know then, but the river had gone from 350 CFS to 8,000, overnight. And it was still rising.

Drenched, I dreamed of lingering over a second cup of hot coffee while sitting and watching the morning light warm our dry desert camp. I pictured birds darting here and there, filling the air with their sweet song. Instead, the birds were all sheltering in the canyon walls, and the air was full of constant, cold, cacophonous rain. We had a set number of miles we had to cover each day, so staying at camp was not an option—we had to keep moving. We figured the rain had to quit at some point, so getting on the river was our best bet.

Under the shelter of the sagging tarp, we made a quick breakfast of hot oatmeal. There was no refuge from the rain except under the tarp, which eventually had to come down. The thought of changing into something dry was futile. I let the dirty dishes rinse in the rain for a minute and then packed them up. We went to our tents and shoved our soaked shelters into their stuff sacks, and the boys stuffed their soggy sleeping bags. We brought our slippery gear bags down the slippery trail of puddles to the slippery boats that floated at the slippery edge of the rising river. It was as if everything had been covered in a layer of slick oil.

Everyone helped Papa and Andrew rig the boats as fast as we could. It was a muddy, messy, miserable morning. There was no hint of friendly sunlight as we loaded up. Everything was rain gray.

It was a quiet departure after Andrew's updated safety talk: stay together, keep your duckies straight, stay away from huge floating trees, tighten your life jackets, and watch for strainers—those beaver-dam-looking piles of debris that can suck you in and trap you beneath the water.

Papa took the lead, the girls huddling together on the front of his boat, trying to stay warm as they were tormented by the rain. The solemn quiet turned to shouts of joy as the boys paddled their duckies out into the current and crested each huge wave and then sailed down into its trough. It was a rollercoaster of waves, one right after the other. Already drenched—the boys were whooping and hollering again—their voices ebbing and flowing with the rise and drop of their duckies. Their squeals of delight sparked a bit of hope in me as I sat like a wet puppy in the bow of our boat.

We brought up the rear, watching the duckies pop up—disappear—and pop up again with each wave. The boys loved it. In the midst of what I thought was miserable, they were having fun. The dangers I saw through a lense of fear, they saw as an opportunity for adventure. I smiled, as their enthusiasm was contagious.

The river began to narrow, and the canyon deepened as the current hurried us along. Soon, the hammering rain turned to a tap and then a drizzle. A Styrofoam cooler bobbed by, and felled trees—twenty feet long—floated in the rising water like alligators.

We rounded a huge bend and the canyon jetted up ten times what it was before. Towering red walls surrounded us. As the river narrowed, the current picked up more speed. Then, as I looked downstream, I saw a massive, stormy wall of rainwater—draped, like a giant tarp, from one canyon wall to the other—and we were headed straight toward it. Wide-eyed, we all pointed to the gray monster ahead. We gripped oars, paddles, and frames with cold, white knuckles. Worried about the boys in the duckies, I wondered if we should pull them into our boat. They paddled hard and fast—without hesitation—facing the wall of water head-on.

I was learning, from my kids, how to confront fear with strength.

The current forced us into the raging storm that filled the entire canyon—whose sheer power blew us upstream. The hard rain stung our eyes and turned the boats sideways. Andrew's glasses made it look like he was in a car wash as he squinted and navigated our boat through the churning water—careful to avoid the duckies who were paddling dangerously close. We knew there was one rapid to look out for on this river, and since our guidebook was stowed away, we weren't sure exactly where we were or how far we had gone.

The girls signaled that they wanted to be on our boat, so I switched with them, not wanting Papa to be alone. Papa and Andrew maneuvered the two boats side-by-side for the trade. River sandals squeaked against the rafts as Naomi and I stood, holding onto each other's elbows, bracing ourselves against the water-filled wind. She looked at me from under her bright red hood—her wet, blonde curls clinging to her smiling face, and said, "Thanks, Mom." Grace switched with a smile as we rose up and down with each wet wave. I took slow steps and made my way to the front of Papa's boat.

Everything, everywhere, was soaked, and we were all chilled to the core. The girls huddled together, turning their backs against the rain that battered their rain jackets and hoods.

Papa decided to put a better rain jacket on, so he tucked the oars under his knees and handed me his waterproof river map through the rain. "Why don't you try to find where we are," he said. I wiped the water from my eyes and the tip of my nose with my dripping sleeve and took the map, orienting myself on the wet page with the tip of my cold finger.

I found Sand Island where we had started the trip, and my finger made a line of rainwater as I followed the map's blue river up the middle of one page and the next to where we had camped. I looked for the start of the tight topography lines that indicated the tall walls of the canyon on each side of the river. I found the symbol for the rapid—and we were headed directly for it.

Shielding my eyes and pointing downstream, I said, "Papa! I think it's right up ahead!"

Lifejacket unbuckled and squinting against the rain, he didn't look too concerned. Then the river slanted a little, and frothy white-water jetted up everywhere. Papa grabbed a rogue oar that had flown out from under his knee and used both oars to stroke and straighten the boat.

"Papa! Your lifejacket!"

He tucked both oars under his knees again and buckled the yellow vest just before we hit the main waves of the rapid. I braced myself and watched the duckies behind us toss and turn with each wave—but they stayed upright. Looks of determination covered the boys' faces as their laps filled with waves of chocolate water, one right after the other. I watched the whole family bouncing and hanging on for dear life and thought to myself, *This is awesome.*

I was so proud of their strength and perseverance through the storm. I would never had gone on the trip if I had been told we would raft through a deluge of rain—but I was so glad we did.

Once everyone was through the rapid, I loosened the tight grip I'd had on the raft frame and unfolded my stiff and frozen fingers to take a headcount. Everyone was safe. The wind and water pushed past us and continued up the canyon, leaving us with a suddenly soft drizzle and a much lighter sky.

Then the most magical thing happened.

It was as if a switch had been flipped. From the plateaus at the top of the canyon walls one thousand feet above our heads—hundreds of muddy red waterfalls formed and plummeted to the river. The canyon walls were alive with water. Everyone stopped rowing, paddling, and talking. Pushing back our drenched hoods lined with wet fleece hats and bending our necks back, we all looked up in awe. Soft sunlight and the tiniest of raindrops touched our faces. An enormous boulder interrupted the moment when it let loose from high above, knocking and bouncing down the tall walls and crashing into the wild water.

"Stay in the middle of the river!" Andrew's voice bounced from wall to wall. "Stay to the *middle!*"

Papa's boat was already in the middle, and the boys paddled closer. We watched the red strands of water multiply across the walls, some thick and thundering, some slim and steady.

It was a holy moment.

None of us could speak.

We knew we had been given a gift, and we lingered in it.

I would do the whole trip all over again just for that moment. The wonder on my kids' faces was something I won't ever forget. Their bright faces delighted in every direction as they craned their necks and looked all around—not wanting to miss a thing. Papa smiled in amazement as the pale sky reflected in his eyes. We were surrounded on all sides by the miraculous. Andrew and I found each other's eyes, and they spoke the same word: gratitude.

The tiny raindrops soon dissipated, and the sun peeked out from its tent, eventually stretching and shining in the narrow blue ribbon of sky between the canyon walls. Each waterfall made its way down, mingling and mixing with the river currents, swirling red and brown as the river churned and rose higher on the red rock walls.

Papa and Andrew paddled the two boats next to each other to regroup and recover. The boys paddled over and grabbed, with shivering hands, the webbing strung along the periphery of the rafts. They steadied themselves and laid their paddles across their laps, enjoying the stability and relief brought by the bigger boats. Our voices filled the canyon as we marveled with each other at the miraculous moments we had just experienced. The quick current pushed our floating mass along, and we looked at Papa's map: the town of Mexican Hat was coming up.

The San Juan River and the town of Mexican Hat border the northern boundary of the Navajo Nation. Mexican Hat has a small historic hotel where we were hoping to get the kids some hot chocolate and find a dryer for their soaked sleeping bags. As we floated along in the busy current that worked to organize its new flow, our chilled and soggy bodies welcomed the wide-awake warmth of the sun.

Just upstream from the bridge that crosses the river at Mexican Hat, we eddied out, pulled the boats up, and tied them to a huge boulder sitting on the shore. We dug out credit cards and any cash we had and climbed up the steep rocky hill to cross the two-lane road to the hotel. A wet and messy group, we climbed the wooden stairs to the front door.

We were seated by a kind waitress with feathered hair and a knowing smile. She had seen our type before: water-logged river rats taking cover from a storm. We ordered hot chocolate for the kids. I found the hotel desk where a not-so-kind older woman in a red flannel shirt insisted that we must be hotel guests in order to use the laundry machines.

"We don't need the washing machines at all, just the dryers," I said. "And only for the wet sleeping bags of our hypothermic children, I promise." I set two damp dollar bills on the counter. She pushed eight quarters my way, grumbling something about how they were the only ones I'd get.

We filled the clean dryers with heavy, wet sleeping bags covered in sand, pine needles, and leaves. This pricked my Type-A laundry conscience (a gift from Ruthie), but it quickly faded as I added our wet clothes. Worrying the machines would break, I watched them turn, round and round. Papa came in, looked at the messy floor piled with wet clothes and sleeping bags, and gave me a smile that said, *If only the woman at the desk could see you now!* Life, whom I had sent to beg for more change, returned with another handful of quarters and a firm message that they were our last.

Andrew and the girls and I said goodbye to Papa and the boys while the sleeping bags tumbled in the dryers. We ran with armloads of still-damp clothes past the office, across the road, and down the hill to where the boats were tied. The sun had started its descent, and we knew we needed to find camp, get a fire going, and start dinner. Andrew tied the boys' duckies to the back of our boat and pushed off. We floated under the tall bridge that held Highway 163 as it traveled across the canyon from one wall to the other.

As our lone boat flowed through the settling waters, the last rays of sun reflected off the red canyon walls and shimmered in the current. With each bend in the river, the sun and the temperature lowered, and a chill set in. While scanning the river's edge for a place to camp, we noticed that any regular eddies were washed out by the storm, making it difficult to find a place to pull off. As we bumped along close to shore, Andrew spotted a camp that would do and dug the oars in and pushed hard so we wouldn't miss it. The girls and I jumped in the chilly water up to our thighs and held the bow line tight as the weight of the boat yanked us over slippery rocks and drowned willows.

Andrew cranked on the oars again, and we eventually pulled the boat to shore. We stirred the blood in our cold bodies by unloading gear and setting up wet tents. The canyon was silent except for Naomi's screams at every spider she saw—shadowed in the sand by the light of her headlamp (and there were many). Andrew got a fire going, and as the color drained from the sky, he scrambled to shore with his headlamp to flag down Papa and the boys before they floated by. The plan we left them with was that we would stop at the first vacant camp we came to—not knowing how far downstream it would be.

Finally, he spotted Papa's bright blue boat floating down the canyon in the last moments of light. "There they are!" Andrew said, waving at the boat as it moved downstream in the fast and flooded current. "Over here!" he yelled to Papa, waving his headlamp back and forth above his head. "Over here!"

With a swish of his oars, Papa turned his boat and backstroked toward Andrew. The shivering boys jumped from the bow and Andrew helped them pull the boat to shore, thankful they didn't miss camp. I saw a big smile on Papa's face as he tucked his oars at his boat for the night. Relief, along with the night, settled upon us all.

Soon, both boats were unloaded and all the tents were set up. Salmon sizzled on the grill and clammy fingers wrapped around hot drinks. Chattering teeth warmed into smiles as we all sat around the crackling fire.

"Well, I'm sure glad you saw us Papa—it would have been a long night if you guys would've kept floating by," Andrew said, sipping a beer.

"Yeah, me too—glad you had that flashlight."

"But Papa—switching jackets in the middle of a rapid?" I said, scooting my camp chair closer to the fire. "That was a close one."

"Oh, I knew where we were the whole time," he said, smiling at me over his mug of hot tea.

"I couldn't believe those waterfalls," Naomi said. "They were incredible."

"And that huge rock that landed—BOOM!—right in the river—that was awesome!" Life said, his smile reflecting in the firelight.

"Those waves this morning were pretty sweet, too," Abe said, sipping the hot cocoa that adorned his smile with a brown mustache.

"I wonder what the river's running?" Grace asked, taking a sip of her peppermint tea.

Stories from the day were relived and dinner was devoured as our tents dried out in the starlight.

The day had been both terrifying and amazing. The storm, with all its rain, rocks, and waterfalls, added a depth and richness to the trip that we would have missed on a safe and sunny float.

There is danger in a shallow life lived without risk—danger of complacency in a life without storms. In choosing what is safe and easy, there is danger in missing out on the courage and character forged by the challenges of life.

The memory of that day on the San Juan River has visited me at some of the hardest times in my life—on days when I wanted to go back upstream and quit instead of facing the storm ahead. I remembered what I had learned from watching my kids on the river: set your gaze strong and steady—and meet whatever challenges come your way with determination and grit.

Thankfully, the rest of the trip was warm and fun. The storm made us grateful for every second of sun. We hiked up side canyons and climbed tall rock walls to high, deep pools filled fresh with rain. The end of the week came too soon, as we had finally settled into the gentle rhythm of life on the river.

But we needed to get back to the ranch. It was homecoming weekend for Grace and Naomi—and also for the cows that we needed to start bringing home from the high country.

And I was interested to see how our niece and Baby Esther were doing.

On the last day of the trip, we floated the remaining miles to the take-out. Sad to leave, but excited to get home, everyone helped deflate boats and load up all the gear. On the red dirt road that climbed out of the canyon to the highway, we slowed to watch a furry black tarantula tap its way across the sand.

The Suburban was silent with sleep as we arrived home just before midnight. Our crew was exhausted. The kids climbed the stairs to bed while Andrew and I unrolled the rafts and duckies in the front yard, leaving the rest of the gear for the next day.

"Well, we did it," Andrew said, as we lay in bed.

"We did it," I said, smiling in the dark. "I'm so tired, but it's a good tired."

"It was a pretty awesome trip."

We fell fast asleep—but not for long—as our lives, our family, and our table were about to change forever.

Chapter 19

It was just shy of two in the morning when we got the call.

"Who was that?" Andrew asked, half asleep.

"We'd better get dressed. Social services will be here in an hour."

I thought of the faces of my kids that rainy morning on the river as we stood on the shore and watched the waves; as they paddled duckies straight through the rapid in the middle of torrential rains; and as they watched the water fall thousands of feet down canyon walls to the river. I remembered the joy that came when I met my fear, face-to-face, and continued on.

And, like that morning on the river, when we could not stop the rain, when we could not stop the storm—how could we not welcome this baby girl who needed a safe place? No matter how scary, inconvenient, or unexpected it would be, I knew that we needed to get in the boat and keep moving forward.

Andrew and I each found our glasses, got dressed, and headed downstairs. My mind was full of questions. A knock at the door came, and we opened the door to see four shiny black boots standing, two gold badges gleaming, and an infant car seat dangling from the hand of one of the officers who stood beneath our porch light.

"Ma'am, we're sorry to wake you all in the middle of the night," he said.

We welcomed them in and the officer set the car seat on the kitchen counter. I lifted the little shade to reveal Esther's big brown eyes staring at me—a pink blanket tucked in around her.

"Hi sweet girl," I said, unbuckling her and holding her close.

She was completely quiet.

I held her against my chest, gently bouncing and swaying as if trying to comfort a crying baby.

The case worker arrived, her eyes sagging just as much as the rest of ours. Andrew stood next to me and put his hand on Esther's tiny back as we listened to the officers and the case worker talk. The moments were brief with little to say for the moment. We were handed a business card and a diaper bag.

"I'll be in touch," the case worker told us.

The door soon closed, and the house was silent. We walked back into the kitchen, the bright lights shining on the three of us.

"Say hello to your Uncle Andrew, sweet girl," I said, handing Esther to Andrew.

Taking the little pink bundle in his huge, rough hands, he held her up to his smile and said, "Well, hello there." She stared back at him, quiet as a little pearl held by an oyster.

My mind immediately went wild with what to do next.

Mom's advice to "do the next thing" came to mind, once again.

Right, okay. I can do this.

I opened the diaper bag on the counter and found a bottle and some formula. I read the directions and turned the water on at the sink.

"I've never made this stuff before," I said, dumping a scoop of formula into the bottle.

"Do you think she's even hungry? She seems pretty happy right now." He found Esther's little hand and she wrapped her fingers around his wide thumb.

"I wonder when she ate last," I said, filling the bottle with warm water. I screwed the lid on and shook the bottle. I tested a drop or two on my wrist. "Let's go back upstairs and get her cozy."

I sat in the old rocking chair in our bedroom and fed her the bottle, which she took without a fuss. Andrew found my stash of old baby blankets in the hall closet and brought them to our room where he made a cozy nest on the floor near our bed.

"I guess we should change her," I said, holding Esther at my shoulder and patting her back. Andrew found a diaper and wet wipes in the bag and set them on our bed. He watched as I changed Esther's diaper and wrapped her in her blanket.

"See, Darlin'," he said. "It's just like riding a bike."

With the little bundle in my arms, I sat back down in the rocking chair. I held Esther at my chest, her little face turned to my neck. I held her hand, and in the quiet, she wrapped her fragile fingers around mine. Andrew switched off the lights, dropped his clothes beside the bed, and climbed under the covers. As I rocked back and forth, I wondered what we were getting into. I thought of changing soggy diapers, clicking tight buckles on a Cheerio-infested car seat, and finding a sour bottle of formula under the couch come Christmastime.

But then I felt her soft breath on my skin as she fell into a deep sleep. I sat in the darkness and watched a pale light appear over the eastern hills as a thin moon slowly rose above the horizon. I thought of the waterfalls after the storm, and I felt peace. Esther and I inhaled and exhaled in the moonlight—the chair rocking slowly back and forth over the carpet, like a ship on the sea.

Ready for sleep, I stilled the chair and found the bed of blankets Andrew had prepared. Careful not to wake her, I nestled Esther's little body in memories of my other babies now grown. I tucked the blankets around her, leaned over, and kissed her forehead.

I joined Andrew, who was still awake, and together we listened to Esther's soft breathing. We prayed, asking God for strength and wisdom in this new chapter of our lives. Andrew soon fell asleep, his breathing deep and peaceful. The small moon and I stayed up together, its gentle light joining me through the window. None of us knew, in those early hours of homecoming day, as Esther slept, calm and cozy, that she had come to what would one day be her forever home.

• • •

The next morning, the house woke to an infant.

And Esther, she woke to our house.

As each of the kids eventually surfaced that Saturday morning, their eyes widened when they saw the thick black hair sticking out from the pink bundle in my arms.

"What happened?" they each asked in their own way.

But they knew.

With river gear strewn and drying all over the yard; huge river coolers filled with trash, crushed cans, melting ice, and remaining food; teenage girls filing in with curling irons and plastic-covered homecoming dresses draped over their arms and slingback black shoes dangling from their fingers; and the table, covered with a cornucopia of pumpkins, makeup, hairspray, baby's breath corsages, bottles, formula, diapers, and wet wipes—my new world felt like a wall of water coming right at me. Thoughts of bottle babies and Adopt-A-Calf powder swirled around in my mind.

Instead of crumpling on the floor in an overwhelmed mess, I did what my kids taught me on the river—I continued on in joy. I changed a diaper, made a bottle, and fed the sweet baby in my arms.

• • •

Months passed as we attended court dates and watched attempts by social services to reunite Esther with the young man who claimed to be her father, even though he had recently been arrested on several drug charges. Our niece made it clear to the court, the lawyers, and the case workers that she wanted Esther placed in our home permanently.

He pushed harder and harder to gain full custody, and whenever I thought of losing the little girl who had become a part of us, I became nauseous and could think of little else. An official visit was planned—the courts would pay his hotel and gas money to visit Esther in Salida.

He did not show.

He offered excuses, and a new visit was scheduled. A DNA test was ordered, and the process continued forward. It seemed hopeless that we would be able to adopt Esther.

Then, at the next court date, it was announced that the DNA test had come back negative.

I watched the case worker lean over and whisper something to our niece—who stared back with her big brown eyes and shook her head no. Having turned seventeen shortly after Esther came to live with us, she seemed only a child herself.

An official ad was placed in the paper of the Arizona town where Esther was conceived. It advertised the dates and details of the situation—noting that if anyone thought they might be the father—they should call the number below.

Seriously.

It didn't seem real.

In the meantime, the court files listed Esther's father as "John Doe" until the real father came forward. The ad ran for the required six weeks. No one called. No father was found. Eventually, John Doe's parental rights were relinquished, formally and forever.

Simultaneously, the Navajo Nation, understandably, did not want to place Esther in a non-tribal home. For months, they explored every other option they could. However, because our niece and her mom fought hard for us, because no other relative on the reservation had filed to adopt Esther, and because we were blood relatives—the tribe eventually agreed. That was a tremendous day.

There was only minor paperwork remaining.

Like waterfalls tumbling down canyon walls after a storm, it felt miraculous.

• • •

Fifteen months after Esther came to live with us, adoption day arrived. The courtroom, usually full of strangers waiting their turn, now overflowed with our family and friends. In a way, we were all adopting Esther together, each person playing a role, however big or small.

"My job is a hard one," the judge said, after he called the court to order. "But on days like today, I love my job. Days like today, they make it all worth it." Each lawyer and case worker presented their last statement for the case, and the judge declared Esther's new, legal name: Esther Hazel Richardson.

After the adoption party was over and everyone went home, Esther took a nap and I cleaned up the kitchen. I wiped pink frosting and cake crumbs from the high chair at the table and tiny fingerprints from the engraved silver cup David and Anne gave Esther.

It was finally all over—and our new life as a family of seven had officially begun.

• • •

One autumn evening, two years later, while making dinner, I looked out the living room windows that faced the fields. The day's end illuminated our cows and calves who grazed the remnants of summer's hay. Cotton-wood trees, lit up golden, lined the edges of the field like a frame. The tender valley held the peaceful picture, open handed, like a feather.

As I washed and chopped kale from the garden, I looked west out the kitchen window to see four-year-old Esther, twirling in her turquoise princess dress—its cape flowing behind her, stirring the fallen leaves and brushing the overgrown chard that bent over the edges of the raised garden beds. She nodded and circled—singing a song all her own—as her bare toes spun in the softness of summer's last grass.

Royalty

Your brown chunky fingers trace
the lines in my pale palm.
You want to be a princess, you say,
and, of course,
I tell you that you are.
You are our little princess,
you whose deep dark eyes shine and see,
the six of us—
our blue eyes smiling back at you.

How do I explain how very royal you are,
how you are many princesses all wrapped in one?

How do I explain that part of you is spicy,
full of cilantro, chilis, corn tortillas,

rolling r's, dancing, and eating salsa?
I imagine an abuelita
whose arms won't know you as little,
but who maybe will meet you one day,
before she is gone—
if she even exists.
But first we must know your father.
I think I hear his mother in the way you say some words,
see her fire in your bones;
with a rhythm only yours.

How do I explain yet another in you?
She is of the earth, the sky, the sun, the water.
If Abuelita were to throw a stone north,
and that stone were carried by a bird
or the wind
over a wall
across a wide river—
it might land where,
before you were born,
when your mother, my niece,
was small,
I met your Shima Sani Hazel.
Tight gray bun
warm eyes like the sun
and a kind face,
the color of you,
she stood short and strong
her earthy hands
resting at the head of her table,

wearing bright silver rings and bracelets,
and a royal turquoise mane—
the color of the sky.
She bowed and blessed Navajo fry bread in the name of Jesus,
the only word I understood.
Your great-great grandmother
lives in your name
and flows through your veins.

Though from a different branch on your family tree
these four in our kitchen,
they share blood with you.
Their blue eyes all laughing
after dinner one night—
when one of your brothers called you Hazelnut,
as you danced around them.
Sometimes you are a little nut—
and he names you because he loves you.

How do I explain the other princess,
the closest to your favorite,
the one you pretend to be?
She is complicated,
pale-skinned and
blue-eyed—
always searching for identity.

Though she comes from conquerors,
in you she hides.
Her blood runs in my palm
and in your finger,

blood that endured
to a shore not its own;
but to that of the others.
No one sees
the pale or the blue
that both dwell in you.

But your sisters,
and you
and me,
we laugh together
our hair pulled up high
in topknots bobbing on our heads.
Pale sisters in dark mud masks
that scare you;
they envy you,
we all do:
your perfect skin,
not blotchy,
not sunburned,
only sun-kissed.

I read you the holy story
behind your name,
the true story of the beautiful girl-queen
who was raised by her uncle,
just like you.
I tell you that your young mother
chose your name
without even knowing the story.

You listen carefully
and trace the letters of your divine name
printed on the white page,
fragile and intricate—
like the wings of a butterfly.

Your perfect eyebrows
the way they arch
and express
as your body dances
and twirls together
all this
blood
beauty
spice
rhythm
laughter
tragedy;
and your steps in the grass weave together
time
land
language
enemies
family
that make you who you are.

Infant princess at our late night door
I hope you treasure
one day
the royalty pulsing through your veins—

you, a swirling of cultures.
One day I will explain to you that
blood is like a river;
some rivers divide,
while others join
creating new beauty—
beauty that dances.

• • •

When the leaves begin to change, I feel a pressing need to get out and see the colors before they fade and fall—before the leaves in their full glory drift in the wind, leaving bare branches to balance fragile lines of snow.

And in this season of life, as the kids grow and leave, I feel the pull to spend time with them. Their lives are changing right before my eyes, and I cannot stop this progression of time, this change of seasons.

Nor would I want to.

Every season holds its own beauty, and it wouldn't be healthy to keep everything, or everyone, the same forever. The fields need a time of dormancy before the demands of spring come again. The garden sleeps during the season of slow decay when manure from the coop and withered leaves of kale add nutrients to the soil. The bare mountains, after a long summer, need months of winter to once again fill the lakes, streams, rivers, and ditches below. A seasonless life—a life without change—is stagnant.

Change is healthy.

Change is growth.

The number of plates at the table these days waxes and wanes like the moon. The empty seats, when they are filled again, share a tenderness that grows gratitude—knowing that life is fragile and often there are places forever left empty at all of our tables and in all of our hearts.

Chapter 20

One morning, in the fall of 2020, we woke to a foot of snow. The week had broken September records for both high and low temperatures—ninety degrees one day, a mid-day freeze the next, followed by a foot of snow that night. Everything was shocked. It seemed everything that year was shocking: from the pandemic to Suzanne's disappearance. Both were unsettling and unimaginable, and both occupied my mind and my routine.

After breakfast that snowy morning, everyone went outside to play and see. What we saw was both magical and tragic: everything was soft, white, and fluffy—including the songbirds who had been enjoying the warm fall days, but who did not weather the storm so well.

Essie and I found yellow warblers and little wrens, stiff, in shadowy pockets of snow, or tucked between the net and the pad of the trampoline. The contrast of their tiny yellow and gray feathers against the stark white snow was somehow beautiful and sorrowful at the same time. Andrew disappeared into his shop for a bit, later appearing with a barnwood birdfeeder. We watched him pound the spindle of an old stair rung into the snow-covered ground in front of the living room windows. I loved that he wanted to watch the birds from inside. He attached the feeder right on top of the spindle and filled it with grain from the barn until we could get to the store for birdseed.

Essie busied herself collecting feathers in her little hand, and I fed the dogs—in an effort to keep them from picking up the feathered bodies from their snowy graves and tearing them apart. The cats meowed, the horses neighed, and our one pig, Wilbur, snorted and ran circles in the snow—I fed them, too. The whole barnyard was talking at me. I checked the hens who peeked out from their coop, but who wouldn't dare stick one skinny claw out into the cold white fluff. Not even the rooster would brave the snow.

"Good morning, chicka-choos," I sang to them as I checked for eggs inside their coop. None, yet. The hens weren't nesting in their boxes; instead, they were clucking around, talking about the storm. It threw them off. Shocking changes did that, and their world had been thrown off-balance by the record-breaking week. They must have wondered what season was upon them.

With the year of masks, social distancing, death tolls, and cases rising, I'd been thrown off balance, too. And when Mother's Day came and Suzanne went missing, my life took on entirely new routines.

At five o'clock each evening, when I would normally be thinking about dinner for my own family, I started meeting people from church and delivering the dinners they had made for Suzanne's family. Other new routines included daily trips to Walmart to replenish searchers' food and drink supplies and midday visits to check on Suzanne's daughters. Phone calls and meetings on the porch with the FBI, the CBI, and our local sheriff consumed hours each week as the search continued.

As I closed the door to the upset henhouse, I whispered, "I understand girls, I understand."

I walked back through what normally was our garden, but what that day was a snow-covered series of lumps and a row of persistent corn that was trying to stand tall amidst broken ears and stalks. I made deep tracks with my black muck boots and stopped at the mounds that I guessed would be the big bushy basil plants I should have harvested before the storm. I decided, right there in the garden, that if there was any basil to snip, I'd make lasagna for dinner.

Digging my leather gloves through the snow, I knew I was in the right spot when the heavenly fragrance escaped to my nose. I breathed in and it woke me more than the strongest cup of coffee. The top leaves were frozen and already blackening, but the leaves of the understory were still bright green. I picked handful after handful, knowing that our growing season was officially over. Lasagna it would be.

The daily routine of making dinner is always on my mind. That year, I had seven mouths to feed every night—and that was if it was just us—which it rarely ever was. Once I have a dinner plan, I feel like I can go about my day with a little more freedom.

With a dinner plan, I find that I look forward to making dinner. The plan allows me the joy of inviting Papa or my dad and Uncle Dan over to join us. But on the no-plan days, there's the frantic look in the fridge as I ward off hungry kids from the pantry while thinking as fast as I can about what I can create with what I find.

With my jacket pockets packed full of wet basil leaves, I worked my way down the row to my new favorite vegetable: dinosaur kale. Also known as Tuscan or Lacinato kale, its leaves are deep green, thick, and bumpy—what might look like dinosaur skin. It's sweeter than regular kale, and since my first taste, I can't get enough of it. I dug and found the tall stems and tough leaves beneath the heavy snow. They perked up as soon as they were freed and touched by the glow of sun through the gray sky.

Was it *really* September in Colorado? Normally September is full of songbird days, perfect and warm. So perfect and so warm that when we are in the mountains cutting firewood and shed down to t-shirts, the idea of needing heat from our wood stove seems ridiculous. But on that morning, there was no firewood stacked neatly for winter, so I added that to my mental list.

As I brushed snow from the kale, I thought of my neighbor, Ann, who introduced me to the superfood. She lives just a mile up the dirt road and walks her dog each day past my house to get the mail from the growing line of boxes on posts along the main road. Essie and I had been to her house for tea and a tour of her year-round greenhouse. Ann is a retired pediatric lung doctor married to a lung pathologist and researcher. They love their work and have projects and research going on, especially with the pandemic.

Ann loves to cook—and I learned this in the best, worst way.

While picking weeds with Essie earlier that year on a sunny spring morning, I saw Ann out walking. We waved to each other and I walked to say hello over the fence. When she asked how we were all doing, I told her about Suzanne.

Ann removed her sunglasses and asked, "Can I bring you dinner tonight?"

I hesitated for a moment. Normally, I am the one who brings the dinner and helps the people going through hard times. And normally, I would say no to help, but this time, I really needed it. I was exhausted.

"Thank you, yes," I told her. "That would be great."

For the next two weeks, Ann appeared at our doorstep each evening with her cheerful voice and her incredible cooking. All masked-up, she delivered meals like Vietnamese stir-fry, pot roast, stuffed cabbage rolls, pork roast, vegetable beef soup, and the best gift ever—her dinosaur kale salad. With a homemade vinaigrette, plump dried cranberries, and smoked almonds, it melted in my mouth. The kids devoured it, and Naomi even requested it as part of her birthday dinner that next week. When I asked for the recipe, not only did Ann bring a huge bowl of salad prepared for the party, but she also handed me a fancy package of dinosaur kale seeds and her handwritten recipe with a few favorite variations. I was so excited to plant those seeds. I babied them more than any other plant in the garden.

• • •

On that snowy September morning, as I broke the thick stems and gathered the green treasure in my arms, I thought of how resilient it was—how the kale had survived the huge storm. I thought of how the recipe called for slicing the kale thin and then squishing and massaging it for twenty seconds. The process softened the leaves and brought out their natural sweetness. I thought of the year, so hard for so many reasons, and how everyone's routines had been upset.

I thought of the day before—when I had returned home from taking food up to Suzanne's family—when my kids were all congregated in the kitchen—when I walked in the door and they stopped talking and snacking and looked at me—when Abe asked how I was doing—when I couldn't say anything—when I just took a step toward him and leaned into his awkward arms and wept—when my son held me.

I thought of how during those two weeks of meals from Ann, we had sat around the table and raved about each dish that brought new flavors and an Eastern European flair to our home. I thought of the empty chair at Suzanne's dining room table and the void her disappearance had created in so many lives and hearts.

I hated to do it, but eventually I told Ann that I needed to start cooking again. Not that we didn't appreciate her generosity and her fantastic meals, but I was starting to get used to it, and I didn't want to impose any longer. I knew my family needed me back home and back in my routine.

And, I needed my routine, too.

Ann completely understood—though she still checked in with me almost daily—letting me know that anytime we needed a meal, she would love to make extra for us. One evening, she even texted, "I miss cooking for you all."

From my neighbor, I learned the value of saying yes to a helping hand. I was shown what an incredible gift a meal can be, because it's really a tangible offering of friendship and love and hospitality. There is no mistake that the word hospital is at the root of hospitality: hospitality is healing.

Life settled back into its routines, both new and old. One thing that helped ground us as a family amidst such uncertain times—the thing that brought us back together at the end of the day—was the table, where we gathered to pray, eat, and share.

• • •

Though there's something comforting about routines, seasons, and the consistency of time, there's also something healthy about stepping out of our routines—like a river trip during a pandemic, church in the woods, feeding bulls at midnight, rafting in the rain, and adopting a child. On a snowy night that Covid fall, Seth added something to the list: riding horses in the moonlight.

It was a blue moon Halloween, and we had just recently seen the season's first dusting of snow. Andrew and I were out working cows with Seth and Susie and our neighbors, Jim and Gina. As the day was getting colder and coming to a close, Seth said, "Moonlight ride tonight. Bring a hot drink and we'll meet at your place once the moon rises."

Jim's eyebrows lifted under his cowboy hat and his mustache bobbed as he said, "It's a plan."

The kids were all in quarantine, so after dinner, Andrew and I left them with a campfire and s'mores in the backyard. The horses stomped and snorted as we neared the corrals behind the house; and Gem and Kelly whinnied as we caught them in the dark. A soft moon glow appeared in the eastern sky, like a sunrise in black. From inside their coop, where they roosted like statues, the chickens watched us as we brushed the horses' rough coats and fumbled with saddles in the shadows. The cats scampered around our feet and dashed after mice that scurried along in the dark.

At the horizon, a tiny rainbow of moon appeared, and we stopped to watch weeks of lunar phases grow in minutes, covering the barnyard in silver light. As we eased bits in place and adjusted stirrups, Andrew's glasses reflected the moonlight, and so did his smile. The horses simultaneously turned and looked down the dirt road—they had heard the others long before we did. After a minute or two, we heard horses' hooves coming in the driveway.

"Evenin'," Jim said, with a moonlight twinkle in his eye, so excited he could barely stand it.

"Evenin'," we said.

"This is so fun!" Gina said. "We had a great ride over."

"And it's not even that cold," Susie said. "It's so beautiful."

"Everybody got your hot drinks?" Seth asked. Everyone did.

Andrew climbed up into his saddle with no problem; but me, I was bundled up so much that I could barely get my foot in the stirrup. I finally made it into the saddle and settled. We turned toward the road, and from our saddles, we all yelled a little goodbye to the kids in the backyard. The six of us rode toward the big pasture where the cows were bedded down for the night, watching their second full moonrise that month.

"The moon's so bright I can barely see the stars," Jim said. And we all looked up, needing moon glasses. It was a quiet night as our long shadows fell across the lighted field. When we reached the herd, the cows started to stir and stand while the calves jumped up to frolic in the moonlight. The mamas called for their calves and the herd grew loud and antsy as we passed through.

"Don't you think the mesa will be too icy?" Susie asked, as we headed out of the field and up the old road.

"Nah," Seth said. "It'll be fine."

I had wondered the same thing. We rode past the grave and the apple trees and turned up toward the mesa. The road was smooth with snow as the horse's hooves clopped against the hidden rocks. Gem's breath puffed and curled like smoke in the bright night sky. As we climbed higher, I was thankful that a horse's night vision is excellent and can see as well as if it's midday.

The horses' sturdy steps stopped as we arrived at the flat top. The view of the peaks was stunning—snowfall from the week before glowed above treeline. The blue moon lit the entire autumn valley and reflected off the river winding in the distance. I had never seen anything quite like it before. We sat in silence for a few moments—a rare time when we were all at a loss for words. Soon, flasks and thermoses appeared from saddle bags, and we toasted each other, the horses, and the moon.

• • •

It is always a little sad when the last leaves let go of the trees and the fall season fades into winter. When I think back to that first fall in our new house, when the garden pumpkins ushered the change in season at the table, and when soup simmered on the stove, I picture the light from the oil lamp illuminating the faces of my family as they delighted in the flavors of the harvest.

I think of the history we have now—the table and I—over a decade of memories and people gathered together. Friends and family have celebrated, grieved, planned, agonized, and played, all while being nourished. Like loved ones, chairs have been added to the table, and chairs have been taken away. Through the sorrows and gifts that change brings to each life, we have grown, and we continue to grow, like thin tendrils on a pumpkin vine.

My family and I have been sanded, stained, and shined by our stories that come from the different seasons on the ranch and from the different seasons of life. Everyone has a story to tell. Sharing our stories with each other allows us to learn from one another's failures and successes. Aren't we all, right now, on this day, whatever season it may be, living stories that are crafting and refining us into something hopefully more beautiful and useful than we were yesterday?

This is the hope, that we are always growing and learning, no matter the season.

Our stories, both good and bad, should not be wasted. Instead, as our experiences shape and refine us, we can share them at the different tables where we sit, allowing them to teach, inspire, and encourage others to live a more abundant life.

WINTER

Chapter 21

Each year on the day after Thanksgiving, as the afternoon fades into a pink winter sunset, Salida officially opens the Christmas season. Lamp posts are twisted with greenery and white lights, and Rotary serves free hot chocolate as downtown fills with its people. The chilly air creates a fog above the crowd as all the children stomp their snow-boots and ask, *When will S Mountain light up?*

S Mountain, with its spiral drive, is also known as Christmas Mountain; and the crowd waits, knowing that the giant-sized tree of lights on the mountain will soon bedazzle their main street view. First the mayor will welcome the crowd and wish a happy holiday season to his town as the bustling slows and the snow boots stop. The eyes of the crowd will turn to the mountain, and the countdown will begin. The children will squeal as number one is reached and the tree of lights is lit—welcoming the Christmas season to Salida.

And when the first substantial snow covers the fields, the ranch welcomes the new daily chore of feeding the herd. Weaned in the fall, the calves are grazing the fields over at Papa's, and the pregnant mamas are at the Sage Place—separate from the bulls.

On the ranch, it's all about feeding.

One freezing winter day, Andrew asked for volunteers before breakfast: "Anyone wanna come feed?" There was a lot of hemming and hawing and a lot of "I went last time," as everyone was either cozy by the fire, still curled up in bed, or late for school.

But me, I love to feed the cows. Though I married a rancher and am allergic to hay, I love seeing the cows and being outside anytime. I spend a lot of time in the kitchen, so any chance I can delegate duties and be outside, especially with Andrew, I take it.

When the kids were little, long before any of them had their driver's license, they loved to go feeding with Andrew. They would bundle up in their Carhartt coveralls, muck boots, wool caps with ear flaps, ski goggles, and mittens to join him in the cold cab of the flatbed pickup where he would let them drive to the haystack to load up. Then they'd drive the loaded truck out to the field and honk the horn, bringing the entire herd running through the powder—majestic mountains towering white behind them (still one of my favorite scenes on the ranch).

Andrew would leave whomever had come with him in the cab to drive—often a vivacious three-year-old—while he fed hay off the back. Bright green against the snow, the hay is always devoured by the cows who run, knock, and fight to get their feed.

Eating is serious business for these mamas.

Abe went to feed one day when he was around six years old. He loved to drive, but on that day, he wanted to stand on the flatbed behind the cab and ride outside. As Andrew was driving along, he took a corner of the dirt road a little too fast and little Abe went flying off the back, landing in the snow. Andrew saw the tiny coveralls sail off the side and was horrified. Abe was just fine—a little beat up—but like any kid on the ranch, he thought it was fun.

To grow up on a ranch has to be one of the best ways to spend a childhood. There's always something going on, and the entire family works hard, together. A ranch kid learns the rhythms of life—and death—and the cyclical nature of the world we live in. A childhood spent on a ranch is spent outside, where there's always something to do; and like most family-run ranches, there's always a gaggle of siblings or cousins to pull into the fun.

These days, instead of driving the feed truck through the snow drifts for fun, the big kids spend their snow days either skiing at Monarch or, if there's snow in the valley, grabbing skis, shovels, and four-wheelers and making snow jumps in the hay fields. The smooth white surface just begs for wheel tracks to be drawn on its blank palette.

• • •

But not all childhood days are full of fun, family, and good memories. Our kids get bored, get in trouble, get grounded, and have to get their homework done, too. But some childhoods are very different.

My parents were divorced when I was eight, and though I saw my dad every other weekend, I mostly lived with my mom. She worked as a nurse, often given the 3-11 p.m. shift, which left me to walk home from school and let myself in. After school, while still living in a small mountain town before we moved down the hill to Denver, I'd walk the mile or so up the dirt road to my house and let my dogs out of their kennel. Our golden retriever and German shepherd were my best friends, and they greeted me with their wagging tails and huge smiles. We'd walk up the hill behind the house to the forest of trees where we would run and play, all three of us equally happy to be out of our respective cages for the rest of the afternoon.

We'd head home, and then, like any latchkey kid in the 80s, I'd grab a snack—a couple of Twinkies, Ding-Dongs, or a piece of Wonder Bread smeared with a thick layer of Welch's grape jelly—and watch TV. Snack in hand, I'd flop down on my belly on the white carpet, elbows propped up, knees bent, toes touching above my back, and I'd watch hours of *Diff'rent Strokes*, *The A-Team*, *The Facts of Life*, and *Three's Company*, while happily nibbling away. Homework never crossed my mind as the sugar and the studio laughter soothed the loneliness deep down. In those moments, I was the one in control of my life, and it made the painful parts—the ones way out of my control, like divorce and addictions—feel far away.

I eventually found my way into college and into the worlds of English, kinesiology, teaching, adulthood, running, rock climbing, and healthy food choices. My life felt fun and in control. I was living on my own and making all my own decisions.

Then I met Andrew.

Both employed as rafting and backpacking guides, our life together began as an adventure. He helped me work through my fears of marriage and divorce—not wanting to repeat history—and we married two years later. He allowed me to see that my life, including my decisions, were my own, and that I was not on some familial wheel I couldn't escape.

I was determined to create a happy and healthy marriage, home, and family. But all of it was exhausting. Morning sickness, nursing, sleepless nights, endless routines, and ceaseless questions—motherhood was coming at me from all angles. Life felt chaotic, and I was just trying to keep up.

My childhood way of trying to control the things I could surfaced once again, and I unconsciously started cleaning up stray Goldfish and Cheerios and eating finger-fulls of cookie batter right along with the kids. Essentially, I ate like a toddler, not a thriving, healthy, self-controlled adult. Food filled some void in my psyche that was hungry for control. After four pregnancies, Life's leg explosion, and losing Ruthie, my life felt completely out of control, and my adult-toddler response to the weight of it all added more pounds to me than I ever dreamed.

Our four kids were growing, too, though in a healthy way. Eventually, one by one, they said goodbye to nursing, diapers, potty training, tantrums, naps, and car seats—and said hello to soccer, friends, jobs, cell phones, and social lives of their own. Andrew and I were loving the new liberation and the new firsts we were experiencing with our maturing family: skiing together, Sunday afternoon naps, family movie nights, horseback riding, and enjoyable car trips.

And then that call came in the middle of the night, and we started again back at the beginning of the game.

• • •

On a December morning, over one year after Esther came to live with us, it was *negative* seventeen degrees outside. Andrew made coffee and built a fire in the wood stove. Once the sun came up, and once the feed truck started, his day of outside chores would begin and he would bundle up and head out to feed the cows. He knew they were waiting for him—their whiskers white with frost. They were waiting to hear the honk of the flatbed truck full of hay that would fill their bellies and keep them warm all through the short winter day.

Life woke early and bumped down the stairs to join us by the fire. Curled up on the couch in a blanket, he looked outside the window, amazed at the lavender sky.

"That's a frozen sunrise, son," Andrew said. "Look at the thermometer."

Life looked and saw −17°. He dashed to the kitchen, setting water to boil. With bare feet and a scalding hot kettle, he walked outside to the edge of the porch and tossed the water into the air. It instantly froze and shattered above the snowy lawn. Frozen droplets of all sizes fell to the ground like gentle snow, and then Life ran back inside to warm his toes by the fire.

By the fire were stacks of books: some were children's, like *The Story of Ferdinand* and *Billy and Blaze*; some were novels, like *A Gentleman in Moscow* and *Great Expectations*; and some were true stories, like *Nothing Daunted* or *Just Mercy*. But lately, there were books on healthy soil, biodiversity, and sustainable grazing practices. As ranchers, we were learning what we could do to become better stewards of the land we love.

It was the cozy time of year when normally I would be baking, wrapping gifts, cross-country skiing, and playing cards with my family; but my reality was far from normal that year. If I moved even a centimeter, my lower back and right leg would flash and fill with indescribable pain—the kind that sends the body into nauseous sweats. Having had back surgery from a horseback riding injury six years before, I was reliving the intense nerve pain. This wasn't just an isolated afternoon of pain on the couch—it was an entire Christmas season filled with dinners delivered each night because I couldn't cook, and disappointing hours in bed thinking of everything I wanted to be doing—but couldn't.

The pain had gotten so bad that Andrew even drove me to Denver for a steroid injection. In a hospital gown, I laid face down on a vinyl table as a doctor and three nurses watched the monitor that showed a live view of the nerves in my lower back. The doctor injected a steroid into the nerve that had ruined my Christmas season. I have never experienced pain like that in my life. I cried out, asking if it was supposed to hurt that bad.

"Usually, we don't get a response quite like this. Your nerve must be very irritated," one of the nurses told me. I wept, and my body sweated as the doctor continued to probe and inject. I thought I was going to pass out.

When they told me that the injection—the torture—was over, I lifted my body off the table and I saw that I was leaving a ring of water, my sweat, around the edge.

I would never go back.

The pain was frustrating because there was no injury this time. I was in my 40s and wondered if I was already getting old. I wanted to be an adventurous mom who could play family soccer games, rock climb, raft, bike, and ski; I didn't want to be the wet blanket strewn on the couch, the one who the kids felt obligated to sit and visit with each day.

There was no injury—and that scared me, because I wanted something other than myself to blame—like a flighty mare bucking me into the air and onto the field. This time, I hadn't been on horseback gathering the last stubborn cow from a pasture while asking too much of the horse who sent me flying in the air only to land on my tailbone. This time, there was no herniated disc that morphine couldn't touch.

No—this time the pain existed for another reason—and it soon became clear that I had become my own worst enemy.

Christmas on the couch came and went. Eventually, the nerve pain subsided after I laid horizontal for days, weight and gravity no longer demanding and pulling on my back. Then, one January day, as I was carrying screaming, tantrum-throwing, thirty-pound Esther up the stairs to her room for a well-needed nap, I felt a pinch of that former pain on my nerve: a warning. After reading a chapter from *Little House in the Big Woods*, Esther and the nerve both calmed down.

It made me sick to my stomach to think that the pain was going to move in again, that the pinch would morph into a stab. I couldn't do it.

I couldn't miss more of my life—more of my family's life—while staying in bed and nursing horrific pain.

Then it hit me.

It hit me that the pain came when I carried Esther. By carrying her squirming thirty pounds—along with my own jiggling *extra* thirty pounds—I was literally carrying the equivalent of a sixty-pound bag of dog food everywhere I carried us. Aside from Esther, I was overweight. My excess weight was causing my pain: the extra pounds on my body were taking a serious toll on my health and my family. I realized that in addition to my back—every joint was beginning to talk to me—my hips, knees, and ankles. Though I could not opt out of carrying Esther ever again, I could surely figure out a way to lose some of myself.

• • •

Our bodies have a hard enough time staying in good health without us adding more obstacles to tackle. I wished there was an easy remedy—a shot or a pill for my problem—and I thought about this as I stood in line at the pharmacy, waiting for Esther's prescription as she had strep throat.

I knew there were miracle drugs and diet fads that claimed to help people lose weight, but I knew the answer to my problem—and it wasn't found on a shelf at the pharmacy. As I waited, I looked at the boxes of medicine lined up behind the counter. There was a huge section of allergy medicines and a few boxes of nicotine patches. Next to those were three boxes that surprised me: a colon cancer test, an ancestry test, and a paternity test. I laughed, because that one little test—the paternity test—would have eliminated months of heart-wrenching foster care drama before we adopted Esther.

Those fifteen months of court dates as kinship foster parents felt very out of my control. Though I had moved on from Cheerios and

Goldfish, my latest *modus operandi* was to never be hungry. And it was that new M.O. that eventually ushered me onto the couch and into that Christmas season of pain.

Adoption day came a month later, on January 13, 2017. I was thankful to be off the couch and in the courtroom for the proceedings. That evening, when I scrolled through pictures from the day, I was dumbfounded. Was that really *me*? Did I really look like *that*? That's when I knew this mother of five had to actually *do something*.

It was time—I had to change something—and it had to be extreme.

Chapter 22

"The beauty of thy peace shines forth in an ordered life.
A disordered life speaks loudly of disorder in the soul."
— Elizabeth Elliot

In the United States, *two-thirds* of adults and one-third of children are overweight or obese. We are consuming more food than ever before.

At the dawn of our nation, the average person in the United States ate two pounds of sugar each year—and by 1970, that number increased to *123 pounds per person*—and now, we eat 152 pounds of sugar per person, per year, which is equivalent to six cups of sugar each week. A study published by Harvard Health shows that "the effects of added sugar intake—higher blood pressure, inflammation, weight gain, diabetes, and fatty liver disease—are all linked to an increased risk for heart attack and stroke."

In my effort to fix my problem of pain, I attended a weight-loss workshop taught by Dr. Evron Helland, a local Doctor of Chiropractic and nutritionist who teaches the pre-med nutrition class for Colorado Mountain College. I already knew what my problem was—it was obvious from watching our cows. I had fed cattle with Andrew enough to know that if he confined a cow and fed it a lot, it gained weight.

To my surprise, Dr. Helland turned most everything I knew about nutrition upside down—including the food pyramid. These were the very basics of his workshop:

- Insulin, a hormone produced by the pancreas, is the "gatekeeper" of the body's fat cells
- If insulin is present, fat cells cannot be "unlocked" and burned by the body as energy
- When a person eats carbohydrates like bagels, rice, tortillas, bread, pasta (as well as Cheerios, Goldfish, and cookie dough), the body turns them into glucose
- For the body to process glucose, it needs insulin
- Carb consumption triggers insulin production, and the insulin delivers the glucose to the cells for energy
- When insulin is called upon by carbs, the fat cells remain "locked up," and fats are being stored in the fat cells instead of being burned

Dr. Helland recommended the following plan: eat only thirty to forty grams of carbs each day. It sounded easy until he told us that the average American consumes over *three hundred* grams of carbs each day. One flour tortilla—or one banana—contains about thirty grams of carbs *each*. I also learned that though fruits and vegetables are carbs, they contain fiber, which helps slow their digestion rate.

The average adult only needs about seventy grams of carbs per day. The idea of the low-carb diet was to "unlock" my fat cells, freeing them to be burned as energy. Dr. Helland said to "exercise hungry" (while the "lock" is off the fat cells) so my body could burn them as I exercised. Lowering my carb intake to thirty grams each day was going to throw my body into ketosis—where the brain would be feeding off ketones and glucose, instead of just glucose (sugar from carbs). Ketones, produced by the liver when we are not eating carbs, are a byproduct of burning stored fat and/or dietary fat, and the brain can use them as a secondary fuel source along with glucose.

When a person eats sugar, the brain's "feel-good neurotransmitter," dopamine, is sent out into the bloodstream. I learned that eating Oreo cookies produces more activity in the brain's center for pleasure than doing cocaine. I thought back to my latchkey days and began to realize that I had grown up as a sort of childhood sugar addict.

One last component of Dr. Helland's program was fasting. He said to pick one day each week and start out with a big breakfast of protein—with foods like eggs, bacon, cheese, and avocados—since fat takes the longest to digest, making the body feel fuller, longer. Then, on just that one day each week, after eating breakfast, skip lunch and dinner. Then, the next morning, I could "break-the-fast" by eating breakfast.

I jumped right in. I told Andrew all about it when I got home, and he became my biggest encourager. He even bought me a scale. We weighed ourselves, and *I let him see what I weighed.* I am 5'6" and he is 6'2", and I weighed two pounds more than him. I was so embarrassed, and he was amazing.

A year later, after diligently working Dr. Helland's program, I had lost over thirty pounds—had gone from a size twelve to a size six—and my body had never felt so good. The food I served at the table was more nutritious and more delicious than ever before. Even the chocolate chip cookies I made for my family were made with fresh-ground whole wheat flour, and they could tell the difference if I was out of wheat berries and had to use white flour.

"They taste empty," Life said one day, after taking a bite of a white flour cookie and asking me what I did differently.

"That's because they are."

My joint pain and back pain were non-existent, and I was strong. I was running again and could do a five-minute plank. I learned how to make creamed cauliflower—which I had never eaten before—and most importantly, I learned that I had just been eating too much. Self-denial had not been a part of my life. I was dealing with hard-to-control situations by trying to control what I ate; while in reality, I was completely out of control, numbed by glucose.

Though the low-carb diet served me well for a season, I knew it was not the way our bodies were designed to be nourished for long periods of time. It was a sort of reset button in my life, and my next goal was to learn how to reenter the world of carbs and make healthy choices. I wanted to be a good steward of the body I'd been given, and I never again wanted to return to my life of painful gluttony. I stopped religiously counting carbs—and I no longer held a five-minute plank. Once I reached my goal, I had to learn how to live life again in a way that was sustainable for the rest of my years. I still ate cauliflower because I loved it; I still ran and did daily planks (though not as far and not as long); and I still fasted every Monday—as it reminded me of one of the most valuable parts of my experience: being hungry for a meal. Hunger also reminded me to pray about specific things and for specific people.

Through my experience, I learned that we do not need as much food as we think we do. Instead, what we need is the right amount of good, healthy food. I learned to value the sugar in fruit as a *nutrient*, not a quick fix for an out-of-control addict. I did not go back to eating a lot of processed foods such as pasta, tortillas, and bagels (or Cheerios, Goldfish, and cookie dough). I learned that white flour is truly not food and is not healthy. Most bleached white flour is made white by carcinogenic chemicals and should be avoided altogether. Eating white flour (which lacks the fiber of the whole grain), instantly increases the body's blood sugar—stimulating an over-production of insulin in our bodies—therefore, increasing the chances for diabetes, inflammation, high blood pressure, and weight gain. Cancer cells also have more insulin receptors than normal cells.

I started eating wheat bread again—making it like Ruthie did—by grinding whole wheat berries. Of course, there were exceptions here and there: birthdays, holidays, or just a hankering for a bagel sandwich at breakfast. Beef, an incredible source of protein, remained a staple of my diet. Whether I ate eggs from our hens, fresh bread from our oven, veggies from our garden, beef from our cattle, or honey from the bees buzzing around our alfalfa fields—moderation and restraint became a part of my life. I felt great.

But then I entered the world of menopause.

Menopause, the evil on which I now blame anything bad in my life, threw me into the world where the availability of tank tops in any season and tampons at any time were a must. Hot flashes, coupled with spastic menstruation and shrinking metabolism, rocked my world. My summer highlights became silvery strands of gray hair. Like an aspen tree whose leaves turn in the fall, I was dramatically changing as a new season approached.

I didn't know if I should replace hormones that seemed to have completely jumped ship, or if I should just push through the craziness. One friend suggested I do what she did and "take everything they throw at you—it's amazing—you'll be back to normal in no time!" Mom said menopause was sort of a non-issue for her and that I should sail through, unscathed.

I decided to just "sail through." In my sailing through, I must have stopped at one too many ports along the way, as the pounds began to pack themselves on again. Not as diligent as I once was, I saw five pounds added to the scale—and then ten. It happened so easily and so effortlessly compared to all the hard work I had done to lose it. Along with the onset of menopause, I wanted to blame Covid—or the fact that we were raising a kindergartener, teenagers, and twenty-somethings all at the same time. But it came down to the simple truth that it was my body and I had no one to blame but me. I was discouraged, and it became all too easy to give up on any sense of order, stewardship, and self-denial.

Then, one windy, snowy day, I got thrown while getting on a new horse—landing me in the hospital for four days with a broken back. Any meager effort I'd given to run, do yoga, and hold short planks was no longer an option. My doctor told me, "Just hold tight for three months. No BLT—bending, lifting, or twisting."

Oh, goodness.

On the other side of those awful, excruciatingly painful three months now, I have a new view of things: be thankful for anything you can do. Enjoy the sun on your face, a walk with a friend, and the increase of your heartbeat as you hike up a hill.

Pain is a tremendous motivator, and I am back to limiting carbs for a season in order to relieve my back, once again, from my extra weight. But it feels like a gentler process this time. Having had my mobility limited gave me a new appreciation for pain-free movement of any kind. I know I will reach my goal again, and I know I will fight harder to stay in a healthy place for the sake of my body and my mind.But in the meantime, during round two, I am a little more patient with myself.

• • •

The fact that I have even needed to give headspace to the concept of limiting my food so that I do not gain weight is a product of my own lack of self-control. But I am not alone. It is also the situation in which we find our nation. We have become a country of no limits and no self-control. We no longer deny ourselves much of anything. Just as my excesses caught up with me, the excesses of our nation have caught up with our world. Just as my lack of self-restraint started to destroy my life, our excesses as Americans are destroying our bodies and our world.

As a nation we are living in excess, and we need to rethink our habits.

There is a tremendous difference in the amount of food we purchase and consume in the US compared with the amount we actually need. We drive, eat, and buy in excess. A USDA report asserts that in the US, "wasted food is the single largest category of material placed in municipal landfills—an alarming 50% of produce is thrown away in the United States."

In order to produce the amount of food wasted in the US, it would require thirty million acres of land, a piece of land about the size of Pennsylvania. Our nation's food waste also uses 4.2 trillion gallons of water and two billion pounds of fertilizer. Global food production requires the use of energy sources, but it also requires high-emission transportation methods to bring us luxuries like blueberries from Peru in December.

We all need to tighten our belts. We need to look at how we live and why, what we purchase and why, and what we eat and why. We need to look at our jobs, our cars, our habits, our diets, our indulgences, and our consumerism, and assess whether we truly believe the science enough to change our lifestyles. Will we actually limit our consumption, change our habits, and rein in our conveniences?

• • •

While our excesses are harming our planet and are slowly killing our bodies, they are also creating another serious problem. According to a recent study from *Psychology Today*, the new epidemic facing 47% of adults in America is loneliness. In our world of easy communication and thousands of "friends," half of us still hunger for meaningful connections with other humans. We are lonely because we are spending more time with a screen than we are face to real face. The average American spends over three and a half hours per day watching TV and almost two and a half hours on social media. Americans are spending an average of six hours each day watching a screen of some kind.

I worry that our excesses have turned us into an unhealthy, wasteful, and lonely nation. We lack self-control. We spend time with screens instead of gathering at our tables for dinner. Many would like to limit the number of cattle who graze instead of limiting themselves. Alongside the global climate crisis, our nation has a crisis of the soul. It would benefit us to do some internal analysis and find what areas of our personal lives need reform and restraint.

Webster's dictionary defines sequester as "to seclude or withdraw." While we look for ways to sequester carbon, I believe we need to stop sequestering ourselves. We need to power-off the screens and spend time outside with our hands in the soil and learn to grow more of our own food. The health benefits of gardening are many. Not only does daily gardening provide healthy food for our tables, it is proven to help reduce dementia by 36%.

Our nation needs to get back outside, and we need to start moving. We need to be reminded that being outside and in nature is good for both the body and soul, reducing significantly the risk of "type II diabetes, cardiovascular disease, premature death, preterm birth, stress, and high blood pressure."

Our consumptive society has been living in excess for so long—shown by how much waste we have and how fat we have become. Our consumerism is contagious, and it spreads like gossip from one person to another. In our pursuit of more money, more food, more experiences, and more things, we and our planet have become sick. There is no easy antibiotic for this infection—no patch or ten-day dose to rid us of our problem.

We need to do some serious soul-searching as a nation and look at the ways we are all living in excess, and we need to begin to value words like *restraint*, *less*, and *deny*.

It's time to lose a little bit of ourselves.

• • •

Andrew and I have been raising hay, cattle, and kids in the Arkansas River Valley for over twenty-four years—and we have watched the slow changes as the land values skyrocket. But, even on the freezing cold days, there's just something special about this life that cannot be bought. Maybe it comes from being active outside, being in touch with where our food comes from, and being with people and animals as we work the ranch.

As human *beings*, the very place we live is one important reason we need to identify the excesses in our lives and start living, not only as good stewards of our bodies, but also as caretakers of the very planet designed to nourish us. As Wendell Berry writes, "The care of the earth is our most ancient and most worthy and after all, our most pleasing responsibility."

Chapter 23

L ately, there's this undercurrent flowing through my days—a consistent desire to linger in moments now—before they become tomorrow's memories. As the mountains are white with snow, I am reminded that the seasons are short. Soon, with the warmth of spring, the earth will stretch and thaw, and the snow will begin its descent into the valley.

On slow winter evenings, when dinner fills our bellies and the dishwasher is humming, I set the kettle to boil for tea. I tidy and sweep up the remnants of day from the kitchen floor: hay from the cuffs of jeans, dried manure from cowboy boots, the morning's crust and coffee grounds that missed the compost bucket, craft beads that rolled from the table, thin garlic coats that floated off my cutting board, a rubber band sent flying from the living room, tiny welding particles that fell from gloves on the counter at lunch, and a random assortment of cat hair, dog hair, and horse dander.

Amidst the messiness of life, I love the time of day when everything's in its place: Essie is fresh out of the bathtub and cozy in bed with a book, Abe and Life are fast asleep after a long day of skiing at Monarch, and Grace and Naomi are both home from college, enjoying the quiet evening by the fire to catch up with Andrew and me. Ideally, boots are paired in their cubbies, coats are hung on their hangers, the mail is picked up and sorted, and the porch light is turned off for the night. It's a wild pace we keep on the ranch, and like the cows, once the sun finally sets, we bed down for the evening.

But then, it happens—and it happens more often than you'd think.

The ring of his cell phone interrupts the peaceful evening as Andrew hops up from his cozy chair to answer in the other room. A minute later he reappears and announces to the entire house, "Sheriff called—cows are out—I need some help!"

Grace, who sits in front of the wood stove with wet hair after a shower, says, "You're kidding." But, after living over two decades of life on the ranch, she knows better.

Naomi stands, stretches, and says with a smile, "There's no place like home!"

Esther hears the announcement from upstairs and her little feet hit the carpet with a thump to join in the excitement. We wake the boys and they groan. Everyone puts on boots and coats and we pile in the pickup and head down the snowy dirt road to the main road. The windows are always down, and the frigid winter air fills the cab, still dusty with summer. The headlights illuminate a few soft snowflakes that fly around us. We squint and see the rogue cows and then spy the gate that was left open after feeding at sunset—and everyone rolls their eyes at Abe, who says, "Hmm . . . interesting." We shine lights on the mamas whose hooves scrape along the slick pavement of the main road as they wander and wonder.

We leave the truck in the middle of our dirt road with the headlights shining on the cows. We spread out and shine our phone lights back on ourselves so the cows can see us. Random voices in the dark spook them, but if they can see us, they are more likely to stay calm.

We speak to them like family: "Come on mamas, come on, let's go," and they waddle their way back through the open gate. The cows know it's better inside the fence—they know there's nothing but barbed wire, slippery pavement, sharp mailboxes, tossed beer cans, broken bottles, and fast cars on the outside—but an open gate is still hard to resist.

Andrew makes sure the wire is tight over the post and we all meet up, our boots tapping on the pavement as we walk back to the truck. The scant snow has stopped and the night is clear. Wide awake, we shut off all the lights and look through the cold night to the Big Dipper, faithfully circling around the North Star, and the path of the Milky Way sparkling across the night to the west where a crescent moon lingers over the mountains

Everything is where it should be, for a moment.

We pile back into the truck and then the house where coats are tossed aside and boots are pushed at the heel and kicked off, landing on the swept floor. Hot water is set to boil for cocoa, mugs and spoons are set out, and the pantry is raided. Wet hair tied up in a bun is set free and warmed by the fire once again. Essie is wide awake, and I know sleep for her won't come for at least another hour, maybe longer, if someone finds marshmallows.

But I linger and love this interruption.

One day, this house will see too many clean, quiet nights, and I know I will long for "the good old days." I know I will somehow miss the unending laundry and the dishes and the daily boots and spurs left in the doorway; the dirt and dust and cups left out; the milk drank straight from the jug that gets tossed in the air before landing back in the fridge with a thump; and the pantry that seems to fill-and-empty, fill-and-empty, fill-and-empty, like the ticking of a clock. These days of homework, soccer, dentist appointments, college tuition, story time, curfews, report cards, and brushing teeth not my own, will one day be a thing of the past.

Abe is a senior this year, and conversations about what he wants to do when he grows up are weighing heavier as time passes, and Life just got his driver's permit, though he's been driving the feed truck since he was a toddler. These days, they are slipping through my hands like water—water I cannot stop from flowing—and like wind—wind I cannot stop from blowing.

This is why I linger.

And this place, this ground upon which our family works and lives, feels more vulnerable with each moment. Open pastures; irrigation water; the herd that grazes; spring branding; riding horses through the fields; long summer days of baling hay alongside cousins, siblings, parents, aunts, and uncles; and delivering lunch and milkshakes with Essie on the four-wheeler—I know these days won't be here forever.

I won't always see Andrew irrigating in his tall rubber boots, shovel over his shoulder, walking through the waist-deep grass.

I won't always hear Life come in from trying to plow and hear him say, "Gotta wait a couple hours for the sun to warm the ground."

I won't always see Abe leave in his camo and binoculars to scout deer from the tree stand up by the Eagles' Nest.

I won't always hear Naomi tell the family how many round bales she baled that day without breaking any: "Sixty-four, you guys! Sixty-four!" she says, slapping her hand on the table while Andrew leans back in his chair, smiles, and nods.

I won't always see Grace rally and wiggle into Wrangler jeans and pull on leather gloves to help work cattle or go on a ride with her dad.

No, these days won't be here forever because generations move on. Like water in the river, time keeps passing by. Like the Camerons and the Sages, new families eventually work the land you have spent your life caring for. Like the Joneses, a family needs change—our bodies age, land prices increase, and our workforce grows up and moves on.

But for now, in this season, I am wallowing in my life as it is. I hope to slow these moments down with my presence, with deep breaths and eyes that stop and see.

I can see it in her eyes and feel it in her thinning coat and bony spine—Molly is languishing. She's slower to rise each day, and her hips catch more and more when we walk. And though I tell her to stay, she still follows. I know she will follow until she can't anymore. Until then, I walk the road so she has less obstacles to maneuver. I wonder with each walk if it's our last.

I wonder what lasts I am seeing pass by me each day without even knowing.

When was the last time Abe crawled up on my lap? The last children's book I read to Naomi? The last time I braided Grace's hair? The last bottle I fed Essie? Did I already drive Life to school for the last time now that he drives me?

And so, I linger amidst being busy. This lingering comes in moments captured like a sunset or a night sky—when I have to stop and watch—or I miss them.

• • •

The first Christmas of the pandemic arrived, and S Mountain had finally donned its Christmas tree, officially ushering in the holiday season in Salida. We bundled up the next afternoon to cut a tree with an ax. We drove up Bear Creek, where the white firs grow, and we hiked snowy hills and crossed hidden streams in our search.

As we hiked, our cheeks rosy with cold and our breath puffing small clouds with each step, I remembered a very special Christmas tree from my middle school years. Before my parents were divorced, our family joined with others and cut massive Christmas trees in the California mountains, so tall they only fit in the two-story living rooms of the A-frame mountain homes of our little community. Ladders were used to decorate the trees and the warm homes were filled with the sound of laughter and Christmas carols, the smell of coffee, and the taste of cookies and fudge. It was a joyous time.

But the tree that I remember the most came to me in a very different way. After my parents divorced, Mom and I moved from the small town in the mountains outside of Denver, down the hill, to the city. We left the big house we lived in—and we left our dogs—and moved into a townhouse.

Mom worked very hard as a nurse, and there was a stretch when she was inbetween jobs and was on unemployment. That stretch happened to fall during a Christmas season in my middle school years. It was December, and I had come home on the bus from my last day of school, as Christmas break had begun. Mom was out job hunting when I got home, and I sat alone in the empty townhouse. It was a sad season as we didn't have extra money for a Christmas tree that year. After the divorce, we started buying cut trees from tree lots instead of bringing one home from the forest.

My habit was to clean the house for Mom, so that at least things were clean and organized in our life that often felt unstable. So I emptied the dishwasher and took out the kitchen trash. I carried the big bag across the snow-dusted parking lot to the large communal dumpster. I swung it back and forth before I let it launch over the edge and into the pile of trashbags.

That's when I saw it.

Teetering on top of all the trashbags was a beautiful, healthy, real Christmas tree. My eyes widened as I walked around the dumpster and looked for a way to climb up. I kicked and climbed my way up and over. I balanced myself on the squishy, snowy, stinky trashbags and stood up, looking around. None of my neighbors were out and about. I wondered who had thrown away a perfectly good Christmas tree? Maybe they were heading out on vacation and didn't want to clean up a floor full of dry needles when they returned.

I grabbed the rough and sticky base of the tree and dragged it over to the edge of the dumpster. Careful not to break any branches, I guided the tree over as it slid slowly through my hands to the blacktop, where it landed with a thud. I leaned the tree against the dumpster and hopped out, my Converse sneakers hitting the frosty blacktop. I looked around again before I dragged my treasure across the snowy parking lot to my home and through the front door.

I lit a paper-wrapped fire log in our fire place and then went down stairs to the basement where I found our tree stand and boxes of Christmas lights and decorations. I brought them all upstairs to the living room. I found a Christmas record in one of the boxes and put it on the record player. The black plastic went round and round beneath the little needle and the living room filled with the sounds of Christmas carols. I made a big mug of powdered hot chocolate with tiny marshmallows and spent the dwindling afternoon decorating the tree.

I did my best to balance the tree upright in the stand, screwing the four bolts into the bark. With Mom's silver pitcher, I filled the base with water for the thirsty tree. With a sense of urgency, I strung lights and hung ornaments as I wanted it to be perfect for Mom when she got home. I fixed the wire stem of the foil star to the top of the tree—the star my brother, Ted, had cut from styrofoam and covered with foil long ago. I thought of Ted, and wondered where he was, as he came in and out of our lives intermittently. I put the empty boxes back in the basement and vacuumed the pine needles that made a path from the front door to the living room.

As the winter sun disappeared over the rooftops and the mountains, the house darkened and the tree grew even more dazzling. The log in the fireplace glowed with a steady line of flames as I sat on the couch, sipped my cocoa, and admired the gift I had been given at Christmas. It was as if God knew how important it was to me to have a tree, and so He provided one.

It was a truly perfect tree.

I heard Mom stomp her boots outside the front door and I popped up to meet her. She walked in and immediately her jaw droppped and her eyes filled with tears.

"Where did you get that tree?" she asked, kicking off her boots and hanging her purse and coat on the hooks behind the door.

"I found it in the dumpster! Can you even *believe* it that someone threw it away?"

She followed me as I led her to the sparkling tree. As she touched the ornaments from my childhood and felt the tender needles of the tree, she looked at me, her eyes reflecting the lights, and said, "I can't even believe it, Lara. It's perfect."

I smiled at the memory as the cold air filled my lungs and froze my nose while my family and I tromped through the snowy mountains to find the perfect tree. There's just something about having a Christmas tree in the house that makes the season extra special.

An opinionated family, it takes us a while to find the right tree each year, as we have to look at all the options before the first whack with the ax fills the forest. Everyone takes turns with the wooden handle and the sharp flat blade, some more adept than others.

"Just push it over," I said, getting cold and stomping my boots in the deep snow. "It's so close."

"Mom, you cannot push a Christmas tree over," Abe said, in between swings with the ax. "You have to chop it down."

Eventually the tree fell, giving the others around it more room and light to grow and flourish. Abe dragged the tall, bushy tree through the snow, its needles doodling all the way back to the truck. He strapped it on with baling twine and brought it home where soup warmed in a big pot on the stove and eggnog waited in little crystal cups in the fridge.

Life untied the tree and dragged it from the truck up the icy stairs to the porch where he sawed its lowest boughs for the mantel and wreaths. He squeezed the tree through the doorway and into the house where the sound of Christmas music filled the living room, along with the smell of the fresh-cut tree. Andrew stood the tree up on its trunk, lifted it into its stand, and turned it this way and that, until we all approved.

The two antique trunks were opened—metal latches flipped up and lids propped open as the cinnamon scent of the season joined the room. It was like Christmas morning as the kids pulled treasures from the trunks they see open only in December: books, stockings, plates, lights, ornaments, candles, the advent calendar whose twenty-five pockets hold tiny ornaments to be hung from its own little tree each December day, and the squatty fat felt birds that would soon stand among the greenery on the mantel.

Strings of little white lights were wound around the soft needles of the fir tree. Years of ornaments and hand-painted glass balls were hung from metal hooks and yarn-covered childhood crafts dangled from the branches. Popcorn flew out of the popper as we made red and white strings for the tree: popcorn—cranberry—popcorn—cranberry. And the star was fixed on top. The seven stockings were carefully hung from the mantel behind the wood stove whose fire warmed us through its windows.

At the table, I unrolled the red and green plaid table runner, centered it, and placed the oil lamp in the middle, lighting its wick. The soft light reflected in the frosty windows that framed the cold, crisp sunset over Mount Ouray and Chipeta, closing the short winter day.

Looking for the herd, I scanned the hay fields, thick with snow. I found them on the far side, lined up beside the shelter of the cottonwood trees, eating bale upon bale of summer's hearty alfalfa that Andrew had fed in the light of the early afternoon. The tender leaves of protein would help keep their bodies warm through the night.

I unpacked the nativity, whose red candles would soon blaze and spin at the table as we sang the season's first carols. I thought of Mom and Rodney, both sick with Covid. Traditionally they come and join us at the table for a ham dinner and load the red satin tree skirt full of gifts; but that year, when many traditions were turned on end, they could not come—and we could not go to them. I was thankful they had each other at home, and I was thankful the virus did not claim that Christmas as their last.

We set the table for eight—white plates and bowls and folded forest-green cloth napkins with a silver soup spoon resting on each. The counting of plates always changes as loved ones and friends come and go. Papa was coming to dinner to see Gracie who was home from college for Christmas. I knew her concept of home was changing. When she is with us, I wonder if she longs to be at her beach home with her four roommates, like when she's in San Diego and longs for her family and home on the ranch.

With the house and the tree all decorated, we gathered at the table for dinner. We sat in worn wooden chairs and held hands as Andrew prayed, thanking God for our family, the meal set before us, and the season ahead. I served the vegetable-meatball soup and started the bread and butter around the table. Conversation with Papa about Grace's future was full of questions and comments as he listened and watched her talk with her hands. Law school? Grad school?

"To me, it's mostly about where you want to end up living, and what you actually want to be doing each day of your life," he told her.

I watched her mind work as she processed his perspective.

I know there is a limit to the number of these dinners—these dinners where Papa drives over in the dark and walks in the door and I greet him with a hug. I know there may come a day when I go to call Mom, excited to tell her something, and she won't be there. I know there will come a day when Dad and Uncle Dan no longer live next door.

And these days, the ones in which none of my children are married, are also numbered. I know that one day the size of our family will start to grow again. And, I know that one morning—and this is the hardest one to think about—most likely, either Andrew or I will wake up for the first time without the other. Only one coffee cup at the table. But I shoo that thought away for now, as that season is hopefully far, far away. Though we have had tragedies and loss in our lives, these days seem easy.

But they are not always easy.

They are full of stress, finances, aging parents, loss, a preschooler, the pandemic, a friend still missing, two college daughters adulting far away, and two teenage boys exploring what's outside the fence.

But really, if I truly think about it, I would not want my life to always be easy and forever the same. I want to experience the miracles that come with risk. I want my kids to grow up and move on and have lives of their own. I want to see if they get married and have kids one day, or not. I want to see what they choose to do for a living.

Growth brings change, and change, like that of the seasons, is healthy.

We are constantly growing—whether that's the value of forgiveness learned in a concentration camp; the need for perseverance and determination in the face of what storm may rage before us; the idea of stewardship as we take care of our bodies and the land around us; the wisdom to get away and reflect on life before it's gone; the faith to risk comfort for what is right; the intention to linger and see simple beauties and treasure the places and people that matter; and the courage to stand alone and afraid under an umbrella of stars, knowing that there is peace to be found in letting go.

Time, like a river, continues to flow; and the mountains, they watch generation after generation pass through. What a privilege it is to be here to experience the moments given to me in this place. When my days here are done, and when I sit at the table prepared for me in eternity, I will be forever thankful for the abundant life I was given. But until then, as the days and years flow by, the table in my home sits faithful and stout, offering a place to gather and share a meal, our stories, and our lives, in any season.

RECIPES

RUTHIE'S CHRISTMAS EVE YULE LOG

CAKE:
6 eggs, separated into whites and
  yolks
3/4 cup sugar
1/3 cup unsweetened cocoa
1 1/2 tsp vanilla extract
Dash of salt
Powdered sugar

FILLING:
1 1/2 cup heavy cream, chilled
1/2 cup powdered sugar
1/4 cup unsweetened cocoa
2 tsp instant coffee granules
1 tsp vanilla extract
3/4 cup Hershey's chocolate syrup

1. Preheat oven to 375F. Grease bottom of a 15½" x 10½" jellyroll pan; line with parchment paper; grease lightly.

2. In a large mixing bowl, beat egg whites at high speed until soft peaks form when the beater is slowly raised. Add ¼ cup of the sugar, 2T at a time, beating until stiff peaks form when the beater is slowly raised.

3. In a separate mixing bowl, beat the egg yolks at high speed, adding remaining ½ cup of sugar, 2T at a time. Beat until mixture is thick—about 4 minutes.

4. At low speed, beat cocoa, vanilla, and salt into the yolk mixture, just until smooth.

5. Using a whisk or rubber spatula, gently fold the cocoa mixture into the egg whites just until blended (no egg whites showing). Spread evenly over paper in pan.

6. Bake 15 minutes, just until surface springs back when gently pressed with fingertip. Sift powdered sugar in a 15" x 10" rectangle on a clean dish towel.

7. Carefully turn cake over onto sugared towel; lift off pan; carefully peel paper from cake.

8. Roll, starting from one short end to the other, towel and all. Cool for half an hour.

9. To make filling, combine ingredients in large mixing bowl; beat until thick; refrigerate.

10. Unroll cooled cake; spread with filling, leaving 1" at edges; reroll.

11. Place seam side down on serving plate; cover loosely with foil. Refrigerate 1 hour before serving.

12. To serve: sprinkle with powdered sugar and drizzle with chocolate syrup (can also decorate with raspberries or sliced strawberries). Serves 10.

BRANDING DAY CHILI

2 lbs. ground beef
1 large white onion, diced
1 poblano pepper, diced
1 jalapeno, diced
1—14 oz can corn or yellow hominy
2—28 oz cans crushed tomatoes
4—14 oz cans dark red kidney beans
Fritos or tortilla chips

5 cloves garlic, minced
2 Tbsp cumin
2 Tbsp chili powder
2 tsp salt
2 tsp pepper
Grated cheddar cheese
Sour cream
Fresh cilantro, diced

1. In a large soup pot, on medium-high heat, combine beef, onion, poblano pepper and jalapeno; heat until beef is browned. Add garlic and cook for another minute or two.

2. Add corn, tomatoes, and beans; stir well.

3. In a small bowl, combine cumin, chili powder, salt, and pepper; add to pot; stir well.

4. Add 1-2 cups of water (or more) to create desired consistency; add more spice to your taste (you can also add a teaspoon of cayenne pepper or a few shakes of your favorite hot sauce to increase the spice). To create a slightly sweet chili, add a teaspoon or two of sugar or a handful of chocolate chips.

5. Turn heat to low; cover; let simmer for at least one hour (stir every 15 minutes and add more, if necessary). Transfer chili to a crock pot and set on low, if desired.

6. Garnish with cheddar cheese, sour cream, and cilantro; serve with Fritos or tortilla chips. Serves 8.

CARRIE McBRIDE'S MAC 'N CHEESE

8 oz small elbow macaroni
1 ½ c (6 oz) grated Gruyere or Swiss cheese
1 c whipping cream
1 c whole milk
3 oz prosciutto, ham, or crispy bacon, diced
3 Tbsp Parmesan cheese
1/8 tsp nutmeg

1. Cook and drain macaroni.

2. In a large bowl, combine cream, milk, ham, Parmesan, nutmeg, and ½ Swiss cheese; add macaroni; season with salt and pepper and stir well.

3. Put in an 11 x 7 buttered dish; sprinkle the remaining Swiss cheese on top.

4. Bake at 400 F for 20 minutes. Serves 6.

• • •

BUTTERMILK WAFFLES/PANCAKES

2 c whole wheat flour
2 tsp baking powder
1 tsp baking soda
½ tsp salt

2 ½ c whole buttermilk
2 eggs
1 tsp vanilla
4 Tbsp melted coconut oil

1. Preheat pancake griddle to 325F; warm oven to 200F.

2. In a large mixing bowl, whisk together dry ingredients.

3. Add buttermilk, eggs, and vanilla; mix well.

4. Add oil; mix well; add more buttermilk if pancakes are too thick.

5. Grease griddle; using a measuring cup, scoop batter and pour onto griddle making circles, letters, snowmen, mermaids, etc; heat until small bubbles appear and pop; flip when underside is a nice golden color; transfer to a large plate or pan and keep warm in oven until ready to serve.

6. Makes about 20 small pancakes (I at least quadruple this recipe for the seven of us).

BONE BROTH

- Olive oil
- Assorted veggies such as onions, carrots, celery, roughly chopped (this is a great time to use any tops and discards from recent cooking)
- At least a few fresh garlic cloves, peeled and cut in half
- Left over meat and bones from a pot roast, steak, ribs, roasted chicken, or soup bones from the meat counter (I freeze leftover bones/meat/trimmings for broth, unless the dogs are underfoot in the kitchen)
- 2 bay leaves
- Kosher salt and fresh ground pepper
- Fresh or dried rosemary, parsley, and thyme

1. In a large soup pot, drizzle a generous labyrinth of olive oil; set to medium heat and add veggies and garlic; sauté until tender.

2. Add meat and bones; cover completely with water, filling pot over halfway full.

3. Add a generous amount of kosher salt and fresh ground black pepper.

4. Add rosemary, parsley, and thyme. I don't measure these, I just shake in a good amount and let them spread across the surface until I think it's enough (fresh herbs are a plus).

5. Cover and set to boil; turn down to simmer for 2-4 hours (or overnight, if you want to use a crockpot). Be sure to check liquid level along the way—adding more water, if needed.

6. After veggies fall apart and meat falls off the bones, using a colander, strain the broth (be sure to catch broth in a bowl beneath the colander).

7. Use broth for sipping, as a base for a soup, or freeze in ice cube trays for another day.

FALL SOUP

1 left over roasted chicken (or four chicken breasts, diced and sauteed)
4 Tbsp butter
2 Tbsp olive oil
1 white onion, chopped
6 carrots, sliced
6 celery stems, sliced
6 garlic cloves, minced
½ c fresh parsley, chopped
1 bay leaf

1 c chopped kale or spinach, no stems
½ tsp thyme
Dash of cayenne pepper
1 tsp salt
1 tsp pepper
6+ c chicken broth or prepared boullion
1 c half and half
1 c freshly grated Parmesan cheese
½ c barley or brown rice

1. In a large soup pot, cover leftover roasted chicken with water; cover pot with lid and bring to a boil; turn heat to low and simmer for two hours, adding more water if needed.

2. Place a colander over a large bowl; strain chicken in colander while saving broth in bowl beneath; set aside.

3. Return empty soup pot to stove; add butter; turn heat to medium high.

4. Add olive oil, onion, carrots, and celery; sautee until onions are soft and translucent; add garlic; sautee for another minute or two.

5. Add simmered broth back to pot; turn heat to low.

6. Add parsley, bay leaf, barley or brown rice, kale or spinach, thyme, and cayenne.

7. Take roasted chicken from colander; remove any leftover meat from bones and shred into bite-sized pieces; add to pot.

8. Add salt and pepper (I like to add a little Lawry's Seasoned Salt); mix well.

9. One cup at a time, add additional broth or prepared boullion until soup reaches desired consistency (Note: the rice/barley will absorb liquid as it cooks; use less broth if you want a heartier soup).

10. Mix well; add more salt and pepper to taste.

11. Cover and let simmer for at least one hour, until carrots are tender, stirring intermittently.

12. At least ten minutes before serving, add half and half; taste again for any needed salt and pepper adjustments; garnish with grated Parmesan cheese.

13. Serve with pumpkin muffins and a crisp garden salad. Enjoy!

ANN'S DINOSAUR KALE SALAD

DRESSING:
2 shallots, thinly sliced
5 Tbsp sherry vinegar or champagne
  vinegar
½ tsp kosher salt
2 Tbsp honey
5 Tbsp extra-virgin olive oil
½ tsp pepper

SALAD:
10 c dinosaur kale, stems removed
1 c chopped smoked almonds
1 c dried berries of any kind

1. In a small mixing bowl, whisk together shallots, vinegar, and salt; let sit for 10 minutes.
2. Wash kale; spin dry.
3. Slice kale in thin strips; add to large salad bowl.
4. Add honey, olive oil, and pepper to dressing; whisk together and set aside.
5. Squish and massge kale in bowl for 20 seconds.
6. Add almonds and berries.
7. Whisk dressing once more; dress and serve.

Variations: *sliced kumquats (only available in winter), chopped tangerines, walnuts, pecans, sprouted pumpkin seeds (the toasted and salted ones).*

CHOCOLATE BIRTHDAY CAKE

1 ½ c flour   2 eggs
¾ c cocoa powder   ¾ c buttermilk
1 ½ c sugar   1 ½ tsp vanilla
1 ½ tsp. baking soda   1/3 c coconut oil, melted
¾ tsp baking powder   ¾ c warm water
¾ tsp salt

1. Preheat oven to 350F.

2. In a large mixing bowl, sift together the dry ingredients: flour, cocoa, sugar, baking soda, baking powder, baking soda, and salt; whisk well.

3. In a separate bowl, whisk together eggs, buttermilk, and vanilla; add to dry ingredients; mix well.

4. Add coconut oil; mix well.

5. Add water; mix well.

6. Grease and flour cake pans (makes one 9 x 13 or two cake rounds).

7. Pour batter into pan(s); tap pans on counter a few times to pop any bubbles.

8. Bake for 20-25 minutes; cool completely before removing from pans.

CREAM CHEESE FROSTING: CHOCOLATE FROSTING:
½ c salted butter, softened   1 c salted butter, softened
3 c powdered sugar   1-2 c powdered sugar
1 tsp vanilla   1 tsp vanilla
8 oz cream cheese   1 c melted chocolate chips

1. In a large mixing bowl, combine butter, sugar, and vanilla; mix well.

2. Depending on the frosting, add either cream cheese or melted chocolate chips; mix well.

3. Frost and decorate cake. Enjoy!

CREAMED CAULIFLOWER

1 head fresh cauliflower, washed and broken into florets
6 Tbsp salted butter
½ c half and half
½ c freshly grated Parmesan cheese
½ tsp black pepper
1 tsp Lawry's Seasoned Salt

1. Preheat oven to 350F.
2. Steam cauliflower florets until they separate easily with a fork.
3. In a large mixing bowl, combine butter, half and half, salt, pepper, and steamed cauliflower; mix well on medium-high speed until creamy; add more salt and pepper, if desired.
4. Pour into a greased, oven-safe dish and top with Parmesan cheese. Bake for 20-30 minutes until golden.

• • •

PUMPKIN MUFFINS

1 ½ c sugar
3 eggs
1 ½ c canned pumpkin (or garden roasted)
½ c warm water
3 c whole wheat flour
1 ½ tsp baking powder

1 tsp baking soda
1 tsp salt
½ tsp cloves
¾ tsp nutmeg
1 tsp cinnamon
½ c coconut oil, melted

1. Preheat oven to 400F.
2. In a large mixing bowl, combine sugar, eggs, pumpkin, and water; mix well.
3. In another bowl, sift together flour, baking powder, baking soda, salt, cloves, nutmeg, and cinnamon; add to pumpkin mixture; mix well.
4. Add oil; mix well.
5. Place in greased muffin pans and bake for 15 minutes. Makes 24 muffins.

NOTES

EPIGRAPH

Austin, Mary. *The Land of Little Rain*. Houghton Mifflin, 1903.

CHAPTER TWO

Petit, Jan. *Utes: A Mountain People*. Revised edition, Johnson Books, 1990.

Everett, George G., and Dr. Wendell F. Hutchinson. *Under the Angel of Shavano*. Golden Bell Press, 1963.

Hovelsen, Leif. *Out of the Evil Night*. Blandford Press, 1959.

CHAPTER THREE

https://www.centralcoloradoconservancy.org/

The Holy Bible. English Standard Version, Good News Publishers, 2001.

CHAPTER FOUR

https://www.chaffeecounty.org/planning-and-zoning-right-to-ranch

https://casetext.com/case/roaring-fork-club-v-st-judes

https://envisionchaffeecounty.org/

CHAPTER FIVE

Ehrlich, Gretel. *The Solace of Open Spaces*. Penguin Books, 1985.

CHAPTER SIX

Leopold, Aldo. *A Sand County Almanac*, and *Sketches Here and There*. Oxford University Press, 1949.

Moore, Kathleen Dean. *Great Tide Rising*. Counterpoint, 2016.

https://usda.library.cornell.edu/concern/publications/r207tp32d

Foer, Jonathan Safran. *We are the Weather: Saving the Planet Begins at Breakfast*. Farrar, Straus and Giroux, 2019.

https://www.fao.org/3/a0701e/a0701e00.html

https://awellfedworld.org/wp-content/uploads/Livestock-Climate -Change-Anhang-Goodland.pdf

www.telegraph.co.uk/news/earth/environment/climaechange/7509978 /UN-admits-flaw-in-report-on-meat-and-climate-change.html

www.epa.gov/sites/production/files/2018-01/documents/2018_ complete_report.pdf

www.greenbiz.com/article/gassy-cows-facts-about-beefs-carbon -emisions-sponsored

www.ars.usda.gov/news-events/news/research-news/2019study -clarifies-us-beefs-resource-use-and-greenhouse-gas-emisions/

www.beefmagazine.com/beef-qualitycould-beef-be-perfect-food -prevent-alzheimer-s

www.nationalgeographic.com/culture/food/the-plate/2015/12/23 /is-more-cattle-grazing-the-solution-to-saving-our-soil/blog .whiteoakpastures.com/blog/carbon-negative-grassfed-beef

www.news.trust.org/cars or livestock which contribute more to climate change

www.pbs.org/ktca/farmhouses/sustainable_future.html

www.epa.gov/greenvehicles/fast-facts-transportation-greenhouse-gas
-emissions

www.eia.gov/tools/faqs/faq.php?id=23&t=10

www.electricchoice.com/blog/50-surprising-facts-on-energy
-consumption/

CHAPTER TWENTY-TWO

http://nationalacademies.org/hmd/Reports/2012/Accelerating
-Progress-in-Obesity-Prevention.aspx

www.health.harvard.edu/heart-health/the-sweet-danger-of-sugar

www.fda.gov/food/consumers/food-waste-and-loss

www.theatlantic.com/business/archive/2016/07/american-food-waste
/491513/

www.psychologytoday.com/us/blog/envy/201902/loneliness-new
-epidemic-in-the-usa

www.statista.com/statistics/186833/average-television-use-per-person
-in-the-us-since-2002/

www.broadbandsearch.net/blog/average-daily-time-on-social-media

www.merriam-webster.com/dictionary/sequester?src=search-dict-box

www.ncbi.nlm.nih.gov/pubmed/16411871

www.sciencedaily.com/releases/2018/07/180706102842.htm

Berry, Wendell. *The Unsettling of America*. Counterpoint Press, 1977.

GRATITUDE

Thank you to Matt Maher, for your song "Alive and Breathing" and Lauren Daigle, for your song "Love Like This."

To Mariel Wiley, for your designs and photos that pulled this whole project together. To Dylan Roth for seeing the design through to the end, and to Jon Rovner and his Western copyediting class for finding my mistakes and making this manuscript more readable than the original.

To Teow Lim Gogh, for your help and enthusiasm, from one writer to another.

To Dr. Steve Coughlin, editor of Western Press Books, for your many edits and suggestions for this manuscript—for finding every big and little mistake down to the apostrophes and indentations; for deepening my faith by asking me to complicate it; and for your enthusiasm in making this new writer's dream come true.

To Ana Maria Spagna, for teaching me how to write about the places, people, and animals I love; and to Dr. Tyson Hausdoerffer, for the gift of metered poetry.

To Dan Pratt, Beth Svinarich, and the crew at the University Press of Colorado for your amazing skills and knowledge—and for making the idea of this book into something I can actually hold in my hand!

To my thesis advisor, Dr. Laura Pritchett, for allowing me in way past the last minute; for all the hours you spent poring over the original words that eventually formed this book; for teaching me to be a real writer; and for offering your writing life as an open book.

To my writing cohort: Kristen Arendt, Corrinne Brumby, and Rita Payne. We did it! I could not have done this without you. Thank you for our past and present time together—you are incredible writers and friends.

To Carrie McBride, Bret and Jenna Collyer, Walt Harder, Dr. Evron Helland, Ron and Jo Jones, Randy Sage, Jim Treat, Katie Turnbull, and Willy Yunikar—thank you for graciously allowing me to add part of your knowledge, lives, and stories to mine.

To Dr. Ann Hallbower, for your kindness, incredible cooking, and dinosaur kale salad.

To Uncle Craig and Auntie Jill—cheers to Covid DNA tests!

To Marj Perry, for your emails, example, and encouragement.

To Aunt Cathy, for your consistent love and incredible packages.

To Suzanne, whom I will never forget; and to your four gifts: Hanley, Holly, Jeanne, and Sheila. To Jonny and Ken—thank you for devoting your lives to justice.

To Jim and Gina, for horses, happy hour, and your endless help. You are truly the "A Team."

To Wyatt and Maddie, we love you both very much, and we are so excited you are starting your lives together in the old house.

To Amanda, Donna, Jane, Janel, Kylee, Nancy, Rebecca, Susan, Susie, and Trista, for your enduring friendship and prayers. I am blessed and inspired by each of you.

To David and Janel, thank you for Mondays, date nights, river days, and all days—I am grateful for you both.

To Uncle Tom and Aunt Julie, for welcoming me into your home for so many summers in my life and for providing an example of a healthy marriage and family when I desperately needed it.

To Gammy and Gan, whose example I glean from all year long.

To Papa, for your wisdom and inspiration; for the perfect place to write; and for letting me row that Big Drop when you should have; to Ruthie, whom I miss each day; to Seth, Susie, Caleb, Ellie, and Daniel, for ranching and living life together; as well as Nancy, Morggan, Matson, Sam, Marcus, Anna, Jack, David, Anne, Ben, Jane, Nathan, and Gideon—thank you all for making Family Dinners mean something special; and to Ben and Jenny—welcome to the family!

To Garrett, Bea, Luke, Nicole, Riley, Asher, Christian, and Sophia— for being such a loving family—"You're awesome! I love you!" (And Lukey, thank you for your hours holding Baby Essie while I made dinner.)

To Thomasina, for your amazing support (and your fry bread); to Tahnee, Coleson, Jordan, and Dorniel—it is such fun when you all visit; and especially to Erin, for the gift of Esther. I am so proud of you. Thank you for being a part of this story.

To Dad, for your love, prayers, and editing—and for adding writing to my blood; to Uncle Dan, for your stories, zucchini bread, and knowing you always have my back; and to Ted, for fighting the good fight. I'm so thankful we live next door to each other.

To Mom and Rodney, for loving, praying, serving, and always saying yes. I could not have done this, and so many other things in my life, without you two. And Mom, thanks for showing me that a mom is always her child's biggest fan. I am so thankful you are my mom.

To Molly, for being the best dog, ever. No walk or run has been the same without you.

To Grace, Naomi, Abe, Life, and Essie—you are my heart and my life—I love you all dearly. Thank you for your encouragement through grad school and this book (for the cups of tea, texts to let me know I've got this, for staying up late and writing papers together, and for your sincere questions about how it's going and what it's about). Thank you for your grace as I stepped back from so much. I still can't believe how God has blessed Dad and me with the greatest kids, ever. (And to Jack, I have prayed for years for the man who would, one day, capture Gracie's heart—and now I know you—and I couldn't be more thankful to have you as our future son-in-law.)

To Andrew, for inspiring, motivating, loving, and encouraging me every day. Thank you for all the nights you did both bath time and dishes and then went to bed alone—still welcoming me beside you after midnight. Thank you for sending me off to write, guilt-free, and for the many surprises of flowers, wine, cheese, bread, and grapes. And thank you for giving me our life and family to write about. I love you and would choose you again, and again, and again.

And to Jesus Christ, my Lord and my God, thank you for loving me and for showing me who you are by what you have made. You are an amazing Creator. Thank you for all of my family and friends, for the life story you have given me, and for each day I have on this earth until I see your face and sit at your table.

"The Lord gives His people strength;
the Lord blesses His people with peace."

Psalm 29:11